SPIRITUAL GENIUS

RANDOM HOUSE / NEW YORK

SPIRITUAL GENIUS

The Mastery of Life's Meaning

WINIFRED GALLAGHER

RANDOM HOUSE and colophon are registered trademarks of Random House, Inc.

Library of Congress Cataloging-in-Publication Data
Gallagher, Winifred
Spiritual genius: the mastery of life's meaning / Winifred Gallagher.
p.cm.
ISBN 0-375-50310-2
1. Spiritual biography. I. Title.
BL72.G29 2002 200'.92'2—dc21
[B] 2001041905

Random House website address: www.atrandom.com
Printed in the United States of America on acid-free paper
2 4 6 8 9 7 5 3
First Edition

Book design by J. K. Lambert

To the handful of unknown great souls
among us who, according to religious tradition,
uphold the world

A man questioned abbot Nistero: "What good work shall I do?" And he answered, "All works are not equal. The Scripture saith that Abraham was hospitable, and God was with him. And Elias loved quiet, and God was with him. And David was humble, and God was with him. What therefore thou findest that thy soul desireth in following God, that do, and keep thy heart."

Verba Seniorum (The Sayings of the Desert Fathers)

CONTENTS

FOREWORD

Only Human

Spiritual genius is the uniquely human ability to seek life's meaning. It's the voice inside us that keeps asking What's it all about? Who am I? How can I make a difference? This inclination to wonder why we exist is not rarefied, or even necessarily conventionally religious, but a basic human trait. Just as we're born yearning for relationships, we're born with a craving to know our larger purpose.

Over three hundred years ago the poet John Dryden observed that "Every age has a kind of universal genius, which inclines those that live in it to some particular studies." Beginning with those of Einstein, the twentieth century had a special genius for exploring the material world—walking on the moon, performing medical miracles, computerizing the global village. At the dawn of the twenty-first century, however, all of this scientific and technological genius has highlighted one of our most ancient questions: Is there something more? Something that underlies and unifies life, including the bits and pieces of our own? That can sustain us through the promise and peril of the new century? The answer calls for spiritual genius, which inclines the individuals in these pages along with many others to "particular studies" of our search for meaning, both as individuals and as a society.

We think of "genius" as meaning both extraordinary talent and the person who has it. The Latin word's original, ancient definition, however, is an "animating spirit" that guides each of us to a special destiny—not just the entries on our résumés, our social roles, or the gratification of our egos but a uniquely meaningful life. To find that larger purpose, that thing that makes it all make sense, we can, like the men and women in this book, use our spiritual genius to do three things.

First we can follow our animating spirits into a hidden reality that exists, as the dictionary wonderfully puts it, "above the categories and predicaments" of the everyday world. Next we can choose to root ourselves in this "ground of being,"[1] whose names include God and the transcendent, Buddha nature and Truth. Then we can express or even embody this mystery in the world as only each of us can—often not so much by what we do as by how we do it. Spiritual genius enables us to do all of these things according to our own lights, which guide us to a unique place within a vast, sacred scheme of things that puts our ups and downs into perspective and illumines even our inevitable sorrows with a peculiar joy.

All of us use our spiritual genius some of the time. We might not recognize it as such, but we tap it whenever we "just know" that something is happening for a reason that, to paraphrase Blaise Pascal, "reason does not know." Spiritual genius tells us that, despite the chaos and confusion around us, everything is all right, so we might as well be nice. It tells us that if we take on a worthwhile challenge, we'll somehow find the necessary strength and help. It tells us that our true self is more than a bunch of personality traits and problems. Like a compass, spiritual genius always points us toward a reality larger than the ego and the status quo. Once we members of the meaning-seeking species find our place in the grand design, we're able to gather up the pieces of our everyday lives, making a coherent picture out of what can seem like an impossible puzzle.

Sometimes, we're most aware of spiritual genius when we lose contact with it. We forget what we "just know," and our sense of purpose. Nothing seems right, and nothing seems to help. Life's joys seem hollow, and its sorrows unbearable. This feeling of meaninglessness brings to mind the ancient Romans' belief in an evil animating spirit, which struggled with the benign genius over a person's fate. The image of this diabolic genius peculiarly suits our own times, when many clever, powerful, cynical voices insist that a human being is nothing but smart meat in search of more stuff.

All of us use spiritual genius some of the time, but some of us use it all of the time. This book explores our human gift through the lives of such spiritual geniuses, because in them we see our own potential writ large. No matter how extraordinary they seem, these men and women differ from us only quantitatively, not qualitatively. Religion has many names for them—saints, *tzaddiks*, *bodhisattva*s are just a few—and describes them as "holy," or intensely aware of the sacred grand design; as "good," which means not just moral but compassionate; and as "charismatic," or able to inspire others. Using different language, psychology describes the same individuals as visionary leaders who share the respected statesman's altruism and social skills and the artist's capacity for transcendent experience. Their terms may vary, but religion and science agree with Thomas Edison that where the spiritual sort, too, is concerned, "Genius is 1 percent inspiration, 99 percent perspiration."

Each of the geniuses here belongs to one of the world's great spiritual traditions. Religion may not be perfect, but it has recorded our search for life's meaning throughout history, which has saved untold millions from starting the quest from scratch. These men and women vary greatly in both personal and cultural ways. They include a low-key Hindu doctor, a passionate Muslim scholar, a sociable Talmudist, a witty Buddhist hermit, a workaholic Christian social reformer. Despite tremendous differences, however, these spiritual geniuses affect us in three fundamental ways. They focus our attention on a reality that's more than meets the eye. They compassionately teach us by words or example how to find and develop our own special roles in the great sacred scheme of things. And they inspire us by demonstrating the ultimate expression of our human potential.

· : · : · : ·

My fascination with spiritual genius evolved through a convergence of professional and personal interests. As a journalist, I've mostly written about behavioral science, whose ultimate reality is the biochemical universe that lies between our ears. At a certain point, however, I began to see that science certainly has some of the answers to the question of why our lives are the way they are, but not all of them. This sense of something missing got stronger as my pursuit of happiness began to feel more and more like a treadmill. Just like the clichés say, having what we want doesn't satisfy us for long. But how, exactly, do we go about wanting what we have? We've all been told that happiness comes from inside, not outside. But how, exactly, do we stay centered when the external world pulls us in a million different directions? Such questions inevitably raise others that lead to the sense of meaning.

Life's meaning has been variously and wondrously addressed by poetry and philosophy, art and music, but it's the principal focus of religion. Embarrassing as it is to admit, it was only when I began to investigate the great spiritual traditions that I started to wonder about the purpose of my own life—not in the usual sense of fulfilling various roles in the everyday world but from religion's vast perspective. What if anything that was special did I bring to this really big party? Something beyond being a wife, mother, daughter, friend, taxpayer, cat owner? It was an interesting exercise.

After some thought I realized that since childhood some animating spirit has led me to be curious about why we human beings do the things we do. As a little kid I just thought about such matters while riding my bike or sprawled on my bed. In college I studied what literature, philosophy, and psychology had to say about our ways. As an adult I write about human behavior. Suddenly I saw that journalism isn't just an interesting career that pays the bills but my window on and contribution to life's grand design, which creates personal experiences and connections with others that would otherwise be impossible. This isn't rocket science, is it? Anyone—teacher, cabdriver, homemaker, Supreme Court justice—could draw a similar conclusion about his or her work. Since I had this epiphany in a teacup, what I do hasn't changed, but how I do it has. On the surface my life looks the same, but inside everything feels different.

That's not to say that just because I've come to regard it as the science of life's meaning, I don't continue to struggle with religion. In our relentlessly secular culture, many of us have a hard time accepting what lies beyond the grasp of our intellects and senses. We want to understand before we trust. One day, however, an encounter with an anonymous spiritual genius showed me that sometimes we may have to trust before we can understand.

On a hot afternoon in India, I was trudging up a hill, feeling very cross and jet-lagged. When the stooped, aged Buddhist monk teetered toward me, hands outstretched, he seemed like yet another person in a poor country who wanted something. As he drew closer, however, I saw that the monk was offering me a cookie from a small packet. At first I was startled by his generosity. Imagine, a person whose reaction to getting a package of cookies was to go out on the street and start handing them to strangers!

When I met the monk's smiling eyes, however, I saw that I was no stranger—and neither was he. Looking into his face was like peering at the sun, yet I couldn't turn away. I was transfixed in the field of awareness and bliss that radiated from this frail figure.

Without a word, the monk did what spiritual geniuses do: remind others of some things that we somehow just know but sometimes forget. He repaired my fragmented view of life's grand design. He demonstrated that there's more to a person—and more going on—than our sometimes shallow or cynical perceptions suggest. He showed me that the sacred isn't just "up there" or in some afterlife but down here, right now. He revealed the Truth that underlies the truths of different cultures. He offered living proof that practice makes perfect. And he made me want to be more like him.

We bowed and beamed ecstatically for a few moments. Then the little monk continued on his way, offering to all comers—none of them strangers—his cookies and his spiritual genius, which, like a magnet, drew their own to the surface.

. : . : . : .

As Dryden observed, different eras have always been associated with different kinds of genius. In our time the spiritual sort, epitomized by the Nobel Prize–winning Dalai Lama, has a huge and ever-increasing appeal among people of all religions and none. This fascinating if little remarked-upon phenomenon reflects several important postmodern social developments. Following history's bloodiest century, our hopes for this new one have already been shaken by appalling acts of terrorism. We're deeply disillusioned with institutions, including religious ones, but we still hunger for the meaning and authority they once supplied. So, for better or worse, we've created a "culture of celebrity," in which the special individual or expert, rather than an organization, is the most trustworthy medium for any messages, including spiritual ones.

Our interest in spiritual geniuses also reflects our skepticism about the secular religions of science and materialism, a questioning that has helped to make spirituality intellectually respectable again. Contrasted to the secular view of the human being as a genetically programmed "consumer," religion's ancient picture of the agent of free choice and seeker of meaning seems newly attractive. Research showing that religious people tend to live longer, healthier, happier lives only increases that appeal.[2] Like high rates of attendance at worship services, the boom in yoga and meditation practices reflects the growing belief that religion isn't just good but good for us. The serenity and joy that certain spiritual geniuses positively radiate helps affirm that conviction.

Finally, the increasing attention paid to spiritual geniuses reflects global changes—from new emigration patterns to the worldwide reach of the Internet—that make the pursuit of insight from diverse sources the rule. In this new climate of intellectual and cultural openness, it's hard to maintain that only one group owns the truth, including the religious sort. It would have been as inconceivable to my husband's English and Romanian ancestors to look beyond their Protestant and Jewish traditions for spiritual teachings as for my Irish ones to venture outside the Catholic church. Now, Protestants, Jews, and Catholics may hear teachers from other traditions from their own congregations' pulpits or take yoga or Zen classes in their basements. When the student is ready, the teachers appear.

· : · : · : ·

Deciding to explore spiritual genius through the stories of living examples was easy. Selecting them was not. Because so many Westerners now look to the East for religious insights, I wanted to do a considerable amount of reporting in an Asian country. I chose India. The world's most religious nation has fostered many spiritual geniuses from different traditions—from Buddha through Gandhi to Mother Teresa—and it especially captures the West's imagination now. Next, I consulted knowledgeable people within five major religions, and they kindly suggested certain names—often the same ones. I eliminated those who were very well known or who seemed authoritarian or self-absorbed, then based my selections on chemistry as well as credentials. For the same reason, someone else would make different choices. No such list, however, could limit the kinds of spiritual genius or numbers of geniuses; it could only suggest their range.

These profiles reflect not only their subjects' different personalities but their different situations. At a seminary I was able to spend a whole semester studying with a rabbi, for example, but at an ashram I could spend only a short time with an *avatar*. A Sufi in Fez gave me a new respect for the word *ineffable,* while a Pakistani activist's life almost communicated itself over the Internet. In one instance I set out to interview a person and ended up captivated by the flexible, almost organic organization to which she belongs.

I hope that the reader will discover that anonymous monk I met in India—and perhaps a greater appreciation of his or her own spiritual genius—in these pages.

SPIRITUAL GENIUS

1. BROTHER

It's immediately clear that waiting is an agony to Brother James Kimpton, a restless, rangy Englishman uniformed in what look like blue surgical scrubs. His long, lanky frame and fidgetiness give him an adolescent air that belies his seventy-six years. It's barely ten in the morning, but the sun has already turned the flat Western Ghats of Tamil Nadu, one of India's poorest states, into a griddle. Car troubles of a complexity perhaps unique to India have stretched a two-hour trip into four, making me late for our meeting. Having written me off, Brother James is just about to depart in his Jeep to visit a "children's village" for orphans recently built by Reaching the Unreached. This nonsectarian antipoverty organization, which he founded and directs, serves some sixty small villages in the district of Periyakulam.

Brother, as he is called, bids me welcome but clearly wants to get on with it. He beckons me toward the Jeep, but after hours on the road I'm desperate for a washroom. Perhaps offering up this small torment to God, Brother white-knuckles it and leads me to the guest quarters.

James Kimpton belongs to the De La Salle Christian Brothers, a Catholic religious order founded by a seventeenth-century French aristocrat to educate the poor. Brother James, who began his career as a teacher, has spent forty years in India, which is home to a full quarter of the world's poor. The country's average per capita income is $350 per year, half of its children are malnourished, and half of its rural students, particularly girls, drop out of school. Brother is no longer simply an educator, however, any more than he is a traditional missionary who trades goods and services for conversions. He is a pioneer in the ongoing transformation of the whole concept of charity.

Reaching the Unreached, which is supported by both secular and religious sources, neither provides handouts nor proselytizes. Its purpose is to help poor rural communities develop the housing, schools, medical facilities, and employment they need to become self-sufficient. The organization serves and is almost entirely staffed by Hindus, and the only Christian teaching Brother James offers is that of example.

From RTU's headquarters Brother guides me next door to Ambu Illam, or Place of Love. The organization's first children's village is an oasis of trees and gardens that's a stark contrast to the baked barrenness beyond its gates. As we speed-walk down neat paths bordered with flowers, Brother observes that this natural beauty is good for the children, of course, but also demonstrates what elbow grease can do with the area's surprisingly good soil. When I say that Ambu Illam's abundant water, spraying from garden hoses and gushing from faucets, must help, too, Brother explains that he's a diviner. Assisted by donations from the American Society of Dowsers, he has sited and drilled safe deep wells in all RTU's villages. This effort has eliminated not only an enormous amount of disease, he says, but much backbreaking drudgery for women, the poorest of whom often walk miles daily for water.

Orchestrating such benign "twofers" seems to be Brother's specialty. As we tear past some of the thirty whitewashed masonry cottages that house "families" of five or six children, he explains that each is headed by a foster mother, who's usually a widow, abused wife, or other woman who would otherwise be homeless and destitute. This particular twofer illustrates Brother's theory that when a poor community does good by, say, helping orphans and other disadvantaged members, it will also do well, notably by creating much-needed jobs. In addition to the foster mothers, teachers, and health aides who serve RTU's children directly, many others work at producing the textiles, food, building materials, and other goods the organization's programs require. According to Brother's brand of economics, compassion is a growth industry.

Visitors to RTU of necessity experience the ancient Christian monastic tradition of hospitality. There's simply no other place to go. I gratefully make a pit stop in one of Ambu Illam's guest rooms, attractively furnished with a hanging mosquito net, ceiling fan, and hand-loomed bedding made here. Brother himself lives in just such a room across the way.

As soon as I reappear, Brother herds me and some visiting Indian nuns into his Jeep, slams it into reverse, and stomps on the gas. "You learn patience in India," he says, "or you go mad!"

Giggling at her old friend as he jounces us over the dirt road's granitic ruts, one of the nuns adjusts her skirt and says that she, too, works among the poor. She explains her busman's holiday: "I always like to see what Brother is up to!"

From a little distance Miriam Children's Village might be a nicely landscaped, tile-roofed retirement community in Arizona. As soon as the Jeep halts, however, children come running from all directions, squealing, "Tata-ji!" Actually, many Indians of all ages call Brother "Honored Grandfather." As the children struggle to attach themselves to his fortunately long limbs, he greets and jokes with them in rapid-fire Tamil, patting the little girls' heads and playfully swatting at the boys' bottoms. "That one is so naughty!" he says, pointing gleefully to one small, mirthful fellow who seems especially delighted by Tata-ji. Brother's teasing British humor apparently translates well. After a particularly noisy chorus of laughing protests, he explains that he has just said that MCV stands for Mental Children's Village. Pleased by the response, he repeats his jest to renewed hilarity.

The "orphans" of Reaching the Unreached defy ready classification. Some are foundlings in the literal sense, having simply been abandoned in a public place. Others are not strictly alone in the world, but their existing relatives are too poor, sick, or old to care for them. Some arrive as infants, or even in the bellies of their unwed mothers, and others later in childhood. All have been subject to adversity, but some have experienced nearly unimaginable trauma. Three children were orphaned when their father, in a rage, set fire to their mother. As the children watched helplessly, she grabbed him and held on until both were immolated. One child seems to be coping, says Brother, but another has tried to burn herself to death, and the third is in a psychiatric hospital.

To describe the RTU children simply as variously disadvantaged, however, is not to do them justice. Laughing with Tata-ji in the sunshine, they are joyful and, oddly, all beautiful. In their lively, lovely company, it's especially sobering when Brother says that his next project is a similar village for abandoned HIV-positive children. The gravity of India's looming AIDS crisis has been hushed up, he says, and partly because of this secrecy he predicts an epidemic worse than Africa's.

Like a benign Pied Piper, Brother leads a tour past MCV's well-appointed playground—"our psychiatric clinic"—the residential cottages, and the airy community center. Its rear wall features a mural of an Indian-looking Christ painted by a Hindu artist; in this religiously inclusive nation, many non-Christians revere Jesus as one of the world's great spiritual masters. The painting neatly expresses the balance between Brother's pride in his own faith and his deep respect for the people he serves.

In forty years in India Brother has not made a single convert. His nonevangelical stance is partly political, in that it allows him to continue his work despite the Indian government's attitude about foreign missionaries, clearly expressed in its prohibition of new ones. Regarding this policy, Brother says only, "We wouldn't want

Indians telling us how to run things in our Western countries." His aversion to proselytizing, however, runs deeper than mere pragmatism. "Our philosophy is Christian," he says, "and the people know that. They know, too, that we don't try to change anyone's religion. God converts people, not us. We just hope to make people better Hindus, Muslims, or Christians."

The next stops on the MCV tour are the day-care center and kindergarten. Illustrating twoferism, both are open to the local community's children. For them attendance means not only an educational advantage but high-protein meals in a region where some children's black hair is streaked with malnutrition's orange. The MCV kids, too, benefit from this integration with the larger community, which they come to feel is theirs.

On a shady porch some foster mothers offer us the *chai*—spiced tea with milk and sugar seemingly boiled all day—that's inevitably given to guests in India. In the wilting heat hydration is essential, and the ubiquitous steel cups of caffeine and sugar quickly become addictive. Several little girls busy themselves grooming Brother. First they comb his scanty locks, which have the reddish cast his temperament suggests; then they adorn him with a plastic headband. While my forehead is being painted with a *bindi,* or ritual dot, I try to estimate aloud how many millions it would cost in America to build a campus that houses and educates 112 children, accommodates their adult caretakers, and also serves the local community. Brother makes some rapid calculations and announces that MCV cost about $80,000. A dollar goes a long way at RTU, where a child can be maintained on $20 per month and 1,000 sponsors pledging $240 per year would cover the children's entire annual budget. When the subject of adoptions comes up, he says kindly, "I hope you don't mind, but I don't believe in foreign adoptions. We only place our children with Indian couples."

The kids are thrilled by my reporter's notebook and insist on putting down their names—R. Nandini, S. Gomathi, M. Ramya—so that they will be famous. Those too young to write sound out their names emphatically so that they can be recorded as well. One tiny, silent child of about two stays glued to Tata's knee. "She has no one at all," he says, gently stroking her shiny curls. "She was just . . . found."

As I watch Brother with the little foundling, it strikes me that the wonder is not the multitude of orphans he has raised and educated over the decades but his regard for *this* one, right here and now. The sight of this odd couple detonates a culture shock that has nothing to do with being a Westerner in India. Back home religion—or, more often, spirituality—is increasingly an aspect of "personal fulfillment," but to Brother, it's a literal response to Jesus' statement "Whatever you do to the least of my brethren, you do to me." For Brother, *whatever* means not just food, clothing, and shelter but a deep, personal, one-on-one concern that must be called love. This little girl may be just one of thousands of Brother's children, but she clearly knows that he loves her, just as she loves him.

While Brother searches for a video of *Home Alone,* a favorite for the children's weekly movie nights, the visiting nun and I enthuse over the pretty, cheerful village. Her far subtler understanding of poverty shows when she commends the thoughtful way in which the doors and windows of MCV's cottages have been positioned to maximize privacy. When children are raised in a crowded single room, she explains, they grow up with no sense of the human right to solitude—their own or others'. Like Brother James, who provides not just houses and schools but also flowers and fountains, Sister knows that poverty can be a spiritual as well as a material affliction.

· : · : · : ·

We return to the Jeep to bump our way back to Ambu Illam for lunch, passing through villages of the sort that constitute the "real India": the small settlements of one- or two-room thatched or masonry houses, connected by dirt roads and paths, where 75 percent of the population lives. Like many dynamos, Brother James is easiest to interview when he's allowed to do something else at the same time, even if it's only driving. Behind the wheel he recounts a little of his history in the region. It began with drilling wells, which allowed him to meet the villages' elders and discuss their priorities, which he found highly sensible. Brother grins, recollecting how the old men told him, "Don't think you're doing anything so grand, after the way you British oppressed us!"

The elders' first concern was medical care. In response, RTU established a clinic that now immunizes all local children and treats 250 patients daily. In addition, each affiliated village chooses a health worker and midwife, who are trained to handle routine problems; these aides are supplied and backed up by mobile clinics, which treat some complicated cases and refer others to the right facilities. Initially, leprosy was the region's leading scourge, says Brother, but since its eradication the main health problem is tuberculosis, which will likely be replaced by AIDS.

The village elders' next concerns were employment, education, and housing. For the ride's duration, Brother switches hats from diviner and public health administrator to architect-planner—a role he seems particularly to relish. To him a decent home is not just a physical necessity but a spiritual requirement. He proudly points out some of the 6,500 free houses that RTU has built for about $500 apiece. Each handsome masonry cottage is designed in the regional style and includes a porch, large central room, and cooking ell. There's a bathing area, Brother explains, but no toilet, which is thought too unclean to be inside a dwelling. The criterion for qualifying for a free home is simple: whether or not Brother could live in the family's present house—usually a decrepit hut mostly open to the elements—for one day. When applicants profess interest in Christianity, Brother smells a rat. "Usually, they just think it will help them to get a new home," he says. "It won't."

A decent place to live "makes a good start," says Brother, but long experience has taught him that there's no single quick fix for poverty. This is especially true in India, where many of the poor are further stigmatized by belonging to the lowest castes, or social classes. This ancient system of discrimination has weakened with regard to employment but still consigns many Indians to substandard housing that's often a punitively long distance from water, schools, and other services. When it took on the challenge of a small village called Samiyarmoopanur, whose inhabitants are low-caste agricultural workers, for example, Reaching the Unreached drilled two wells, then provided the community with ninety new homes, a day-care center, and a grain-drying floor. "You can't just do housing," says Brother. "Or water, or medical. You have to address all aspects of a village's development—the whole thing." One of Samiyarmoopanur's most important new buildings is its meeting hall. As soon as possible in RTU villages, says Brother, "the people run things themselves." He regards this emphasis on self-determination as a major reason for the organization's longevity and success. "There might be a little slump at first when the villagers take over the administration from us," he says, "but then things go fine."

· : · : · : ·

Brother James lives like a Tamil, so there's very little furniture in the room where, along with visitors, he takes his simple Indian meals. In a concession to Western joints, however, low benches line the walls, which are hung with very fine portraits of RTU children done by Brother, who began his career as an art teacher.

We serve ourselves from a sideboard, and Brother makes sure we salt our spicy food to ward off dehydration. Only someone made of very stern stuff would fail to comply. The mail brings Brother a photo magazine filled with shots of scenic England, which evoke some reminiscences of his life before India.

Brother was the second of five children in a Catholic family and grew up in Chester. He likes to say that he was "born in the church," because when his father and pregnant mother were traveling in search of employment, a priest took them in—just in time for young James's arrival. He "always knew" that he had a religious vocation. He became a lay brother rather than a priest, who can say mass and administer sacraments, because he was deeply impressed by a De La Salle brother who visited his school. "He was so tall and aristocratic and charismatic that I was hooked," says Brother. "Perhaps if someone from another order had come, I would have joined that one instead!" At thirteen, with his parents' blessing,

James Kimpton began his religious training in a monastery on the isle of Guernsey.

In the De La Salle tradition, Brother has devoted his life to children. When his training was completed in 1952, he left Europe for Sri Lanka, where he taught, eventually becoming a headmaster. As a skilled calligrapher and printmaker, he was able to start a school for deaf, mute, and blind children, who learned the printing trade while operating a successful press. In 1964, however, a new government dismissed all foreigners from Sri Lanka. Brother resettled in India at Madurai, an ancient Tamil city about ninety minutes from RTU. "Something just clicked," he says. "I knew I had come home." He founded a huge orphanage in Madurai, based on the Nebraska Boys Town model, but soon began to dream about a new kind of work in the rural villages.

One Sunday after mass the priest confronted Brother with four orphans, whose father had just starved to death trying to feed the already motherless children. Brother explained that Boys Town couldn't accept a family that included girls.

When he was halfway home on his motorbike, Brother says, a voice told him to go back for the children. In the tradition of innumerable biblical figures who heard this voice, he first reacted by protesting that he simply wasn't able to do what was being asked. "Hire a woman to do it!" said the voice. "Go back!" From those four destitute children, says Brother, "we now have five hundred." His initial rejection of the orphans taught him a powerful lesson: "Institutions build invisible walls. We must look over them to discover people's real needs. Sometimes, we just don't *see.*"

Later I meet with Brother in the RTU office. For someone from a culture in which young children and the aged are increasingly consigned to "caregivers," it's hard to imagine being him even for a day. He's the guy everyone for miles around calls with the bad news. Battered woman? Disabled orphan? Tubercular HIV-positive husband? Abandoned widow? Find Brother James! When I ask him how he copes with the seemingly bottomless need, he gives a little sigh. "We just keep taking what we see under our noses," he says, "and doing what the government asks." He's encouraged by the fact that RTU has greatly improved the quality of life in the surrounding villages. His main resource, however, is spiritual. Without time for prayer, Brother says simply, "I couldn't go on." Adopting the biblical prescription for charity, he "tithes" 10 percent of the day for his personal religious life, which includes mass at 5:45 A.M. "Prayer refreshes me," he says, "and gives me the grace to step into the dark."

Brother is too busy living the gospel twenty-four/seven to talk about religion much. When pressed, however, he speaks about God as simply and unself-consciously as if describing his next-door neighbor. When I ask if he often feels "guided," he says that one day, before RTU's real growth spurt, he was standing on a hillside surveying some of the organization's first houses. Suddenly, he says, "Christ was standing next to me. It was as if we were one, with these streams going out from us. Christ said—said in my mind—'You will reach out as far as you can see.' I said, 'No, Lord! How can I do that?' He said, 'You will.' I said, 'Lord, does it have to have anything to do with religion?' He said, 'No. Just do as you're doing things now.'" Brother describes this experience as "almost a vision" and allows he has had "two or three" like it.

· : · : · ·

Brother James personifies many ingredients in the alchemy of genius in general and the spiritual sort in particular.[1] Behavioral research shows that—along with intelligence, ability, and a maverick creativity—extraordinary achievers of all kinds share certain personality traits. These include independence, curiosity, and a healthy ego, of course, but especially a tremendous drive that fuels their seemingly superhuman dedication to their work. As Thomas Carlyle put it, genius is "the transcendent capacity of taking trouble, first of all."

Where spiritual genius is concerned, the inclination toward prayer and meditation that religion regards as a sign of holiness is an expression of the capacity for transcendence that also allows poets, musicians, painters, and cyber-whizzes to "lose" themselves in "a different world," in which "time stands still." Spiritual geniuses who are particularly drawn to contemplative practice are known as mystics. Mysticism, which emphasizes direct awareness of and communion with the sacred, is especially esteemed in the East, but all religions have forms of it. The Christian *unio mystico* described by Brother, Jewish *devekut,* Muslim *fana,* Hindu *samadhi,* and Zen *kensho* manifest the same intense consciousness of ultimate reality's underlying unity and goodness.

If spiritual geniuses share certain tendencies with artists and "dreamers," they're able to put their special visions of reality into practice and enlist others to help because of traits they share with beloved politicians, coaches, and executives. Like these "can-do" secular leaders, they're great communicators who are gifted with warmth, altruism, confidence, ambition, optimism, magnetism, and other-directedness. Spiritual geniuses who strongly express these qualities, which religion calls goodness and charisma, seem less like mystics and more like social activists—a type epitomized by Brother and greatly favored in the West. Still other spiritual geniuses are, like Francis of Assisi and Gandhi, mystic activists or activist mystics, who resemble the medieval Sufi master described by a contemporary thus: "He had something about him that won the hearts of children. But kings, too, sought to gain his friendship."

· : · · : ·

One morning Brother James inspects 488 elementary and secondary students hurrying to the main RTU campus for a weekly assembly. (Toddlers and preschoolers have their own day-care facilities, where the malnourished soon grow plump on special high-protein "health food.") In a few minutes they'll gather to raise the flag, sing the national anthem, say multicultural prayers, and hear reports from the class leaders. "If they're not neatly dressed with their hair combed," says Brother gleefully, "I send them right back home!"

Brother James carries on the De La Salle order's prescient tradition, admired by the American educator Horace Mann, of using education to empower the poor. RTU's students master the principles of personal finance in the school's own bank, for example, and girls as well as boys learn electrical wiring. The typical youngster graduates from high school, then goes on to professional education in a field such as nursing, teaching, or engineering. Slower children receive vocational training so that they too can be as self-sufficient as possible. Girls receive dowries, which they may keep, regardless of marriage, after completing their education. Many of the boys and girls raised together eventually marry—weddings involve six hundred guests feted over three days—and produce "RTU grandchildren."

Brother introduces Mr. Ilango, a warm, inventive Hindu educator who's one of RTU's three top managers. All two thousand boys and girls who are served by the organization are under his aegis, but he has a special bond with the residents of the children's villages. Calling them "very sensitive," Mr. Ilango says, "They always want love. We try to help them get over their backgrounds by giving them foster mothers, trees, flowers, and other nice things. We make sure they're always busy and never lonely, because that makes them sad. We can't pamper them, but stern words can make them withdraw for days."

As far as Mr. Ilango is concerned, his main responsibility is to be an "*appa*—a father." He describes one boy who wept bitterly when anyone asked about his father but wouldn't or couldn't explain why. "I told him that I was his father now," says Mr. Ilango, "and that when anyone inquired, he should say that his father works in the RTU education office. That made him feel much better." Slowly increasing opportunities for poor women have inadvertently helped create a new kind of gender crisis: the marginalization of men who can't or won't work and the consequent breakup of their families. For an increasing number of children, says Mr. Ilango, "Brother and I are the only male role models."

In the West sexism can seem academic, but in India it's an everyday matter of life and death. Mr. Ilango escorts me to a meeting where RTU's village health aides, proudly wearing their special violet saris, are discussing a particularly gruesome problem: female infanticide. Girls' second-class status derives from the fact that they require a dowry and then become their husbands' families' property; boys are their parents' social security, but girls are financial drains. Poor village women particularly suffer the consequences, including domestic violence, which is very common but rarely reported or prosecuted. The most notorious example is "bride-burning," in which women who have displeased their husbands or in-laws are "accidentally" incinerated in their kitchens after being doused with "spilt" kerosene.

Of all Indian females, however, the youngest and most helpless are the most endangered. India is among the few nations that has more male than female births. In cities many parents who can afford the prenatal testing meant to detect birth defects use it to determine a fetus's gender, then abort the females. In the villages, where an infant's sex is revealed only at birth, unwanted newborn girls are poisoned—or even throttled, burned, or buried alive. The rationale often given is that it's "better to suffer a short time than for a whole life as a girl."

One of the RTU health workers rescued a baby girl from death just a week ago. "People criticize families that have too many daughters," she says. "They ask the parents, 'How can you manage?'" Another aide says that in her village the husbands insist on the killings, which are carried out by women—usually not the mother. Recently, she says, a baby girl was given an overdose of a sedative; then her family maintained that she had gotten sick and died. "This was a crime," says the aide, "but it was covered up by the whole village."

Later, when I talk with Brother about the health aides' meeting, it's clear that he sees kindred spirits in the hardworking, child-oriented village women. To assist them in feeding their families, RTU not only employs many women but also promotes schemes to help them earn—and protect—money. In one village, for example, thirty women formed a self-help group and saved upwards of $600, which they loan to each other in small amounts at very low interest to support their cottage industries.

My tour of RTU's educational facilities ends with a visit to a source of the real hope for rural Indian women. The Girls' Hostel is one of two such boarding schools for secondary students, whose families pay a tuition of thirty cents per month. The bright-eyed teenagers in their flowing *choridors* beam upon hearing about the stunning success of Indians in the global computer industry, which has recently established a stronghold in Bangalore.

One the way back to the guest quarters, I stop to chat with one of RTU's managers. "Brother is our guru," this Hindu says. "Our teacher in our hearts. He reaches the God within us, the God inside people. Here, there was no concept of helping someone for no reason. But Brother always says that when we serve the people, we serve God."

· : · · : · ·

At dinnertime I joke with Brother about treating him to a nice steak; then we head for the dining hall. There are several European visitors, including a German college student who's something of a religious seeker. His remarks remind me that, in the West, rather than Christianity's "corporal works of mercy," such as feeding and housing the poor, the growth industry is in the spiritual mercies, which include comforting the sorrowful and counseling the doubtful. Like him, I'm experiencing one of the underremarked revelations of a trip to India. Despite our material prosperity, Europeans and Americans often hunger for a sense of life's meaning and community in a way that many poor Indians do not.

When the conversation turns to comparative religion, the German youth describes his eclectic experiences, including a Zen retreat, which required extensive periods of meditation each day. "You mean you just sit there for hours and do nothing?" says Brother incredulously. "I'd hate that!" Someone else mentions a very famous Indian guru of mixed repute. Brother laughs. "I stay away from him!" he says. "He gets in people's heads!" I confess to feeling overwhelmed by India's throbbing, syncretic, omnipresent spirituality, which seems to relativize and blur religious distinctions. Hinduism is renowned not only for its genius in incorporating elements of other religions but also for influencing them. Just as it gave birth to Buddhism in the sixth century B.C.E., it's the wellspring of the vast modern movement known as the New Age.

I ask Brother if he's still the same traditional Catholic he was when he arrived forty years ago. He says, "Yes."

Considering his actions-speak-louder Christianity and orthodox theology, it's somewhat surprising when Brother contributes fond recollections of Father Bede Griffiths. For some thirty years before his recent death, this Oxford-educated British Benedictine monk lived and taught in India at his Ashram of the Holy Trinity. Father Bede is admired by New Agers for his explorations of the underlying unity of the world's religions and his efforts to combine Eastern philosophy and Christianity. Nonetheless, Brother describes Father Bede as "a wonderful man—a scholar—who ran a good ashram that mostly attracted Indian students. He was Christian, but *Indian* Christian. The church hasn't done well here because it has been too Westernized."

His restless temperament, British reserve, and infinite to-do list must sometimes make socializing a trial to him, but Brother is a considerate host who's particularly zealous about his visitors' rest and hydration. He chats for a while longer, but inevitably his seemingly continual awareness that somewhere nearby someone is miserable and he could help breaks through. India's vast population makes it easy to think in generic terms, such as "the poor." Brother, however, thinks about individuals—the foundling at MCV, the baby just rescued from infanticide, the mother of eight who cut up the wedding sari that was her only possession to make little skirts for her naked daughters. To him these aren't "cases" of "suffering humanity" but particular persons whose fate preys on his mind.

All day Brother has been preoccupied by a sickly, destitute woman who just smiled when he asked why she hadn't taken her blind children to a doctor. "Her face was so hopeless!" he says. Looking strained, he adds that in India the combination of so many problems and no resources can make suicide seem like "an easy way out." From his concern anyone would think he was brooding over one of his family and, of course, he is.

This particular woman belongs to an impoverished group that's so far down on the social scale they don't even have a caste. India's

50 million dark-skinned indigenous folk, known as Adivasis, come from the same stock as Australia's aborigines. Many speak their own languages and practice their own animistic variations on Hinduism. For thousands of years they lived in peace in remote wooded regions of no interest to farmers. In the past few decades, however, India's soaring population has created an agricultural expansion that has consigned many Adivasis to what amounts to slavery. The blind children's mother, for example, is one of ninety tribal people who had been illegally "bonded" to a rich landowner. They were forced to work to reduce loans they could not repay—sometimes for generations—because of exorbitant interest. A government official finally discovered the group, who had been hidden away in the jungle. Reaching the Unreached was asked to help them make new lives on a piece of ground donated by the Forest Service.

In India there are many shades of "poor," some of which are much more tolerable than others. Brother explains that this group of tribal people isn't just impoverished but utterly destitute. Enslaved, malnourished, illiterate, sickly, hopeless, despised, isolated, limited to close intermarriage, they have been unable to lead human lives. Two weeks ago they moved into twenty-five houses built for them by RTU. Tomorrow, says Brother, we'll visit their new village, bringing clothes, food, and soap. "I should be beyond shock by now," he says, "but I was shocked by these people."

· : · : · : ·

En route to the new tribal village, we stop to buy a hundred kilos of rice. The money comes from Brother's emergency kitty, which somehow, he says, almost but never quite runs out. "I never worry about the financial side," he says. "If you're doing God's work, money just comes, as does a good staff. God will provide."

Much like welfare in America, charity has become a controversial matter in India. By the end of her long career, social changes in the developing world meant that even Mother Teresa was criticized for encouraging the poor's dependence and passivity. Brother James could be the poster boy for empowerment, but even he insists that sometimes old-fashioned charity is necessary. As usual, for him this is not an abstract idea but one that calls to mind two children who were recently hospitalized too late to prevent their deaths from starvation. "Once they're established, with homes and some sheep and a school for the children," he says, "poor families here do well. But, like these tribal people, they may need some help getting started."

The mention of Mother Teresa evokes Brother's fond recollections of his old friend, for whom he built a women's shelter in Madurai. "People criticize charity," he says. "But destitute dying women? Or our beautiful HIV-positive children, who die in weeks? Someone has to do that work. Mother Teresa's way was to attend to such immediate needs. If she saw a person who needed something, she'd leave a conversation with a bishop." With some amusement Brother recalls watching Mother Teresa cut off the philosophizing of a trendy theologian midsentence with a brisk "Thank you, Father!" He remembers, too, the toll exacted by her ceaseless work: " 'I'm so tired,' she once said to me. 'I want to go to heaven so I can rest.' " Offering his ultimate compliment, Brother says, "There was no nonsense about Mother Teresa. Nothing soft at all!"

In a very Western way, Christianity celebrates such heroic individuals. Its veneration of exceptional men and women as saints dates from the patristic era (200 to 500 C.E.), when the tombs and relics of early martyrs, such as Stephen, were enshrined and honored. The assumption that if anyone attained salvation it would be the person who died for the faith was seemingly confirmed by portentous signs, especially healings, near the martyrs' bones. (There are parallels between pagan hero worship and the veneration of the saints, but the Christians' new enthusiasm for things associated with death, such as graves and relics, greatly disturbed pious Romans, as well as Jews.) Miracles also suggested that the saints—real people who were now with God—were ideal go-betweens for human beings wishing to approach the divine.

As Christianity became increasingly respectable, its concept of sainthood broadened. The pious were no longer persecuted, so they gave up life's comforts rather than life itself. Replacing martyrdom with asceticism, some Christians left the cities and their earthly things behind in order to "die to the world." Their monastic communities developed a new vocation that combined personal spirituality, based on prayer and an austere way of life, with social service, particularly to the poor so markedly favored by Jesus. The martyr's heroic death was replaced by a life of "heroic virtue," exemplified by Mother Teresa and Brother James.

A drive in rural India, on roads shared with *saddhus* (wandering ascetics) and elephants, trucks decorated with goddesses and bullocks with gaily decorated horns, can be a surprisingly pleasant experience that a friend describes as "rolling *prana*"—life force. As we pass through villages that have been involved with RTU over time, it's easy to see the organization's enduring effect on the region. Compared with neighboring raggedy villages, the RTU communities have a prosperous, settled look that bespeaks the residents' sense of responsibility about maintaining the organization's standards.

On a beaten track that passes for a road, we stop in a small jungle village. An indescribably unsanitary *chai* stall is pleasantly situated in a clearing embellished by a shrine and large paintings of a lion and a guru. As the proprietor pours, Brother advises sotto voce, "Don't look at the shop, just the tea." It's not exactly a café on a Roman piazza, yet something of the same gay *dolce vita* air obtains. The local men hanging about are pleased to see Tata-ji and schmooze with him in Tamil. As I cautiously sip, he breezes through one of India's numerous lively daily journals, which fearlessly juxtapose headlines such as MAN USES TRAIN TO AMPUTATE LEG with reports on the latest doings in Bollywood and commentary on the Vedas, Hinduism's oldest scriptures.

Back in the Jeep, we head toward a distant mountain range. Atop one of the peaks is Kodaikanal, a lovely hill station in the cool, misty tea country that might be on a different planet from the blazing ghats. Kody is an old missionary town, and Brother James looks forward to his visits there each year during Holy Week. The displaced tribal people's village is nestled in a pretty spot by a river that offers a nice view of the mountains. The white masonry houses trimmed with chrome yellow paint sparkle in the sunshine. After a brief tour, however, one notices that this brand-new place has the air of a ghost town, seeming more haunted than lived in. Inside the houses there might be a few scraps of cloth, a plastic bucket, a tin pot holding a little plain rice, but none of the food stores or personal things that turn four walls into a home.

The thin, listless men and women who live here seem like ghosts, too. Breast milk gives most of the babies a healthy look, but some children's hair is raked with orange. Brother first calls on the desperate woman whom he has been brooding about. His quick inspection shows that the beautiful three-month-old daughter is not merely blind: she has no eyes at all. He's more hopeful about the older sister, who has one eye that might respond to surgery.

Brother is right. These people are shocking. Their reaction to the gifts of rice and masala, clothes and soap suggests something of the gulf that separates them from society. Far from becoming excited, even pushy, they remain passive, almost indifferent, when the RTU staff begins opening the sacks and boxes of goods for distribution. Even when the staff members pile the new shorts and saris in their arms, they are subdued. The sight of people so unaccustomed to getting or having that they aren't even greedy stuns me. "They can't understand why anyone would help them," explains Brother quietly. "After all, no one ever has."

As the mother of the two blind daughters receives her goods, Brother says, "Her children will need special schools if they're to have a real life. But just out of the jungle, she couldn't even consider that kind of separation yet! Even getting them to a doctor will be delicate." He shakes his head again over "that look of hopelessness in her eyes." (Brother's anxiety was justified. The woman would die within the year; RTU placed her older daughter in a school for the blind and the baby with a personal "grandmother" at Ambu Illam.)

The people take their new goods, including the makings of a decent supper, to their houses, then return to the new community hall. Their shy smiles suggest both lighter spirits and the effort of assimilating the huge changes they're undergoing. Even in this battered community, a few individuals already stand out as more than mere survivors. The spunk of one happy-go-lucky little boy, wearing only a colored thread, has already attracted Brother's admiration. An older woman, who arrives on the scene balancing on her head a day's work—a huge load of firewood that will bring her a dollar—has the gravitas of the mother of the Gracchi. She's emerging as one of the group's leaders, says Brother, and has already spoken publicly about their plight.

Despite his private worries for them, Brother sits on the hall's stoop, joking and laughing with his new loved ones. His joviality is partly motivated by the fact that he wants the villagers to get to know and trust him, so they'll accept his help and advice, particularly about the medical care that will at first inevitably alarm them. But his sunny mien also reflects the South Indian people's tonic effect on him. When he teases the tribal women that tonight they must make "cockroach curry," they at least pretend to be greatly amused at his wit. He plays with the children, tickling chins and ruffling hair (long habit keeps his hands from straying to his own face—an easy route to dysentery). Learning that one little girl is called Pushparani, he beams at her. " 'Queen of the flowers'! I think that's such a lovely name." She beams back.

After even a short time in Brother's company, it's impossible not to wonder what a man of so many parts would have become in "the world." Architect, entrepreneur, designer, economist, painter, doctor, expert on social service or education? Somehow, by making a career out of serving others, he has become all of those things, and something else as well. I ask one of RTU's top Hindu administrators how the district's people regard Brother James. "They say that Brother is a living god," he says, as if stating the obvious. "Who else would do such things?"

Brother James may not be Jesus, but he's the next best thing. The children who once seemed destined for slavery and who are already clustering around Tata-ji on the steps will grow up in a world their parents can't yet imagine. When they face prejudice in the larger community, they'll have a powerful brother to defend them. They won't be hungry. They'll be clean and clothed. They'll be immunized and when they get sick they'll receive treatment. The handicapped will have the necessary surgery, rehabilitation, special education. All the children will read and write, and some will go to college. Because of James Kimpton, they will live as human beings.

2. TEACHER

A postcard-perfect New England village, dominated by a classic white church on the green, isn't the first place one would expect to find a Jewish mystic. On a bright winter day, however, I drive around Sudbury, Massachusetts, looking for its teacher of Kabbalah, and eventually end up at a gray clapboard Yankee version of a *shul*.

Congregation Beth El is a Reform synagogue named for the place where Jacob had his famous dream of a ladder. Much of the building seems to be a bright, modern, progressive school. Beth El's reputation for serious study as well as affecting liturgy attracted so many Jews from the greater Boston area that the congregation feared for its sense of community and voted to limit membership. Here, religious education starts before kindergarten and extends through high school into adulthood. For almost thirty sometimes tumultuous years, Lawrence Kushner has been Beth El's day-in, day-out shirtsleeves rabbi, or "teacher." Beyond Sudbury, Rabbi Kushner is well-known for his teaching and writing about Jewish spirituality. *Invisible Lines of Connection* and *The Way into Jewish Mystical Tradition* are unambiguously Jewish books, yet they speak to anyone who has ever had an intimation of the sacred.

Rabbi Kushner, a fair, trim, quick man who looks younger than his fifty-six years, waves me into his office. I hand him a brown bag that greasily encloses two muffins, purchased at the restaurant where I've just had a pleasant lunch. In many years of reporting I've never brought a gift to a "source" before and can't imagine why I'm doing so now. The rabbi says they'll come in handy the next morning, when he must head for the airport first thing.

Before long I'll see the muffins as an illustration of one of the rules for the game of life that Rabbi Kushner has discerned: There are no accidents. Maybe the whole point of my driving six hours to meet with him today was to bring these muffins. Maybe he's sick of cereal and eggs, but if he skips breakfast tomorrow he might be grumpy to the stranger seated next to him on the plane who needs to talk with him. As far as the rabbi is concerned, in the game of life everything is here for a reason and connected to everything else. To win, you have to figure out why things are as they are, how they're connected, and what it all means for you. You get points not only for puzzling out the big picture but also for helping others to do so. All great religions offer strategies for playing the game, and in the rabbi's opinion Judaism's ultimate guide is Kabbalah, a system of mystical theology.

Before our meeting I'd heard many things about Rabbi Kushner. "He's a strange bird," said a prominent American rabbi. "Sells Hasidic mysticism to Reform Jews. A *tzaddik,* maybe." "His stuff about light is really great," said a priest. "He really knows what he's talking about." "I like him," said a man who belongs to Beth El. "He has a lot of energy." The man's wife said, "He could be more of a people person."

Five minutes into the interview, all of the above seem potentially true. Rabbi Kushner says his job is "helping people make sense of life's transformative moments by using ritual, prayer, and study. I also help them come together in their common quest for the presence of the holy. Really, what I do is teach Torah." Specifically, the term refers to the five Books of Moses, which Orthodox Jews regard as God-given revelation; broadly, Torah also includes the whole body of Judaism's classical scholarship, much of it collected in the Talmud. "For other people, words only approximate reality, but for Jews, words create reality."

Rabbi Kushner's reputation as something of an iconoclast is rooted in a view of his duties that harks back to an earlier time. "Many of the rabbis I grew up with were baby kissers who worked the room and glad-handed," he says. "I was repulsed by that! I don't go to parties—even bar mitzvah or wedding receptions. There's an older, nobler rabbinic tradition in which the rabbi stays put and the people come so they can learn together, and that's what I do."

As rabbis are wont to do, he stops to tell a story. This one concerns Beth El's preschool religion class, which was meeting with him in the sanctuary. "I wanted to take out the Torah to show them, but we ran out of time," he says. "I told them that next week I'd open the curtains that hang in front of the ark and show them something really special. Back in their classroom, they talked about what this thing could be. One kid—the rationalist intellectual—said, 'Nothing.' But another said, 'A giant mirror.'" The rabbi laughs. "In fact, that's what I teach—that the sacred text *is* a mirror, because you meet yourself in it, as Abraham or Miriam or the mountain or the sacrifice or even the pharaoh."

At high-minded Beth El, even the ridiculous can be sublime. Rabbi Kushner produces a Hanukkah T-shirt that was designed by David Mamet, who also contributed to this year's Purim play. The shirt shows a cartoon drawing of a droll reindeer and the Hebrew letter *aleph*. I stare at it blankly until the rabbi obligingly sings "Rudolph the Red-Nosed Reindeer," stressing the phrase "aleph the other reindeer."

It's not often that a clergyperson stays in one place for thirty years. I ask the rabbi what he has learned from all that time on the job. "It's your ego, stupid!" he says. "God is mysteriously the source of our true self, which is mirrored in the heavens, but we can't possibly understand that until we learn how to let go of our egoistic self. In being swallowed up by the divine—either through mystical union or by taking on the yoke of the law—we retreat from ego and find God. The funny thing is that it's only when you let go that you get it."

Among well-educated people trained to be skeptical, such as many of the rabbi's congregants, religion in general and God in particular are often challenging subjects. Concerning the latter, says Rabbi Kushner, "the problem is the idea of the all-powerful God up there and us down here. I try to help people see that that model is seriously flawed. The Hasidic 'heresy' is *Alles ist Gott*— it's all God."

Suddenly, as I'm scribbling in my notebook, the rabbi morphs from a genial clergyman who might be mistaken for a college professor into a firebrand from the Bible's books of the prophets. His face flushes, his eyes glitter, he leans forward. "God is in everything!" he kind of yells at me. "Do you hear me?" My startled nod fails to assure him. He reaches over and starts flicking my notebook with his pen. "God is in this! In everything! There's nothing 'up there' to see, because we're *within* the divine! God is 'the one through whom being is made'! We don't try to have a 'relationship with' God! We try to become aware of our presence within the divine!"

Not with but within God. At least for the few moments that I'm able to hold the huge thought, there are words for something sensed but seemingly beyond articulation. I wish I could find a quiet place to think, maybe with a cold compress on my head. This is an interview, however, not a retreat, so I ask the rabbi how he tries to convey this mystical vision of God.

First, Rabbi Kushner mentions some ways that God *can't* be communicated. It's bad enough, he says, that we must resort to words to try to materialize the sacred, but images—the damage done by movies such as *The Ten Commandments*! His favorite teaching tools are stories, repetitive movement, and melodies. It's not that these three staples of organized religion produce astounding new insights but that they remind us of what we know down deep but forget or can't quite express. "There's nothing religious that I need to tell you that's a surprise," he says. "The question is whether you can construct and say it to yourself in a way that makes you realize it's true and real in your life. That's religion's job—to hit us in the forehead with a brick."

If that's the job, I think, here is the man for it.

"There are only a finite number of great religious ideas," says the rabbi, "and I think that every religion has them all." He points to a picture of him and the Dalai Lama. When they met, says the rabbi, "he said to me, 'Who wrote the first Torah?' That's the whole kazoo! I said, 'Black fire on white fire,' then winked. He smiled. He got it! The different traditions are exciting and beautiful. Your degree of religious tolerance is a barometer of your spiritual development. If you're secure, you like to do religion with everyone."

Before I leave, Larry, as he says I may call him, invites me to visit his class for rabbinic students at Manhattan's Hebrew Union College Jewish Institute of Religion. Philosophy/Theology 158 is described as "Introduction to Kabbalah: Elements of a Personal Jewish Mystical Worldview."

By the time I leave snowy Sudbury, I know a lot about Larry Kushner, because this Gestalt, what-you-see-is-what-you-get interview is the way he plays the game. He's fast, intense, humorous, impatient—even irritable. Most of all, he's ready to share life's deepest secrets—"the whole kazoo"—with anyone who has ears to hear.

· : · : · : ·

A few weeks later I head to Greenwich Village to attend Larry's first class. In the seminary's handsome modern building on the NYU campus, fifteen students, mostly youngish men and women preparing for ordination, are gathered around a long conference table. Larry looks professorial in tweed jacket and challis tie, complemented by the kind of Middle Eastern cap that seems to have become more fashionable than the smaller yarmulke. He apologizes for the grisly hour of 8:00 A.M., adding that "for this material, midnight would be more appropriate." When someone asks how he gets to New York on time for class, Larry says, "I channel down from Boston the night before."

Kabbalah is an esoteric system of interpreting the Bible. By its lights, the scriptures' every word and letter, number and accent, has a hidden meaning that must be pulled out of the text. In Exodus, for example, there are three verses in a row each of which has seventy-two letters; not coincidentally, God's mysterious real name is thought to have seventy-two letters. Esoteric knowledge of such things is said to confer miraculous powers on those who possess it. In this course, however, the emphasis is not on secret formulas but on Kabbalah as a tradition that balances Judaism's formal, legalistic dimension with mystical spirituality.

Kabbalah's principal text is the Zohar, which was written by Moses de León in the thirteenth century but is based on much older oral teachings originating with the Bible. According to this tradition, our souls—indeed, all things in the universe—are "emanations" from God. The closer each of these divine fragments is to its source, the greater its goodness; the farther away, the greater its potential for evil. By cultivating certain virtues, we can both move our own souls closer to God and advance the cosmic goal of gathering all the emanations back into divine unity.

Kabbalah's golden age was the medieval era. Between 1500 and 1800, says Larry, even average Jews were as familiar with the Zohar as with the Talmud. Like religious traditions generally, Kabbalah was influenced by other ways of thinking—particularly Neoplatonic philosophy and Gnosticism—and has also been influential outside Judaism. For example, Christian scholars of the fifteenth century studied Kabbalah, discovering what they interpreted as references to the Trinity and Jesus' death. Gradually a popular form of this mystical tradition degenerated into a kind of magic in which letters and numbers were used to predict the future or ward off evil—much as they are by today's pop Kabbalists. At the Enlightenment, when the West embraced rationalism, mainstream Judaism disparaged Kabbalah as shameful superstition: hocus-pocus nonsense and folklore about golems. From that time to this, outside the Hasidic citadels of Eastern Europe, Jewish mysticism remained tainted.

Many American Jews are unaware of Judaism's mystical spirituality. When he was a rabbinical student in the 1960s, Larry says, he had to learn about Kabbalah through independent study. The subject simply wasn't taught in respectable seminaries. To help explain why, he reads from a text by an eminent late-nineteenth-century Jewish historian who calls mysticism a "new sect" and "a daughter of gloom," and derides the Hasidic mystic masters as dirty, backward, and disgusting. "This is the guy who set the tone for twentieth-century Jewish thought about mysticism and spirituality," says Larry. "So it's not surprising to hear Jews say, 'We don't have that mystical stuff.' Historically, however, Kabbalah was mainstream."

Larry shows us a 1790 edition of the Zohar, which he found in a pile of rubbish in the back of a synagogue. He calls the work a "magical mystery tour of a novel that describes encounters with all these weird people—donkey drivers and panhandlers—who spout wisdom, then disappear. Encounters in which people's brains are freed." This freedom comes from mysticism's assertion that "the world's apparent brokenness conceals a hidden unity," says Larry. "Religion is an organized way to remind us of that. At least what I call 'disorganized' religion is about that. It's a spiritual anarchy that says we should trust everyone at every moment."

As the old book is passed around the table, certain faces reflect mainstream Judaism's ambivalence about Kabbalah. Larry responds by underscoring that mysticism "is one way you can do a religion. The mystic brings to the tradition some heightened stuff. But mysticism can't be done outside a tradition. You study Kabbalah only after Bible and Talmud and observing the tradition."

To signal the end of introductory small talk, Larry leads us in a few minutes of singing a wordless, lai-lai-lai-lai Hebrew melody. Then it's time for study, which in Judaism is always done in reference to a text. The students work on a passage from the Zohar, which was written in Aramaic, an ancient cognate of Hebrew. Finally, one guy raises his hand and translates, "It is the light of the eye." The words send Larry off on one of his big themes.

In Genesis, on the first day, God says, "Let there be light." This primordial light, created before the sun, is central to Kabbalah. As

Larry puts it, "After the big bang, there was only this electro-magnetic energy. When the hidden of all hidden wanted to reveal itself, there went out from it a thought, which made a point, an Einsteinian singularity. A holy hidden spark, a dot of light, which was eventually trapped in gross matter, as in $E=mc^2$. The sun, the moon, Adam—everything was contained in this light, which is all. The sum of all knowledge." Larry pauses while we struggle with these huge ideas, then says, "A mystic wants to see and know what God sees and knows."

Another student translates the next bit of text: "Lift up your eyes to the heavens to see who created them." When the mystic looks to where the Hubble telescope finds God's fingerprint, he or she asks the ultimate question, says Larry: " 'Who?' The answer is the ancient hidden one, clothed in radiance, who made the whole world because He wanted to. God! But there's nothing to see! The infrastructure of creation and all knowledge can't be described or named, except 'Who.' "

The mystic's question is "Who?" Mine, however, is "Why? Why did God bother to make us at all?"

The answer lies in the next text: "Who was there with Me [God] with whom I could share My secret?"

Larry acknowledges our dazed expressions by allowing that discussion of such things "push the mechanics of how we know what we know to its furthest edge." Then he underscores the mystical principle that God is the one through whom everything is connected to everything else. Pointing to his watch, he says, "What makes something meaningful is its connections—the more, the more. If this is not only my watch but a gift from my father, and also was once owned by a great teacher . . . We can describe the sense of connectedness as wholeness, consciousness, ultimacy, truth, reality. Light is a metaphor for all that. It's neat to know about and to help others know, too, right?"

Pretty neat, all right.

This light, however, is tricky business. We do some *midrash,* or interpretation, of a line from Psalm 31: "How great is your goodness, which you have treasured away for those who fear you."

What could this mean? That God favors the righteous? That God tests them by concealing things from them? Larry's reading is more provocative: "Knowledge of God is dangerous. Too much of this light can fry you."

The light that is the sum of all knowledge can be dangerous in another way. "When ultimate awareness comes too soon or to the wrong person," says Larry, "there's a mess—even evil and destruction. If we could see as God sees, we might use it to play the market! Considering that Adam couldn't even follow one lousy *mitzvah*, God had to do something about the light." The divine problem was that, although the light can be dangerous, without it the world would collapse. The divine solution: conceal the light from most of the people most of the time.

Among those with whom God shared the light, Moses stands out. For him, says Larry, "God made exceptions." According to Kabbalah, God gave the light to Moses for three months before Moses confronted Pharaoh to demand the Hebrews' freedom from slavery. Then God took the light away again until Moses ascended Mount Sinai to receive the Torah. From that point, which established the connection between ultimate awareness and revelation, Moses kept the light all his days. The Israelites couldn't draw near him unless he covered his face.

We consider Moses' face. Was it physically so bright that looking at it was like looking at the sun? Is there something so overwhelming in the eyes of an "enlightened" one that it makes others look away in awe? Larry throws out another possibility: After he told his congregation that he planned to be arrested for civil disobedience during the Vietnam War, he learned that "people avoid you when they don't know what to say."

Making one of his sublime-ridiculous segues, Larry describes a party following one of his lectures. When the host couldn't open a jar, someone joked, "Give it to the mystic!" To be a good sport, Larry waved his hands over it, and the lid popped off. "No one would talk to me for the rest of the evening!" he says. "I. B. Singer said that we all do magic tricks, but some people do them often enough to attract notice. If they decide to become professional magicians and make a living at it, they become charlatans, because then they must simulate something that naturally comes and goes." Pointing to the battered two-hundred-year-old book, he says, "You have to be a *mensch* to study this material."

· : · : · :

One day, curious about this Reform rabbi's deep involvement with a spiritual tradition that has been kept alive by ultraorthodox Hasids, I ask Larry about his religious background. He was raised in middle-class Detroit in a "classical Reform home" where family life revolved around the synagogue. Describing his parents as "pious Reform Jews," he says, "that might sound like an oxymoron, but they were very serious about it." As a third-generation member of the movement and father of a daughter who's a rabbi, he considers himself a Reform "blue blood": "The Kushners are in it for the long haul."

Most American Jews continue to identify with the modern Reform movement, but interest in the stricter Conservative and Orthodox traditions is increasing. Larry is exasperated by internecine battles over which branch of Judaism is superior. "They all have good and bad congregations and rabbis," he says. "Being a *serious* Jew is what's important." To him, *serious* means prayer, study, and repairing the world—the three major activities at Beth El. "There's no bowling league, sisterhood, fund-raising, plaques for big donors," he says. "It's a radically egalitarian community. The downside is that this congregation doesn't have as exciting a social life as some others do."

Beth El is known for the quality of its liturgy, and it's not surprising when Larry recalls worship in the synagogue of his youth as "almost high church." To the extent that this accent on spirituality and ritual was a reflection of a minority group's attempt to be "fully Americanized," Larry says, it had its drawbacks. "I couldn't get married there because they wouldn't allow a *chuppah*—too Eastern European, low-class. That was what I lost. But what I got was an abiding sense of sacredness and community and wonderful memories of being with my family in a special place."

It's not uncommon for people raised in a strongly religious environment to rebel or end up feeling wounded or estranged. Looking back, however, Larry recalls "very little spiritual abuse or people getting beat up or oppression—other than you should always be well-dressed and clean-shaven!"

Orthodox boys often attend *yeshivas*, where they become steeped in Hebrew and Jewish studies. Larry wishes he had had such an immersion but says he has "come to terms with that. If God wanted me to be a Hasid, I would have been born on Eastern Parkway. I also think I should have been the quarterback for the 49ers. But God said, 'That slot is taken. All we got is being the rabbi of this small town near Boston. Do you want it or not?'" According to the rules of the game, he says, "This is who I am and what I've been given. I have to figure out why—what I'm supposed to do with it."

Larry can pinpoint the moment when he decided to become a rabbi. In ninth grade he went to a special service at his temple that was attended by six guest rabbis. "I never saw so many in my life!" he says. "It hit me like an epiphany that rabbis actually got paid to be good people and to help others to be good people and make sense of their lives. What more noble calling could there be? And they get paid for it! It still seems to me the greatest deal going."

But, I say, doctors and therapists can also be good people who improve others' lives. "They help people get better or figure out what to do," says Larry, "but clergy go for the core stuff—life's ultimate truth and meaning. When you talk about God, you're talking about what connects everything to everything else. A rabbi tries to help people see that—make sense of that—especially at crucial times. Most people miss out on the insights of some powerful life passages, because no one is there to help them put what's happening into a large meaning system. I try to open a little window at that sacred moment so that people can tell themselves the truth about what's going on."

In going about the business of being a rabbi, Larry relies on advice from a teacher who said one's best chance of staying spiritual lay in treating the rabbinate like a job. "It's a funny job," says Larry.

"No heavy lifting! But being a rabbi is what I do for a living. I work hard at the office, but I don't bring it home." As a husband and father of three, he's especially sensitive to the plight of rabbis' families, who "have to deal with everyone watching them to see if they do what the rabbi says, as if that were the only measure of his integrity. We never asked our kids to do anything that any regular Jew in America wouldn't do." On the subject of his wife, who is a psychotherapist, he says, "Karen is the most spiritually important event in my life. She's naturally spiritual—I just do it awkwardly. And I can't imagine anything I've ever said or thought about relationships that I didn't learn from her."

I ask Larry about his own sense of personal spiritual progress after so many years of helping others achieve greater awareness. He grins wryly. "Religious insights can't be given," he says. "They must be earned. Unfortunately, most of them must be earned every day."

· : · : · ·

My fellow students will soon become rabbis, and from time to time Larry gives them an old hand's advice. This morning our first bit of text is short: "Listen to my voice, and I will counsel you." In fact, Larry says, the most important element in counseling is "to get the other person to listen to your voice." Awakening their future congregants to the beauty of Torah will depend less on their brilliant exegesis, he says, than on their wholeheartedness. "Much of your education has trained you to ignore your little voices—the personal religious ones. Instead, you should cultivate them. When you teach, all people want is for you to tell them what moves you in the text. That's it!"

Dov Baer of Mezrich, the legendary mystical rebbe known as the Maggid—the Storyteller—said, "I will teach you the best way to *say* Torah. Be unaware of yourself at all except as an ear that hears the *davar*"—the "big thing," another student kindly whispers to me—"speaking in him." In other words, says Larry, "as soon as you begin to hear yourself, shut up. You say Torah when you speak from a place where it's not clear that it's just the rabbi saying it." Recently, Larry says, he looked over his sermons for the big holy days of the past fifteen years. "They're all the same! That's my Torah! It's all about finding your Torah. That's *saying* Torah. Speaking without a net, living on the edge. You can't know it's you saying Torah."

We turn to a text from the Zohar and hear the voice of an old man, a "grandfather," who explains that he's trying to help people who are all mixed up. Some don't see the way of truth—the inner core of Torah that is Kabbalah—and others fail to love it "seductively." Lest there be any mistaking the analogy, Larry says, "This text says that people don't want to make their heads come. Torah calls out to them, 'Hey, beautiful!' But they're afraid to let anything happen in their heads."

Having secured our attention, Larry says, "Why believe this stuff in the Torah? Why isn't it just a bunch of silly stories? That's the big question. The whole point of your work as rabbis is to get people to the point where they really want to kiss the Torah because it's so beautiful!"

The day's texts are full of sexy imagery. For those who know her and are known by her, Torah takes a word from her "sheath," reveals herself through it, then immediately hides again. "Peekaboo!" says Larry. "You're reading along, and suddenly, you startle. Then you say, 'Nah, it couldn't be.' But there's more than meets the eye, and Torah is a way to get to that inner core. To the only thing that can restore and renew." A sound religious background gives the student of mysticism the insight and confidence to look again after startling. Before studying, says Larry, "get your head ready. Say a blessing, assume the text is smarter than you, expect to be chastened. You prepare as much as you can, then you turn down the lights and wait for the peekaboo."

Reading on, we learn that Torah is like a beautiful, voluptuous princess who hides in her palace. She has a secret lover who hasn't even declared himself yet. She knows of him, but he doesn't know that she knows. He passes her gate all the time, hoping to glimpse her. "The poor bastard," says Larry, shaking his head. "She calls all the shots." He remembers a teenage friend who used to sit in a car parked in front of his girlfriend's house while she was at camp. "A primary human experience! There was this woman who raised an eyebrow—an eyebrow—at me, and that was it! I was gone! It's okay, I married her! So this poor guy is staring up at Torah's gate. What does she do? She opens her door a little, reveals her face, then immediately covers herself. Like one of those Magritte paintings? Only the lover notices. His guts flow out after her! You've all been there, both in love and in Torah study, or you wouldn't be here!"

Here in a citadel of New York's cerebral, academic Judaism, Larry's voice rises and his face flushes. Amidst some startled, even embarrassed looks, he says, "Torah knows she has aroused, awakened, her lover, if only for one instant! She knows someone who has a heart, is devoted, and keeps passing her gate. Only the lover, body and soul, goes after her. You!"

Smiling fondly in recollection, Larry says, "Remember how when you fall in love, you don't mind traffic jams? You give the panhandler a dollar? There's beauty and meaning everywhere. That's the goal of teaching Torah. You're going for that gesture you see someone make"—Larry takes off his glasses and, as if overwhelmed, rubs his eyes—"when the text has just reached out and poked him."

As in a romance, the developing relationship between student and Torah is filled with ups and downs, impasses and revelations. "For her lover's sake," says Larry, "Torah reveals herself, drops hints, resists advances, picks fights. His knowledge of her comes and goes. She gives him easy words at first, until he begins to see. Torah raises him to a new level, then she immediately hides. When you don't understand a passage and feel stupid, that's a personal message—a high level of intimacy. She's saying, 'Dummy, come close to me so I can have a word with you.' Through layers and layers of scriptural awareness, she speaks first from behind a curtain, then a thin veil, then wearing a negligee. Finally, when her lover has become accustomed to her, the princess says, 'Take off all my clothes.' He's master of the palace. She has no secrets from him anymore and tells him anything he wants to know."

Now Larry, red-faced, leans forward and hollers, "She says, 'You saw that hint in the text when you were fifteen and now you're seventy-four and I'm going to give it to you!' "

Sitting back in his chair, he says, "That's enough for today."

· : · : · : ·

One morning, Larry e-mails his translation of an old mystical story:

> And some say that the Holy One does this in order to appear to a person that He is distant, that the person should strive to get very close. The Baal Shem Tov, his memory is a blessing, used to tell the following parable before the blowing of the shofar: Once there was a wise and great king. He made an illusory [castle with illusory] walls, towers and gates. Then he commanded that [his subjects] should come to him through [the illusory walls and] gates and the towers. Then he scattered before each and every gate royal treasures. [In this way] when someone came to the first gate, he took the money and left. And so it went [with one seeker after another] until the beloved son came with great determination and proceeded [to walk through one wall after another] right up to his father the King. Then he realized that there was nothing separating himself from his father. Everything was an illusion.[1]

Larry's writings often refer to death. When I ask why, he says, "Religion is basically about what you do with the fact that you're going to die. Good religion keeps reminding us that, despite our illusions, we're not God. That our self-awareness is fleeting, but that there's a greater self that we can be part of. We can either 'get it' when we die, or we can experience that reality daily with a *petit mort*. For me, the thought that this might be the last day of my life isn't morose but liberating and glorious. I say, 'But I'm not dead now! There's something more that I want to see, say, do.' "

Larry is not very concerned about what might or might not happen following death. "We Jews don't do much with the afterlife.

My friend says that when you die they put you in a big comfortable chair in front of a giant video screen with quadraphonic sound and show you the movie of your entire life, over and over again. Heaven? Hell? You pick."

· : · : · : ·

On a sleety, gray February morning, 8:00 A.M. seems especially early for a two-hour class. A few stragglers hurry in, shedding damp coats, while the rest of us blearily nurse paper cups of coffee. No later than 8:02, Larry tells a little story that sets the tone for today. Once, while traveling on a plane, he heard a nearly deafening pop that was accompanied by a blinding blue-white light. His first thought was "Who?" When the stewardesses explained that lightning had struck the plane, he says, "all the passengers nodded and said, 'Oh, it was lightning! Sure, we understand.'" The class has barely begun, but Larry is already excited: "We understand *nothing!*"

If even natural phenomena can be hard to comprehend, the mystics' efforts to grasp ultimate reality push brains and language—and religion—to the breaking point. Until quite recently mainstream Judaism has not much concerned itself with theology, or the study of God, considering this an impossible, even irreverent task. Instead, its focus was on how Jews should live. Nonetheless, over many centuries Jewish mystics quietly developed what Larry calls "a diagram of the DNA of the universe. Or a psychoanalytical diagram of God."

On the blackboard Larry quickly renders a sketch that resembles a tree. The branches and peak symbolize Kabbalah's ten *sefirot,* or mysterious emanations, which function in several ways. They can be thought of as God's personality traits, for example, and as manifestations of God in the material world. They can also be seen as virtues that we should cultivate in ourselves, and as rungs on a ladder of spiritual awareness and development.

At the very top of the sefirotic diagram is *ayn sof,* or the profoundly mysterious divine "nothingness," which is sometimes symbolized by *aleph,* the first letter of the Hebrew alphabet. The greatest thing we can conceive of is something like "all of being throughout all of time," says Larry, but *ayn sof* may be more than that; it's so utterly incomprehensible that no words apply to it.

We turn to our first text, which a student translates: "You [God] are one, but not in counting." Only something that is "one"—that has no parts—can encompass all being, says Larry, "and for the mystics, God is all of being. God may be more than that, but all we can comprehend right now is that God is the holy one of all being through whom everything is connected to everything else."

We are neither the first nor the only ones to shake our heads and rub our eyes over these huge ideas. Larry quotes the legendary Kotzer rebbe, who "pulled a Columbo by asking, 'Why would God tell Moses to come up on the mountain and be there?' Where *else* would Moses be?" Likewise, says Larry, "our heads break when we ponder why God, who is one and everything, would be anything. Or how one becomes many and many, one."

Beneath *ayn sof* and the *sefirah* called *Keter,* or "crown," which represents the ineffable aspects of God, come *sefirot* that connote two kinds of knowing: *Binah,* which Larry describes as "wombed" intuition, and *Hokhma,* or penetrating insight. Below these are *Gevurah,* justice or power, *Hesed,* or love, and *Tiferet,* harmony and beauty. Next come *Hod,* or majesty, *Netzah,* endurance, and *Yesod,* foundation. Finally comes *Malkhut,* or *Shekinah,* which refers to God's presence in our world.

Like the Taoist concepts of *yin* and *yang,* the *sefirot* have male and female aspects and represent elements of a whole that are meant to be kept in balance. "We can talk as if they're separate," says Larry, "but they're not. How can God, who is one, have ten parts? If we had six fingers instead of five, maybe we wouldn't have figured out that there are ten *sefirot,* commandments, trials of Abraham, and utterances at Sinai."

Someone asks about the enigmatic expression of "entering" into the *sefirot.* "It's anyone's guess," says Larry. "They're a psychological diagram of God, who is the self of the universe, so in finding your true inner self, you find God. For us, the point is to keep all the traits in balance, so it's not too much *Hesed,* say, and not enough *Gevurah.*"

Circling back to being in the plane struck by lightning, Larry says that we think that when we impose words on things, we understand them, "but we understand squat. This diagram is a guide to the world seen and unseen. We're talking here about the code of how all things are connected. The grand unified theory of the universe. The infrastructure of being. Or DNA. Or the inner life of God. We can say some things about the lower emanations of the divine, but not its white-hot center. We think we see what's going on, but we only see what our limited perception allows. The question is, How much stuff—how many connections—can you take into your head and process?"

It's only 10:00 A.M., but many faces around the table look exhausted. Larry says that the Hasidim have always balanced their wild theology with strict orthodox observance: "The further out you go, the more you need tradition to keep from flying away."

· : · : · : ·

I tell Larry about a strange experience I had on the day of my father's funeral. Although it was early December, the temperature in New Jersey was a record-breaking seventy-two degrees. On my way home I went into the ladies' room at a busy highway rest stop. Oddly, it was empty except for an attendant. As I washed my hands, she said to me, "What a beautiful day!" I said, "Yes, it's beautiful, but it's a sad day for me, because I just buried my father." I noticed that, although she was a very dark-skinned black woman, she had bright cobalt-blue eyes. She looked at me intently. "You read the Bible?" she asked. "You know the story of Lazarus? Your father will walk on earth again, just as he was." I walked back to the car, telling myself that she was just an eccentric Bible lady with some weird contact lenses.

Larry, who has written about the way we insist on seeing miracles and revelation as accidents and coincidences, loves this story. "If some clergyperson told you that, you wouldn't have heard it," he says. "It's always the person you least expect."

· : · : · : ·

There are no accidents, and Larry begins the next class by addressing a question that has been puzzling me all week: What's the relationship between "our" *sefirot,* here in the funky material world, and God's?

Hitting us right between the eyes, Larry says, "Everything a person does affects all being. His or her raison d'être is to give strength to God. To bring about the unity of all that exists, which was sundered in the Garden of Eden. That's the point of prayer— to reinvigorate the upper sefirotic layers from whence light issues to the lower ones." According to the Maggid, the creation of the world from *ayin*—the divine nothingness—was "a big deal," says Larry, "but what *tzaddik*s do is a bigger one, because they create *ayin* from the world of something." Suddenly, in this rabbinical class, I have an insight into other traditions: maybe Buddha and Jesus could do what they did because they balanced the virtues— justice and mercy, or *Gevurah* and *Hesed*—so perfectly that they operated in the *ayin.*

There are no shortcuts to the *ayn sof.* One must ascend all the sefirotic rungs. "What has to happen to you to get you from who you are to what you want to be?" Larry asks. "To bring about true change? There's a moment when the egg isn't just an egg anymore, but it's not a chicken yet, either. That's scary, but how badly do you want to be a chicken?"

Larry does a good existential chicken. After the laughter dies down, however, he moves from this homely image to one closer to the phoenix. "We Jews are always talking about death, transformation, rebirth. You walk into the Red Sea, and you drown—as slaves, as your former selves. To become a new thing, you have to be willing to die. To be dead. To become like an ingot in the blast furnace. Here's a new definition of God—the annihilator! If you want to be with the one who can't be contained, don't bring any containers!"

Next, we read my favorite story from the Hebrew Bible: Moses' encounter with the burning bush, from which issues God's fiveword autobiography: "I am who I am." When Larry invites *midrash,* I say that maybe the burning bush is a metaphor for Moses, who could be with God—know what God knows—without burning up. Larry likes this. As the "slow student" in this class of Hebrew readers, I blush with pleasure.

To Larry, Moses-as-bush means that God doesn't just hear our prayers "but prays them through us as well. There's a huge transformation when you forget your self and realize that your hands and eyes are God's. Once you're with, or the same as, God, you aren't praying for your own needs, because you have none." As if defining holiness and goodness, he says, "You're just praising the divine and praying for others."

The point of liturgy is to help us create our own burning-bush experiences. By putting us on autopilot, says Larry, ritual allows us to stop thinking and let go, becoming the spiritual equivalent of "a drop of water that falls into the ocean." He tells the rabbis-to-be that "people will come to you wanting these unique weddings. But the best way for them to go is to stick to tradition and become just another bride and groom, another Adam and Eve. Lose the self and go with the experience!"

· : · : · ·

Judaism forbids imagery of God but permits certain religious symbols. The most potent is the *merkava*—God's chariot, which the Bible says is carried across the heavens by an eagle, a person, a lion, and an ox. "If you're a Jew and you have a mystical experience," says Larry, "you see the *merkava*. If you see Jesus on the cross, call your rabbi immediately!"

The *merkava* first appears in the Bible when God is first represented as mobile. "The Jewish people are in exile," says Larry, "so God rides a motorcycle. Here he comes! There he goes!" Because God is *ayin*—boundless and beyond everything—God can never be contained in a temple or any other thing that has borders—*yesh*. In *ayin,* discrete existence is "annihilated," says Larry. "If you cleave to *ayin,* you're a manifestation of God. If you think you're something—*yesh*—you're nothing. I can't help thinking how the *merkava* is the opposite of one of our big permanent synagogues."

It's not the *merkava* that comes and goes, of course, but our awareness of it. In the day's first text we read that there's a big difference between someone who thinks of God some of the time and someone who does so all of the time. Larry is a passionate sailor, and he quotes his boatyard's mechanic: " 'Rabbi, any damn fool can sail a boat in a hurricane. It takes a real sailor when there's no wind.' Can you only pray on Yom Kippur or *shabbos*? Or also on the subway and at a meeting?"

Returning to *ayin* and *yesh*, God and us, Larry says, "God's thinking of us each moment is what sustains us, here in this classroom, as the ocean does the waves. A drop in the ocean is everywhere in the ocean. If that's true, we're all God. To be a mystic is to believe it's possible to be a drop in the ocean. That's the Hasidic heresy—*Alles ist Gott*. But to see that, you have to forget your self and your autonomy."

Great souls who live in the continuous presence of the divine have their problems, such as learning how to function simultaneously in the world. The rest of us face other challenges. "You might have a huge encounter with tremendous wisdom and fulfillment," says Larry, "yet it's beyond language. How do you know that you know what you know? That it wasn't just something you ate or drank?"

· : · · : ·

One day, during an interview, I get a personal sense of Larry as a congregational rabbi. It's unprofessional, but I blurt out that for months—since my father died, now that I think of it—I've felt that life is just one damn thing after another. So many people seem to have unrealistic expectations of me! I just want to be left alone! Larry considers this. "Winifred," he says, "it's hard to be a Jew!"

Okay, okay, I say. Moreover, Larry continues, "I don't think it gets easier. If you made a list of the twenty people who are squeezing you, you'd see that you wouldn't want to remove any of them from your life. It would turn out that you love them all. They're important."

But what about the just plain miserable parts of life? I say. What about Dad's last round of chemo? Larry says that according to the God-up-there model that obtains in most people's heads and on the surface of much of the Hebrew Bible, bad things happening to good people is a problem. Things like cancer and plane crashes "drag people into the whole theodicy trip," he says. " 'Who caused this? It must have been God! How could He?' That whole point-less Punch-and-Judy show."

The God model that Larry advances, however, puts life's bad things in a different perspective. "If it's all God, and we're within the divine right now," he says, "even though life has things we don't like or that strike us as evil, the problem is our own myopia. I don't mean to trivialize cancer or other terrible things, but what's the alternative? The devil did it? I don't want to be a Pollyanna about it. There have been the usual terrible medical things in my family, and most of the time I was a basket case. But there were moments when I could say, 'Somehow, God, this is supposed to be this way. I can't see it now, but for a split second, I can see that maybe it's okay.' That doesn't make all the pain go away, but it does take away the existential-meaninglessness monster that's really the worst part of those moments—that feeling that everything has fallen apart and nothing means anything anymore. No. Things still mean something, even if you don't like them and you can't stand on a tall enough ladder to see what's really going on. It's not that everything is sweet and nice, but that everything is con-nected."

Our conversation illustrates the blurred borders between post-modern religion and psychology. Each week Larry counsels six to twelve people, during sessions that last from ten to sixty minutes, on subjects ranging from family and career to "you name it," he says. As to how he distinguishes between spiritual and psychologi-cal problems, he says that, although he's not "a sophisticated me-chanic, I know something about cars, and I can tell a noise you don't have to worry about from one you should take to a me-chanic. I don't see anyone more than three times. After that, I send him or her to someone else."

How does what Larry might say to a couple in a troubled mar-riage differ from what a secular counselor might say? "What I get to do, as a religious person, is to say, 'The reason your marriage is busting up is because you're a shit,' " he says. "I get to say, 'You have to quit treating the other person like that,' and 'I want you to do better.' That's what I'm supposed to do—yell at people. I'm very old-fashioned about marriage. I tell people that the chances of finding happiness outside this thing are worse than within it. What they need to do is go deeper. There's something that they saw in each other once, and they have to find out what that is and trust something deep inside them."

At the end of our talk I suddenly announce that not only did Dad die, but he left me with the responsibility for my stubborn, aged mother. "With the trained ear of the congregational rabbi," says Larry, "what I'm hearing is that your struggle lately is really about the mother. It takes one to know one. I'm in a similar situation, and I've decided that as many more years as God gives us together, I'm going to try to figure out what our relationship is about. It's a new sacred job for you! Why, of all the people in the world who could have been instruments of your birth, did God chose your parents? What the hell was He thinking? There must have been a reason. If your father or mother was nice, or difficult, there's a reason for that. Things you're supposed to learn from that about what you're supposed to be and do."

On the other hand, says Larry, "mothers are grown-ups and have a right to screw up their lives. You can help her, but if she insists on killing herself falling down the stairs in that big house, that's not your responsibility.

"That'll be ten dollars."

· : · : ·

Today Larry introduces one of the reasons for mainstream Judaism's antipathy toward mysticism: the potential for misunderstanding Kabbalah's ethical implications.

In *ayn sof,* everything is equal: life and death, good and evil, land and sea. "It's not like how life is most of the time, when we're in the *mikveh*"—the ritual bath—"holding on to the lobster and thinking about the rent," says Larry. "You're no longer subject to the laws of linear logic and time. You can march, like Moses, right into the Red Sea. It's very dangerous, because you could go mad or become unethical. At this level, it's not that you have to be religious to be good but that you have to be good to be religious."

Our first text cuts right to the chase by suggesting that, like good, evil works for God, who is, after all, the master of all things. It tells the story of a king who warns his son to stay away from a certain wicked woman. The son agrees. Then the father hires the seductress to tempt the son. The young man, however, resists her advances, and his good character is duly honored by his royal parent.

In all religions, good and evil—deliberately malicious behavior—are serious business, and this is particularly so in Judaism, with its intense focus on "the law." Larry speaks to this class of rabbinical students in a way that he wouldn't from his synagogue's pulpit. "What makes this story different is that here the hooker works for the king," he says. "At the end of the week, the king is the one who signs her paycheck. If it weren't for the hooker, the son wouldn't have been honored." Even at this table, faces take on uncomfortable expressions. "That God is one," says Larry, "means there's a oneness at the core of all being in whom everything, even evil, converges."

Voicing the question that immediately springs into everyone's mind, Larry says, "Where was God at Auschwitz? In the ovens. We're talking human wickedness. God doesn't interfere in human affairs without human agency." Like many a liberal clergyperson, Larry says, "God doesn't have hands, we do. When we act as if we were God's hands, then God acts in history." Like a teacher of Kabbalah, however, he also says, "All our behavior is God. Some is very close to God and some is excruciatingly distant."

A look around the table proves that I'm not the only one grappling with concepts perhaps more readily grasped by the heart than by the cerebral cortex. It's impossible not to question the ovens, slavery, AIDS. Perhaps by way of an answer, Larry says that the Hasidic master Reb Yehuda Lieb of Ger taught that the exile occurred so Israel could collect its lost sparks and converts. "Even in an anti-Semitic hellhole," he says, "we're to raise everybody up."

Turning from the larger world to the inner one, Larry says that, like the king's son, we have instincts toward both virtue and vice. "When you get a lascivious thought in *shul,*" he says, "the harder you push it away, the harder it pushes back. The Hasidim would say that the thought is a buried part of yourself that pops out." Larry does a Dr. Strangelove, vainly trying to control, then chop off, an arm that seems to have a life of its own. It's almost as good as his angst-ridden chicken. Rather than try to cut off our "bad" parts, he says, the Hasidic solution is first to acknowledge them as part of the whole package.

By the lights of Kabbalah, evil occurs when a whole—from a person to a nation to the human race—is divided up into parts, some of which become alienated as "the other." If we accept the other instead, says Larry, "we neutralize the potential evil in what was never really other, and thus redeem it. Even a lascivious thought has potential for good—it's part of the procreative urge. Put your prayer shawl around it!" According to Tsaddok haKohen of Lublin, says Larry, "even a wet dream is a manifestation of the divine. Can we learn to see the whole world like this, as a unified psyche? It's a different option from shooting evil on the spot."

One student, who radiates a quiet, thoughtful sweetness, raises her hand. "But doesn't all this mean . . . Like it doesn't make any difference what we do? What keeps us in line, if all is God?" Larry tells her, "Go ahead, do anything you want! Go on, be immoral! Murder! Steal!" He pauses, then asks, "You see?" Another student shakes his head and says, "But you can't go around saying that!" Larry says, "To the bar mitzvah class—or half the members of your congregation's board—no, of course not! But here, at this table, it's okay."

We keep trying to digest this new way of thinking about good and evil, but it's too big.

Look, says Larry. "If we say that evil isn't working for God, we're fueling dualism. On the other hand, if you know the harlot who tempts you is working for your father, she loses her power over you. This is very dangerous, but not off the wall. It's some-thing like giving yourself permission to eat all you want, instead of all the denying. Maybe you won't want to overeat! The strategy of the 613 *mitzvot* is to get you to see that *Alles ist Gott.* It requires finding God more and more frequently in increasingly less attractive places."

Maybe, I say, God doesn't care about good and evil as much as we think. Maybe we project a lot of judgmental stuff on God. Maybe, as with a parent and child, God mostly just likes to share existence with us.

"Job's great epiphany is that God chose *him,*" says Larry. "The trick is to find the divine in everything. There has to be a part of you that knows that, at the end of the day, it's all working for God. The bumper sticker for today is: 'In the way a person wants to go, they will lead him.' "

The important Jewish concept of *teshuvah* is often translated as "repentance." But, says Larry, *teshuvah* doesn't mean just sorrow about wrongdoing but transformation, to the point that even an intentionally evil act from the past can be redeemed. "The healing of sins is to realize that *Gott ist Alles,*" he says. "That's what takes you out of the guilt-trip Punch-and-Judy show in your head. You're sorry, but you get out of the past and on with the present. You kick someone, make *teshuvah,* then become best friends. It's the closest that Judaism comes to what Christians see in Jesus."

I have to leave class a bit early today, and as I gather up my things Larry begins speaking in Yiddish. When I reach the door, he says something that sounds like "*Gesundheit,* Winifred."

· : · : · ·

Larry is very little impressed by his reputation for being a mystic. "They'll say that about a lot of people," he says. When I bring up miracles, he says, "I believe in them. But they're not so much a change from the natural order as times when the sacred unity that underlies all being erupts. Sometimes, it happens with volcanic force, and we're astonished to see it."

As to whether he has ever seen a miracle, Larry says, "I see them all the time, and I'm not being cute. I held one in my arms last Saturday. The mother was orphaned as a child—has no relatives. She and her husband tried for eight years, with all the technology, to get pregnant. Before giving up, they tried one more thing, and it worked. I get choked up when I talk about it. Who says God doesn't answer prayers?"

Only once, however, has Larry felt that he was the agent of a miracle. "One Saturday," he says, "a young woman rabbi and a doctor who never came to the same services did. Before I left the room, I leaned over and told the doctor the rabbi's name and that she wasn't married. That August I did the wedding. There's no doubt in my mind that I was an agent of something much bigger. To this day, I don't know why I did it."

But what about parting the Red Sea, I say, or the time-traveling attributed to the mystic masters we study in class? "If someone knows about that stuff," says Larry, "he'll deny it. If he doesn't, he's a fake. Gifts exist, sure. People have all kinds of gifts. You know the joke about why it's a good thing there are computers now? Because before, no one knew what to do with the geeks."

· : · : · ·

Larry has just returned from a big conference on physics and religion that included speeches by Steven Weinberg, the Nobel laureate, cosmologist, and atheist, and John Polkinghorne, a Cambridge University physicist who became an Anglican priest. Over lunch with the two men, Larry was delighted that when he asked Weinberg how it felt to be the warm-up act for Polkinghorne, the Nobelist said, "Remember, John, the first rule of vaudeville is 'Never follow an animal act.'"

Getting down to business, Larry says that today's subject is mystical experience—events described by William James as passive, transcendent, noetic, and ineffable. To Larry, spiritual experience is to religious living as love is to marriage or a refund is to income tax: "You don't get the one without the other."

Our first two texts complement each other. One student translates, "I'll sing in praise to enter the doorway to the field of apples." Another offers, "Man sanctifies himself, then the angels sanctify him from above." To Larry, these readings suggest "an interplay between the two worlds, so that you can tickle and massage things from the other world—not 'up there,' but 'other' and entered through *kavannah*"—attention—"that you never expected were possible."

Larry explicates even the most heavenly texts with earthy analogies. He combines insights from mystical masters with those of old Jewish ladies—a rich mine—as well as sailors, former teachers, and daily life. Larry has lately been struggling to learn to play the clarinet. He always stops at the bar lines, he says, although his exasperated teacher keeps telling him they're not really there. And so it is when it comes to reality: "What most of us see is full of measures. We have to struggle, to learn, before we can perceive the true world's seamless unity."

The promise that if a person makes an effort, something greater will take over, is even more explicit in our next text. When you cling to God, it says, you become a prophet—another kind of being. That's how Aaron somehow or other became not just Moses' brother, says Larry, but Israel's first priest, and even the angel of the Lord of Hosts. Once again I think also of Buddha and Jesus. "First, you do the law," says Larry. "You act ethically. You set the table, then you wait."

The means by which mortals enter the "field of apples," the other world, is *devekut*. The term means "to cleave to or fuse with God," says Larry. "To want what God wants." Once a person attains the holiness of *devekut*, he says, "God's right hand takes care of you. Even when you're attending to the body's requirements, your soul is with God. If you're flesh and blood, achieving such holiness is a gift."

Our next text says, "You will see the difference between the holy and pure person." In Judaism, *pure* means keeping kosher and other things that Larry calls "the body stuff." But unless it becomes an opportunity for *devekut*, he says, purity has nothing to do with being holy. "For the holy person, the cemetery isn't just something that requires purification but an opportunity for transformation. The holy person is 'dead' while alive, because he has relinquished his self to God. He has transformed himself into the scene, the locus, for the holiest acts and events."

Unlike the Holy One and his holy ones, most of us "crash and burn with each tragedy," says Larry, because we can't see life fully, much less trace each event back to its roots or forward to its consequences. He tells us that he just met a rabbi's wife who's recovering from a radical mastectomy. She told him that in the course of treatment, although it wasn't strictly indicated, her surgeon decided to order a bone scan. The test showed an unrelated benign brain tumor that would have caused a fatal aneurysm within a week. The woman said, "Thank God for the breast cancer!"

To be evolved spiritually means to be able, like this woman, "to see the funeral in the wedding and the tragedy in the birth, yet also the joy," says Larry. "It means knowing that I could die at any moment, but that I'm not dead. Going back and forth is the price we pay for being human."

Periodically, Larry reminds us that he's not talking about just the *devekut* of great saints of blessed memory. "Since the temple's destruction, you are a priest, your table is an altar, and your eating is a holy act. If our forefathers drew the *merkava,* so can you. You wouldn't be here if you hadn't at least had glimmers of this gift, this holiness. It comes and it goes."

· : · : · ·

On the morning of the last class, Larry begins by referring to an event that had horrified New Yorkers the day before: a youngish husband and father, a hardworking man much respected in his community—a *mensch*—had been randomly pushed in front of an oncoming subway train, which severed both of his legs. The tragedy happened at the subway station right beneath Larry's hotel, just as he was arriving from Boston. As he talks about it, he starts to cry.

Our first reading is from the Maggid, who was perhaps the most radical of the great Hasidic rebbes. Jewish tradition holds that only the holiest people can be heretical. Turning pink with laughter, Larry says that he once confessed to Alexander Altman, a distinguished British rabbi and scholar, that he was afraid he had become a heretic. In clipped tones the great man said, "Relax, Rabbi Kushner. You're not smart enough to be heretical."

Returning to Dov Baer, we read, "I picked up a teaching: The person's steps are ordered by the Eternal, and He delights in your way." This doesn't mean that God is a puppet master up there, pulling our strings down here, says Larry, "but that all is God. It means that, as Buddhism also says, suffering comes from thinking things could be other than they are. It means that, really, your only choices are to be here now or pretend you're not."

For the rest of our final class, we focus on what seems to me the course's most profound piece of text. Oddly, it concerns business travelers. First, the Maggid gets their attention, and ours, with a quotation from Isaiah: "My [God's] thoughts are not your thoughts." He goes on to say that these travelers assume that they themselves are responsible for the decision to go on a trip, that it's for commercial reasons "that they're wearing out their shoes."

The Holy One, however, is not thinking thus, says the Maggid. Sometimes, a man has a loaf of bread while traveling—that precise loaf at that time and place—that's important for his soul. It's to complete his soul that his steps are directed to wander far away! Sometimes, the vital bread is destined not for the businessman but for his servant. How could such a one get this bread, unless the businessman takes him on the trip? No matter what the master may think, what causes his will to travel to that exact place is that his servant should fill his belly there! So, says the Maggid, even a business trip is God's will, ordained to gather together all the parts of a soul.

Lest we restrict the Maggid to the pre-business-class era, Larry tells us to imagine that our work has brought us to the Dallas–Fort Worth airport. There we are, waiting for our flight, eating a Twinkie. We're not just mindlessly chomping, however. We're thinking, I'm not really in charge here. I'm supposed to be eating this exact Twinkie. Maybe the reason I had to come to this airport today is to smile and say, "Thanks, that's nice," to the lady who sold me the Twinkie, because otherwise, she wouldn't have been able to go on. Maybe it's because I have to give someone this stupid souvenir I just bought.

Like us most of the time, says Larry, the Maggid's businessman thinks he's just taking care of business. He has no inkling of the cosmic gears and wheels spinning him along on his seemingly quotidian journey. "This is how God works," he says. "It's enough for us to know that God is to the universe what your subconscious is to your daily life."

Today's bumper sticker seems to be: Something else is always going on. "Ha!" says Larry to the graduate students in the throes of their dissertations. "I bet you thought you were just doing a thesis! Oh no!" Once, at a very busy time, he says, he unaccountably took two days off and went all the way to Detroit to help his widowed mother buy a car. The whole thing made no sense to him until he got there and suddenly realized it was time for his father's *yahrzeit*—the anniversary of a loved one's death. "Something else was going on!" he says. "Once in a while, you have one of those nee-nee-nee-nee *Twilight Zone* experiences that gives you a hint of what that might be. But if you could figure out all of what's going on, you'd be God. The One through whom all other things are joined in some larger system of meaning."

If we can just get into the habit of thinking about what else could be going on, says Larry, we'll start acting like the holy ones of old. "Everything offers an opportunity to be present with God, followed by doing a *mitzvah* to commemorate it. This is easy on Yom Kippur or even *shabbos* dinner, but not so easy after the father gets his legs cut off on his little subway business trip."

Something else, we hope, is going on.

· : · · : ·

The summer shoots by. I ask Larry if I can visit Beth El during the fall High Holy Days. He e-mails back that at Rosh Hashanah he has wall-to-wall duties. As Yom Kippur looms, his congregants all get crazy and think they're going to die. We settle on the more low-key Sukkot, the harvest festival. The word derives from *sukkah,* Hebrew for "booth," which recalls the shaky shelters in which the Jews lived while wandering in the desert. During the holiday observant Jews still live—or at least take some meals— outside in *sukkah*s, albeit usually backyard models.

On a rainy Saturday morning in late September, I join some fifty people gathered at the synagogue for their weekly study session. The discussion will focus on text from Ecclesiastes, which is the customary reading at Sukkot. Larry is cordial but red-eyed and pale after the rigors of Rosh Hashanah and Yom Kippur. He introduces Karen, his wife. She's a pretty brunette in jeans and sneakers who exudes a quiet warmth. I think of Larry's frequent analogies between Torah and the beloved.

At nine o'clock we move into a classroom and do the folksy humming that helps produce the right frame of mind for study. Beyond the large windows, rain falls in cataracts. First there's some discussion of Sukkot. Calling it Jewish Outward Bound, a man says that he and his family have lived all week in their *sukkah,* sleeping in sleeping bags, cooking on a barbecue, and even making do with a latrine. Sounding like a Buddhist, he says that this exercise "teaches us about nonattachment to results."

Jews are commanded to take a meal in a *sukkah* during this holiday period, so the problem of bad weather has been exhaustively considered by the rabbis. Their decision: You can go indoors if it's raining so hard that your soup is diluted. "If you notice the soup is watery and stay," says Larry, "they say that you're an ignoramus. If you don't notice, you're a mystic."

Next, we read the beginning of Ecclesiastes, which purportedly records the words of Kohelet, "the gatherer of the congregation," another name for Solomon, the wise king who built the great Jerusalem temple. This piece of "wisdom literature" is filled with phrases and aphorisms that we often employ, although we may be unsure whether their provenance is Shakespeare, Homer, or the Bible. "Vanity of vanities. All is vanity! For all his toil, his toil under the sun, what does man gain by it?" Larry translates the Hebrew word for vanity as "*Pffft!* Like vapor!"

We read on. "What was will be again; what has been done will be done again; and there is nothing new under the sun." The words seem rather Confucian. Certainly they might have been written by a Greek Stoic philosopher of the third century B.C.E., which may in fact be when the Hebrew text was recorded. The biblical writer goes on to observe that futility is the lot of the good as well as the wicked, and that even the pursuit of understanding is ultimately in vain: "Much wisdom, much grief," we read. "The more knowledge, the more sorrow."

As Larry points out, "Ecclesiastes could be called Been There, Done That. We study it on Sukkot because, like the *sukkah,* it's about transience. The flimsiness of life. The theme is stoical, glum, and bummed-out, and borders on saying that we should make hay while the sun shines. Yet this text made it into the Hebrew Bible. Why?" He opens the floor to his extroverted congregation.

First, Karen raises her hand to pose another question: "How can we read this when we're commanded to be happy on Sukkot?"

"It's freeing," someone says.

Another sees a connection to the paradoxical "happiness of Yom Kippur. When you're bankrupt, have nothing, there can be a happiness in that."

"It's Jewish happy," says a woman. "*Oy!* I'm so happy!" Everyone laughs.

We move on to the chapter that famously begins, "To everything there is a season . . ." At least for me the words have been drained of power by endless rounds of Judy Collins. Larry doesn't linger over the too-familiar text, saying only that to him they mean that "you should dance whether you feel like it or not. Get your money's worth." He then excuses himself to meet with the day's bat mitzvah girls and their families for a half hour before the regular *shabbat* service. An older congregant takes over the study session.

At Beth El members assume functions that elsewhere would be exclusively the rabbi's. Once, when I was griping to Larry about the struggle to fulfill both religion's spiritual and its practical components, he said, "If you're a hermit, you're in big trouble. In a congregation, however, the odds are that there'll be some people who are strong in matters of the heart, or prayer, of the hands, or repairing the world, and of the head, or study. In different times of your life, you might do more of one or another, but the community keeps the balance. That's the main reason I can think of to be in a congregation!"

Our final text says that the earth abides, but we come and we go, and end up in the grave. In light of the ultimate futility of our grand designs—what Buddhists economically call impermanence—Karen seems justified in concluding, "Our reward is to live right now with all our might, as opposed to waiting for some reward, like heaven."

Outside, the fall day is as gray as February. Inside, too, the holiday is tinged with melancholy. Larry has recently announced that he's leaving his position here in order to teach and write full-time.

· : · : · : ·

At 10:30 we file into the red-carpeted sanctuary for the morning *shabbat* service. Over the ark there's a line from Psalm 36: "By Your light do we see light." One wall is almost all windows, which frame a patch of sky, trees, and a *sukkah*. In most respects, the large space resembles a modern suburban church, except that what might be a choir loft is a library instead; Judaism blurs the line between study and prayer. As does the gray clapboard siding, the *shul*'s Williamsburg-style chandeliers add a New England touch.

There were few Jews in and around Sudbury till the 1950s. The town's first congregation, which met in the Methodist church, assembled in the 1960s. Larry, then twenty-eight, arrived as the first full-time rabbi in 1971. His tenure has been stormy at times. In 1974 the renewal of his contract was approved by one vote. "They figured out who I was," he says, "so it was a reasonable thing to do." Some of the friction was generational: the young rebbe led services in Levi's and had a beard and long hair. Then there was the newspaper incident. When Larry got to Sudbury, he was interviewed by the young editor of the local paper. They hit it off and talked honestly. One of the things Larry said was that Reform Jews are "pretty tight-assed," which of course became the story's headline. When he contemplated publishing a retraction, his friends in the congregation said that only the tight asses were upset, and that if he recanted, *they'd* fire him.

At heart, says Larry, the problem was his conviction that "you should be able to talk about religious things in the same real, enlivening language, including 'bullshit,' as you do other things. To me, the most potent, revolutionary, and dangerous thing you can do is simply and lovingly to tell the truth, without worrying about where the chips land. And religious institutions are full of people who lie all the time. That's why so many people don't take them seriously—they lie!"

Over the decades in Sudbury, Larry has mellowed in the sense of what he describes as "realizing that I didn't have to try as hard as I was trying. I was in your face, pushing all the time, and a lot of nice people just couldn't stand it. I began to understand that you can get the same results with more gentleness. I've learned to trust my innermost vision, so that even if I don't grab you by the lapels and tell you what I want you to know, you'll figure it out."

I asked Larry if there had been special events during his rabbinate that inspired him to go on. "It has been just the opposite," he said. "For thirty years I've considered myself barely surviving as a rabbi. Hanging by a thread! If the slightest wind had blown, I would have dropped down and gone somewhere else. That this has never happened—that each time I was about to bag it, something came from somewhere else to bolster me up—is actually one of the few proofs for the existence of God in my life. By all odds, I shouldn't have survived as a rabbi. I say the wrong things. I do the wrong things. But somehow it always works out."

The service begins, and it's immediately clear that Beth El's liturgy is not conducted for spectators by professionals. I follow along in a prayer book called *Purify Our Hearts,* which was written here and is now also used elsewhere. Much of the service is in Hebrew and is mostly sung, by either a cantor—a lovely gray-haired woman who seems to have great human as well as musical instincts—or the whole group. Everyone enthusiastically joins in to sing Psalm 118 in Hebrew to the tune of "Amazing Grace"—only in New England! When it's time for the *Sh'ma,* which is usually a big aria, we all sing the prayer softly over and over, almost like a mantra.

Congregants do the readings and offer commentary. One man observes that "it's harder for us to be joyful on Sukkot than self-denying on Yom Kippur. Maybe Yom Kippur is just a preparation for Sukkot, which we're twice commanded to celebrate, as opposed to only one mention of Yom Kippur. But before we can enter into joy, we must give up our guilt."

Other than wearing a snazzy Hasidic silver-trimmed prayer shawl, Larry avoids the impresario role and seems like one of many people who are making the service happen. When the bat mitzvah ceremony begins, he says, "From Sinai to Rachel! From Sinai to Sarah!" and hands the Torah scrolls to the two girls, surrounded by their families on the *bimah*. One grandmother is on a walker, another in ostrich feathers. To stress further Judaism's familial nature, not just the girls but also their parents read Torah portions; parents can choose English or Hebrew. One girl panics partway through her reading and begins to alternate Hebrew with strangled little sobs. Larry and the cantor direct laser looks of support, willing her through. When she finally finishes, the relieved congregation is about to applaud, but behind his back Larry raises a hand for quiet.

When he and the girls ascend to the ark, he has a few private words with each, then puts his hands on each head in blessing. He must reach up to do so for the tall, willowy twelve-year-old who could pass for eighteen, which inspires him to do a little double take. To the tearful one, he looks as if he's saying, "Don't you let all the pressure and a few tears take away what's important about today!"

As we leave, a handsome lawyer in a dark suit who had been sitting next to me says of Larry's departure: "We're having a tough time adjusting. There are a lot of complex feelings."

· : · : · : ·

A month later I meet Larry in New York for a final interview. I get off the subway at the stop where the *mensch* lost his legs and head to a lounge in Larry's hotel. It's happy hour. Big television screens blare sports and news. I ask Larry how he defines holiness. "Standing in the presence of God," he says. "Everyone has it, but some people seem to have more of a knack for accessing it."

We talk a little about how mysticism is often paradoxically dismissed as silly vapors when it really concerns "knowledge of the truth," says Larry. "Since ninth grade, I've just wanted to know what the truth is. Scientists want to know facts—data. But there's another kind of truth, which is about how it is, really. It's hard for me to imagine that someone interested in that wouldn't be led to mysticism. Sooner or later, you'd get there. The minute you get it, of course, it disappears. But you're changed, so you start all over again."

So what is truth? I ask. "The meaning of life," says Larry. "That it has something to do with God. That it's all God. It's all connected. And you're gonna die. That's pretty much it. There's something else going on. You shouldn't have to struggle so much. It'll happen anyway. Something else is going on here. In moments of religious meaning, you get a glimmer of that."

Larry Kushner's genius lies in his ability to keep alive an ancient tradition not just by talking about it but by being it—and in an utterly natural, timely way. Like his mystic predecessors, he teaches with stories. Now he tells me one about waiting for a ferry; like much of his writing, it doesn't seem particularly religious at first. He and Karen, who were traveling in the Pacific Northwest, got to the pier early. There were only four cars ahead of theirs, including one belonging to a man who had just missed the previous boat. "This guy was fuming and cursing," says Larry. "As fate would have it, he was parked next to a vacationing rabbi from Massachusetts. He said to me, 'Dammit, I just missed that boat!' I said, 'You wouldn't have made it even if you had left earlier. There would have been a traffic jam or a flat tire. That boat didn't have your name on it. If it did, you wouldn't be here talking to me now.' The guy said, 'Huh. Really? Thanks! I feel a lot better.' He just needed to understand that he was supposed to be here now. To remember that even though he thought he was running things, he really wasn't! The older you are, the more you realize that."

I had just finished reading Larry's book of *midrash* on Genesis

28:16, called *God Was in This Place & I, i Did Not Know.* I ask him about his most recent thoughts on Jacob's great line. He says he has been studying a difficult text written by Mendel of Rymanov, an eighteenth-century Hasidic master, who suggests that all God said at Sinai wasn't even "I"—the first word of God's ten utterances there—but the first letter of the first word: soundless *aleph,* which signifies "self," as well as the divine nothing that made everything. When one meets God face-to-face, as Moses did on the mountain, "the *aleph* in you sees the divine *aleph,*" says Larry. "In that moment, you lose the self, but find the true self. You see yourself in the heavens, and the heavens show themselves to you. So, the *midrash* would be, 'God was in this *face,* but I, I did not know.' The holy ones of old tried to walk through life and only see the name of God, which made it unlikely that they'd do something hurtful or stupid. They tried to see the divine face everywhere, in the face of everyone."

Larry is producing an epiphany, and it's hard to meet his gaze. "So I could look at your face right now," he says, "and you could look at mine. . . . That's very dangerous, honestly. But that's the holiest thing we could do. Do you understand?"

3. EXPLORER

Bowing slightly to the Englishwoman in the maroon robes of a Tibetan Buddhist nun, I say, "Ani-la, I've come a long way to see you."

"I know," says the Venerable Tenzin Palmo, smiling and taking both my hands for an instant. Her pale, glittering blue eyes are striking, particularly here in the brown-eyed "Tibet" established by refugees in the Indian foothills of the Himalayas. Three small circular scars on her shaved head, left by burning cones of incense during her *bhikshuni,* or monastic, ordination signify that this *ani,* or nun, has the same status as a full monk. In the Buddhist world, however, Tenzin Palmo's distinguishing feature is neither physical nor social but experiential. She has spent most of twelve years— three of them uninterrupted—in solitary retreat in a remote Himalayan cave at thirteen thousand feet.

No woman has ever been recognized as one of history's many "living Buddhas." This title is given to someone who has become fully enlightened, or, as Tibetan Buddhists say, "realized," which is short for the permanent realization, or achievement, of the mind's true state of selfless, blissful, infinite awareness. Tenzin Palmo is discomfited by such talk, because it sounds pretentious, but it's said that she has vowed to become realized in a female body—no matter how many lifetimes it may take—not for her own sake but to support and encourage women on the spiritual path.

Tenzin Palmo prefers the hermit's life, but her unusual vocation has a public dimension as well. Her forty years' experience of Tibetan Buddhism, including associations with legendary figures such as the Dalai Lama and Trungpa Rinpoche, and her flair for presenting this complex tradition to Westerners, make her an increasingly sought-after, if reluctant, teacher and writer. Moreover, this mystic's commitment to Buddhist women who, like her, are determined to develop their full spiritual potential has compelled her to become an activist as well. She recently established the Dongyu Gatsal Ling Nunnery, whose first twenty-five novices from the Himalayan region, aged fourteen to twenty-six, are training in borrowed quarters here at the Tibetan Buddhist monastery at Tashi Jong. Land has been purchased nearby, and construction of the nunnery building is to begin within a few months. Unlike the majority of *anis*, who take only novice vows and receive little formal religious education, these young women eventually will, like Tenzin Palmo, receive *bhikshuni* ordination and study Tibetan Buddhist philosophy. Some will, like her, go further, learning esoteric practices that help direct all of a person's emotional, intellectual, and physical energies toward realizing Buddhahood.

Along with her maroon robes, Tenzin Palmo wears the mother superior's invisible mantle of command. Remembering the reverend mothers of my youth, I straighten up and try to smooth some wrinkles engraved into my clothes by several days of hard, hot travel. Thoughtfully, Tenzin Palmo offers a chair, tea, and small talk about the people I've been interviewing. After my descriptions she asks in her English drawl, "Why would you want me? I'm so ordinary."

Tenzin Palmo is down-to-earth, but she's not ordinary. She may be a nun, but she belongs to another venerable sisterhood as well: that of adventurous British women, such as the Ladies Jane Digby, Hester Stanhope, and Isabel Burton, who escaped staid England for the mysterious East. Like her predecessors, she has the knack of appreciating Eastern culture while retaining her own British qualities—the grit required for the hermitage, the combination of humor and reserve needed for monastery life, her way of putting esoteric religious concepts into plain King's English. While sipping tea, Tenzin Palmo casually sums up Buddhism thus: "Here we are, and there are difficulties. Despite whatever we may have, we're insecure. We strive for happiness, but we create problems. Something is wrong, but it's not out there. It's inside us, in the form of negative emotions, especially delusion, egocentricity, and grasping. There's a cure, however. We can get beyond all that negativity to the unconditioned, unprogrammed state of pure awareness that Buddhists call mind, which is our true nature."

Mind has inspired as much abstruse, one-hand-clapping discourse as any subject in Buddhism. Tenzin Palmo, however, says that there's no need to make a big fuss about it, because we experience mind whenever we see things as they really are: "If we can just stand still and let go, we've got pure awareness! It's so easy, because it's who we really are." To her, mind is like "a great blue sky that's generally clouded over by our usual thoughts and feelings. We identify with those clouds, instead of the vastness behind them. When we think, 'Who am I?' we answer 'angry' or 'calm,' 'American' or 'Chinese,' or whatever is going through our heads at the time, instead of identifying with the simple, naked awareness that's our true nature."

Tenzin Palmo doesn't care to hear any whining about the difficulty of getting in touch with mind. "We don't believe how simple it is, so we insist that it's hard," she says. "We don't need to do hours and hours of practice, but we don't believe that. We have to travel around the world to realize that we already have what we're looking for." She smiles and sighs. "It's very difficult for most people to realize that there's nothing to do."

I for one have just traveled around the world. Two days of

flights were followed by twelve hours in a ludicrously named sleeper train compartment with a handsome, irritable Kashmiri whose twenty questions began with how much money I made and my opinion of Mohammad. When he demanded my view of Western men who drink in nightclubs and go with women, I offered him an antacid and switched off my light until we reached squalid Patankot, a military town on the volatile Pakistani border. Several hours in a Jeep through the lush, green province of Himachal Pradesh brought me to Dharamsala, home of the Dalai Lama and capital of the Tibetan diaspora. After some sleep it was a mere two or three hours' drive to Tashi Jong.

Tenzin Palmo explains that she reserves her mornings and Sundays for spiritual practice and solitary work, but most other afternoons, starting tomorrow, we can talk for an hour or so. Then she sends me along to the monastery's guesthouse for a much-needed wash and rest.

· : · : ·

Tenzin Palmo was born Diane Perry, the gifted daughter of working-class parents in London's cockney East End. At eighteen she became a librarian at London University and began her spiritual search in earnest. Photographs from this era show a slender, attractive gamine who, in the staid 1950s, must have seemed awfully cool. She began to read about Buddhism and was soon drawn to its Tibetan tradition, which was then regarded as a superstitious folk religion. She studied the Tibetan language at the university and met the first of her remarkable mentors, including the young, unknown Trungpa Rinpoche; this lama, or monk regarded as a spiritual master, would later become a highly influential guru in the West. At twenty Diane left high heels and boyfriends behind and boarded a steamer just ahead of the wave of young Europeans and Americans who would soon pour into India on spiritual quests. She joined the Tibetan refugee community in North India, where she taught English to young *tulkus*—recognized reincarnations of important lamas.

On her twenty-first birthday, Diane's life changed irrevocably when she met the eighth Khamtrul Rinpoche. She immediately recognized this powerful lama as her root guru, or the teacher who reveals the nature of one's mind. (The Khamtruls are important figures in the Drukpa Kargyu sublineage of the Kargyu tradition; Tibetan Buddhism's three other branches are the Sakya, Nyingma, and Gelug traditions.) The rinpoche in turn recognized her as a close associate from previous lifetimes; in fact, some of his monks remembered a very old painting in Tibet that showed a blue-eyed, tilt-nosed lama who strongly resembled the Englishwoman. Within the month Diane Perry was a nun called Tenzin Palmo and the Khamtrul's secretary. Although she lived amidst one hundred monks, she was barred by gender from much of monastic life, including its formal religious training. Technically, Buddhism regards women and men as equal, because both have genderless Buddha nature. For all the usual reasons, however, the thousand Buddhas of this aeon have somehow all been male, just as the Buddha was in all of his past lives—even as a rabbit or monkey.

Almost immediately Tenzin Palmo determined that education was the key to unlocking the riches of Buddhism for women. With characteristic gumption she sought private instruction and studied until she was ready to travel to Hong Kong for her *bhikshuni* ordination—called *gelongma* in Tibetan—which few Buddhist nuns outside China receive. Her early frustration as a devout woman struggling against the status quo to fulfill her religious potential shaped her vocation: she would not only strive to achieve Buddhahood as a woman, no matter how many lifetimes that might take, but also work to ensure that the women following in her footsteps would face fewer obstacles.

After eight years Khamtrul Rinpoche told Tenzin Palmo that she was ready for solitary retreat. From fall through spring she lived alone in her tiny cave, completely snowbound for most of the year, returning to Tashi Jong monastery only for teachings in summer. After nine years of this rigorous preparation, she undertook a three-year-long unbroken retreat in her cave. This experience in particular has linked her with Tashi Jong's nearly mythic *togdens*—the Tibetan term for people who have become enlightened, or as they say, realized—who were among her early mentors.

Togdens are elite yogi-monks, especially associated with the Kargyu tradition, who from youth direct their whole physical, mental, and emotional being toward becoming realized in a single lifetime. During many years of training, in isolation even from other monks, *togdens* master all types of meditation and esoteric forms of yoga that cultivate subtle psychophysiological energies. Most of these practices are secret; the only one generally spoken of is *tumo,* in which the practitioner can raise his body temperature until soaking sheets wrapped around him in freezing temperatures steam-dry. The *togdens* are said to be very strong, fast, and agile into old age and to have metaphysical powers. The few who really know anything about such matters are very circumspect, making only vague allusions to what one person calls "that matter-energy, emptiness-form stuff." The only outward signs of the *togdens'* special status are their red and white robes and uncut hair, which is braided into long coils and bundled turban-style around the head.

Since the Chinese invasion of Tibet, *togdens* have become an endangered species. Seven of the yogi-monks escaped with the eighth Khamtrul Rinpoche, and the three who still survive at Tashi Jong are among the few *togdens* left in the world. To keep their tradition alive, these elders are training eight young monks high above the monastery. Within a restricted area roped off by prayer flags, the trainees live in isolation and extreme asceticism for at least twelve years, often dwelling in caves and eating and sleeping only sparingly. One day an *ani* suggests something of the rigor of their practice when she mentions that the young men sometimes wear deep grooves into the wooden planks on which they do prostrations.

Ajam, the senior *togden* who had served the seventh, eighth, and ninth Khamtrul rinpoches, whom he described as "all the same," died last year at the age of eighty-seven. His death was a momentous event still being discussed at Tashi Jong. When he was cremated, his ashes contained *ringsels,* or little seashell-shaped objects of great portent; photographs were sent to the Dalai Lama. In

Tibet, Ajam had spent thirty years in retreat, six of them in a small cave where he subsisted on water and *tsampa,* or ground barley. To ward off sleepiness during meditation, he sat on the edge of a Himalayan cliff. His memories of Tibet included *togdenmas,* or female *togdens.* "If you ever saw a *togdenma,*" Ajam said, "you wouldn't even look at a *togden.*"

Following the long years of retreat that have associated her with the *togdens,* Tenzin Palmo revisited Europe and her cultural roots. She spent six years in Italy, living as a Buddhist nun while reading voraciously and immersing herself in Western art and classical music. She then returned to India to fulfill her promise to the eighth Khamtrul Rinpoche to build a Drukpa Kargyu nunnery that can "grow *togdenmas* from scratch."

It's rumored that Tenzin Palmo is a *togdenma.* She dismisses such talk as both embarrassing and ridiculous. Moreover, she is very circumspect concerning her personal religious life and never behaves in any sort of not-of-this-world way. Even the *ani*s who are her closest associates can only speculate about what she experienced in the cave and its relationship to something one occasionally glimpses in Tenzin Palmo's eyes. "When she gives you that blue look," they say, "that's when you see it."

· : · · : ·

Life in a monastery quickly dissipates any notions of otherworldly precincts inhabited by ethereal beings. At Tashi Jong, the membrane between town and gown is highly permeable. For much of the day the monastery grounds bustle with the comings and goings of a hundred and thirty monks, aged eight years to well into the eighties, and, while the novices are in retreat, about twenty *ani*s, including the nunnery's team of Tenzin Palmo, three Scottish, Canadian, and American nuns, plus a staunch Australian lay volunteer. Adding to the clerical mix are visitors, Tibetan and Indian villagers, and animals ranging from wandering Hindu cows to the temple's fierce guard dogs.

The monastery complex was built by the eighth Khamtrul Rinpoche. In 1969 he led a group of monks and laypeople to this small Indian village to make a permanent home in exile. On a hillside they all pitched in to construct the *gompa,* or temple, prayer hall, primary school for monks, institute for higher studies, and other buildings, including the guesthouse. (Although it's oddly situated between the barn, with its vast manure pile, and a long row of "squatters," or seatless toilets, used by the monks, the rooms are comfortable and, considering the private baths with hot water, a great value at four dollars per night.) The lay families settled into the mazelike village below, in single-story masonry row houses and the odd villa. Several small shops and whimsically named cafés serve villagers, visitors, and monks alike. The Tashi Jong community has become known for its Tibetan arts and crafts and especially for its festive ceremonial lama dances, which are held twice a year.

The monastery day begins about 4:30 A.M. with choruses of birds and monks chanting in the cool, soft light. For that matter, chanting of some sort goes on till dark. The young monks' schooling is based on group recitation, performed at full throttle for long periods throughout the day, interrupted by equally energetic recesses for cricket or football. Monks they may be, but the little fellows are as wiggly and grubby as any country boys. Even the smallest ones, who sometimes tote a battered plastic plane or water pistol, appear to thrive in their cheery fraternal environment. Certainly these youngsters prove that robes are no impediment to an active life. After a few days among shorn males and females of all ages wearing long maroon skirts and stoles and red or yellow sleeveless shirts, I begin to think that perhaps everyone should wear this flattering, timeless drapery, which highlights faces and downplays body consciousness.

Each morning and evening villagers come up to circumambulate the *gompa,* reciting mantras and spinning handheld prayer wheels just as they did back in the old country. Like the Japanese, Burmese, Thais, Koreans, and other peoples, the Tibetans have evolved their own variations on the theme of Buddhism, which readily accommodates such cultural customization partly because it's less a conventional religion than a theory about the mind and how it works.

In India in the sixth century B.C.E., the Hindu aristocrat who would be known as the Buddha set out to find a solution to suffering. After six years of fruitless meditation, fasting, and following of other disciplines relied on by spiritual seekers of his time, the young man gave up on asceticism and had a profound mystical experience. Emerging in a state of perfect equanimity, he began to teach others what he had discovered: the Four Noble Truths concerning the nature of suffering, its origin, its cessation, and the way to achieve that surcease.

Buddha determined that we suffer because we become attached to natural phenomena—not just people and things but thoughts, emotions, and life itself—which are by definition impermanent. To free ourselves we must first realize the folly of binding our well-being to what can only change and disappear, then cultivate the one entity that doesn't alter and will never die. All sentient beings have this "Buddha nature," or mind, but human beings, who can choose what to do, are best equipped to realize it fully, achieving enlightenment.

The Buddha, however, was not merely a remote intellectual or chilly stoic. If wisdom is one half of his *dharma*—teachings—the other is the compassion for all beings mired in *samsara*—the world's endless cycle of birth, suffering, death, and rebirth. After he perceived his cure for human pain—relinquishing attachment to the impermanent and freeing the true, changeless mind from the churning thoughts, emotions, and personality quirks that usually obscure it—the Buddha devoted the rest of his life to teaching his Eightfold Path to enlightenment. To emulate his generosity, devout Buddhists take the *bodhisattva* vow, by which they dedicate their practice to free all sentient beings from suffering.

· : · : · : ·

One morning Tenzin Palmo accelerates my education in Buddhism by dispatching me to meet the ninth Khamtrul Rinpoche, who embodies some of religion's more challenging principles. Like the eight who came before him in a lineage founded around the fifteenth century in eastern Tibet, Khamtrul Rinpoche, twenty-one, is known simply as the Khamtrul and addressed as Rinpoche, the title accorded a very special lama. His immediate predecessor—a strapping man described as both sweet and awe-inspiring—spent his first thirty years in a simple room in a monastery in Tibet, although he reigned over several hundred monasteries and thousands of monks. When the Chinese incursion finally forced him to flee, the eighth Khamtrul and a few companions escaped on horseback; dodging enemy troops, they rode clear across the Himalayas to India, where he reestablished his tradition before dying of diabetes at forty-seven. Even Tenzin Palmo sounds like a schoolgirl when she talks about the man she calls "my lama." To convey something of his power, she recalls a night while she was working as his secretary; he entered the office unexpectedly and happened to catch her eye. His unshielded glance, she says, "hit me like a thunderbolt." The chagrined lama apologized to the quivering nun for this accident and sent her home to recover.

Since he was two years old the ninth Khamtrul has been raised in the monastery built by this formidable predecessor. At the appointed time I arrive at his house to participate in his daily English lesson, which is conducted by Ani Chozom, a winsome young nun from Canada. With its curtained windows and heavy carpets, the Khamtrul's somber parlor seems more appropriate for a dowager than for such a young man. As an important *tulku,* however, he has long been accustomed to a sheltered life, at a remove even from other monks.

Khamtrul Rinpoche's frequent shy smiles don't disguise a seriousness that bespeaks his scholar's reputation. First, the proprieties—for Buddhists, prostrations and a ceremonial giving and returning of a *kata,* or white silk scarf—are observed. Chozom gracefully flattens herself on the floor three times. I bob and duck a bit, then offer my token gift of a protein bar, which makes the rinpoche laugh. He then invites us to sit on carpet mats before his book-littered divan for an hour of conversation in English. Like most language students, he would rather listen than speak, but Chozom tactfully prods him into answering to my questions.

Asked about Tenzin Palmo, whom he met when he was just two and a half, the rinpoche says that his first memory of her is "walking and talking in English. Ani-la is especially generous, as one can see in her dedication to building the nunnery."

Next I inquire about his rather special life, wondering if it's lonely. "No!" says the rinpoche, laughing. "I like it. I like to study." He seems pleased to hear that people praise his strong intellect and say that he's a "mind incarnation" of the eighth Khamtrul. Chozom asks if there's anything he likes to do just for fun. He's puzzled at this idea, then says that he enjoys picnics—a popular monastic festivity that involves not just special snacks but games. Perhaps in reaction to his own isolated boyhood, the rinpoche goes out of his way to chat and play with the little monks from the primary school.

A series of seeming accidents has led me halfway round the world to Tashi Jong, and when I remark on my surprise at being here, the Khamtrul immediately says, "Karma!" We all laugh, then Chozom and I explain that many Westerners would chafe at the notion that everything that happens to us has been predetermined by our previous actions, in this or an earlier life. The rinpoche's interested, nonjudgmental reaction to this viewpoint makes it plain that, even in his august company, one can speak one's mind frankly about religious issues.

Emboldened by the open atmosphere, I ask the Khamtrul if he finds any particular Buddhist doctrine difficult to comprehend. He shoots back, "Emptiness!" We all laugh again and shake our heads at the thought of this "pregnant nothingness." When I allow that reincarnation is a stretch for me, the Khamtrul says matter-of-factly that "some people remember their past lives."

The rinpoche doesn't meet many Westerners at out-of-the-way Tashi Jong, and he is interested in Christianity. Perhaps it's not surprising that, as a ninth reincarnation, he wants to know about the born-again phenomenon. He's also curious about Jesus' resurrection, which doesn't seem as unlikely to the rinpoche as it does to many postmodern Christians.

When the hour is over I ask the Khamtrul for a blessing. He immediately shifts from diffident ESL student into authoritative lama. Placing a little bronze statue of White Tara, covered in pearls, on my head, he prays for quite a few moments. The rinpoche's manner suggests what he'll be like as he matures into his formidable role.

· : · : · : ·

Later, Tenzin Palmo illuminates some of the Buddhist principles raised by my visit to the Khamtrul in a way that suggests why she's an increasingly popular Buddhist teacher. First off I say how impressed I was by the open nature of religious discussion in his presence. "We think doubts are bad, but the Buddha didn't," she says. "Buddha is not a god but someone who realized his—and our—total potential as a human being. The *dharma* is based not on dogma but on experiment and experience. Whenever I expressed doubts about certain things, my lama said to just put them aside, perhaps until later. Question marks are okay, as long as we don't solidify them or feel threatened by them."

I'm pleased to report that even the Khamtrul is challenged by emptiness. Tenzin Palmo says that "like space, emptiness contains everything. Its nature is awareness—not in the 'I'm aware of something' sense, but naked awareness itself." When I ask if we all have a little piece of this big mind inside us, she says, "We have the whole lot! The only difference between most people and the Buddha is that he realized that and we think we're just ordinary!"

Meeting the Khamtrul has put a form to many aspects of Buddhism that seem mysterious to me, starting with past lives. Rebirth as a human is not so rare in itself, says Tenzin Palmo, "but to be reborn in an environment where you can find a genuine spiritual path and teacher? And with the intelligence and desire to follow it? There's nothing comparable to such a rebirth in its preciousness and rarity! How many of the billions of people are even interested in a path? How many of those are able to follow it or get someone to guide them?"

As to exactly what "comes back" in a reincarnation, Tenzin Palmo first says that any person's fundamental nature isn't the ego but its opposite: the indivisible, subtle consciousness of mind. Apart from this boundless awareness, there's a "mental continuum that carries certain propensities," she says. "If you were very musical in one life, for example, you might be very musical at an early age when you come back."

To Tenzin Palmo, the ninth Khamtrul "is and isn't" the eighth Khamtrul. While not his predecessor's clone, the young man shows the same intellectual bent and marked equanimity. Even when the young Khamtrul was two and a half, she says, he was "just as he is now—very centered, sweet, gentle—not like an ordinary child at all. When people came to see him, he would sit calmly and quietly on his seat, sometimes on and on, until they left. Then he'd get down and start playing. If someone else came, he'd leave the toys and sit patiently again. You can't teach a tiny child that."

To Buddhists, of course, such precocity is the result of *karma.* Where monotheists see a separate Creator-being, says Tenzin Palmo, Buddhists see a universe in a constant state of evolution and dissolution that's generated by the *karma* of its beings. "Things scatter," she says, "then *karma* brings them together." *Karma* on this cosmic level seems more palatable than the predestined, individual sort that seems to doom some to a miserable existence. But, says Tenzin Palmo, "just because someone might 'deserve' a hard lot in life doesn't mean we don't do all we can to help him, because maybe that's his *karma,* too. To be helped."

With her gift for putting Eastern concepts into Western language, Tenzin Palmo says that, in the end, *karma* is "all about choice. *Groundhog Day* is a Buddhist movie! We can choose to develop awareness or to pursue selfish pleasure, which allows us to be responsible agents instead of helpless victims. We are reaping the seeds of our earlier choices now, which means that much of what happens to us is unavoidable. But we can create our future with the way in which we respond now."

Even if one comes back as a rinpoche, I say, reincarnation seems something of a Pyrrhic victory, obliging one to keep on enduring the indignities of infancy, adolescence, and old age. But, says Tenzin Palmo, the cycle gradually becomes less painful, "because eventually you realize the changeless naked awareness that's your true nature." Much of our suffering derives from our identification with the finite self, she says, so that whatever threatens it, particularly death, elicits great fear. Once one has truly realized the mind's true nature, however, "the ego is no longer this solid 'I' that's set apart from everything else that isn't I. All that goes. Instead, you just see incredibly expansive interconnection. Then, what happens doesn't seem so solid, but more like events in a dream."

> *Row, row, row your boat*
> *Gently down the stream*
> *Merrily, merrily, merrily, merrily*
> *Life is but a dream.*

Tenzin Palmo's perspective invests the old nursery rhyme with both Buddhist wisdom and compassion. Part of the pleasure of listening to her has to do with the fact that, perhaps because she left Britain before the arrival of pop culture, her English is wonderfully correct and full of old-fashioned words like *purity* and *devotion*. Most appealing, however, is her honesty and way of speaking from the heart. Indeed, her integrity is such that even when she talks about phenomena that overtly contradict the laws of nature, one wonders if their scientist-formulators have perhaps made some mistake. For example, her mother, Lee Perry, was a spiritualist, and Tenzin Palmo says that "séances were no big thing—just what we did on Wednesday evenings with the neighbors. One night, there I was, nine or ten years old, watching a big gateleg table—with a great big woman sitting on it—just flying around the room, because my mother had told the spirits that they weren't very strong!" She laughs delightedly at the memory. "I'm very grateful for my early upbringing," she says. "From spiritualism I got an awareness of many different realms of being. That there's more than meets the eye everywhere around us. A total conviction of life after death."

Segueing neatly back to rebirth, Tenzin Palmo says that reincarnation "helps us see the vast, spacious quality of mind versus ego.

Like actors, we're just playing roles, which we shouldn't overly identify with. What happens to us now isn't that important. What's important is our response."

Although Tenzin Palmo has little tolerance for signs of low-mindedness, laziness, willful stupidity, and other sorts of bad behavior, she's never impatient with others' spiritual struggles and questions, however simple they must seem to her. I complain that as soon as I feel some sort of a grip on, say, emptiness, it evaporates. "This life is just a tiny thread in a vast tapestry," she says with an encouraging smile. "We don't have to do it all this time."

· : · : · ·

All Buddhist traditions uphold basic principles of the *dharma,* such as the impermanence of all things, the need to cultivate mind, and the importance of compassion. Yet in other respects Zen, Korean, and Thai practices, say, look quite different. With its countless deities and complex rituals, Tibetan Buddhism seems particularly "other." One afternoon, with her customary clarity, Tenzin Palmo arranges the Tibetan details in the larger Buddhist picture.

We meet in her all-purpose private room, just off the nunnery's office. It occupies the ground floor of a handsome stone building that was once the home of the eighth Khamtrul Rinpoche. The intellectual Gelupkas are known for their scholars, such as the Dalai Lama. The Khamtruls and the other practice-oriented Kargyus are epitomized by the mystic Milarepa, who spent most of his life in caves, taking advantage of the emptiness that Tenzin Palmo considers Tibet's single most impressive feature. Outside Lhasa, she says, "you can go for days without seeing a person, even a tree, in this vast"—or "vaaahhhst," as she pronounces a favorite word—"mountain landscape with its vast horizon and sky."

Tenzin Palmo draws a parallel between Tibet's seemingly limitless geophysical spaciousness and the "empty mind" of what were, until the eighth century, its simple agrarian tribal people, who had little in the way of literature and other cultural accomplishments and were cut off from the rest of the world. "And then they went to India and got the *dharma,*" she says, savoring the word until it sounds like "dhaaarma." "Ever since, they don't leave a square inch empty, either in their paintings or in their Buddhism! It's full of incredibly subtle, profound philosophies that take decades to unravel, of meditations that are mandala inside mandala inside mandala."

If Zen Buddhism is less, the Tibetan tradition is more. Its richness partly reflects the fact that, well into modernity, a whole culture channeled virtually all of its energy, intelligence, and creativity into its religion, which was also the wellspring of its art, science, literature, music, and government. Then, too, the Tibetans who traveled to India between the eighth and twelfth centuries brought back not only the *dharma* but yoga and Hinduism's Tantra. Its simplistic identification with sex notwithstanding, Tantra is an esoteric discipline concerned with the interrelationship of all things; its aim isn't sensual pleasure but an ecstatic union of the human spirit with transcendent reality. To this heady religious mix the Tibetans added elements from Bon, their earlier animist religion. The result is the so-called Vajrayana path, or "diamond way," which uses all of a person's resources—even what are usually regarded as problems—to achieve enlightenment in a single lifetime.

In her practical fashion Tenzin Palmo compares following the diamond way to launching a rocket into space. "You need enormous amounts of fuel to get it beyond the earth's gravitational pull," she says. "In the same way, if you want to get to the unconditioned mind, you need everything you've got, including so-called spiritual obstacles, such as the body's senses and negative emotional states."

To help very different individuals make the most of their resources, what Tenzin Palmo calls the Tibetan "*dharma* supermarket" offers a huge range of spiritual practices: prayers and mantras, hand gestures and prostrations, circumambulation and silent sitting. In short, this Buddhist tradition has something for everyone—intellectuals drawn to formless meditation, yogis who plumb the body's subtle energies, or devotional people attracted to deities called *yidams*.

At first glance *yidams* don't seem to fit into Buddhism, which is a nontheistic religion. On one level, says Tenzin Palmo, these gods and goddesses embody various aspects of human nature, so that Chenrezig and Tara, for example, are the male and female representations of compassion. On another plane, however, "these kinds of entities really exist," she says. "The perfect crystal of ultimate reality is transparent, but when you shine light through it, it produces rainbow lights—like the deities, who come in rainbow colors! Pick your favorite—sweet or wrathful, male or female—even couples."

There's no need to choose just one type of practice from the *dharma* supermarket, and Tibetan Buddhists typically combine several. Tenzin Palmo describes a hypothetical morning observance that begins with setting out ritual water bowls, lighting a lamp and some incense, and doing three prostrations. Next the practitioner would "take refuge," or recommit to the *dharma,* and renew the *bodhisattva* vow. Then would come deity and guru practices, during which the practitioner visualizes, then meditates on, and finally merges with the *yidam* or teacher, with the goal of striving to embody that ideal in daily life. Next comes a quiet meditation of paying attention to the present moment. The whole ritual, which might take between thirty and sixty minutes, sets the tone for the day, during which the practitioner will revisualize him- or herself and all other males or females, including animals, as Chenrezig, say, or Tara. "If the person is very keen," says Tenzin Palmo, "he or she might recall that all his or her thoughts are the play of Chenrezig's or Tara's mind, and all words and sounds those of a mantra."

As a Westerner, I'm both intrigued and a little shocked by the thought of visualizing oneself as a god. I'm also struck by the markedly positive tone of the regimen Tenzin Palmo has outlined, which contrasts sharply with the "sinners in the hands of an angry God" mentality that influences much of Western religion. Tenzin Palmo says that *of course* Buddhist practice is positive: We all have Buddha nature, so what else could it be? Demonstrating compassion, she adds that all faiths profess that "our true nature is not just our temporal form. Jesus himself, for example, said that the kingdom of heaven is within us. It's there, but it's ignored in the Semitic religions in general, except by mystics."

Even as a small child in Britain, Tenzin Palmo felt she was living in the wrong place. When she was nine she watched a TV show about Thailand that showed frescoes of the Buddha's life, and she asked her mother about him. "She said he was a sort of Oriental god," she recalls, "but I thought, No, that's not right, because he had a life, like Jesus, so he must be a person. Then I said to my mother, 'I'm a Buddhist.' She said, 'Are you? So then, who's the Buddha?' And I said, 'I don't remember.' But I knew that I knew!"

· : · : · ·

One day I get a demonstration from Tenzin Palmo herself of the Vajrayana way of using a negative emotion as spiritual fuel. The social highlight of the nunnery staff's day is the vegetarian lunch served in the office lounge. This day I'm invited to join the group. While waiting for the food to be served, we talk about music. I mention that I enjoyed *Amadeus,* a movie about Mozart, who's Tenzin Palmo's favorite composer. She's as outraged as only a Briton can be. Anyone, she says, who knows anything about Mozart, history, music—in other words, who isn't a complete ignoramus—was appalled, just appalled, by the film. Unfortunately, the food is now on the table, so I can't creep off and hide. Within seconds, however, Tenzin Palmo turns this awkward little incident into an impetus to be especially kind throughout the meal. Later I'm invited to join the staff for lunch every day.

Tenzin Palmo often talks about anger, and she's a spirited woman. In the Tibetan Buddhist scheme of things, however, even negative emotions such as anger, lust, and greed can be turned into spiritual resources. Later that afternoon, when we meet in her office, she says that "when all goes well and everyone is charming, we don't learn anything. We think that we have no problems and are quite nice, happy people. When life is difficult, we're shown where we're really at, and that's when we can really practice with our negative emotions." The trick is to stop identifying with the destructive feeling—"I'm an angry person"—and just observe the emotion itself without becoming attached to it—"Hmmm, there's an angry thought." In that moment of awareness, says Tenzin Palmo, "the feeling can dissolve."

Anger is no mere academic subject in a community of Tibetans. Unspeakable things have happened to nuns and monks since the Chinese invasion, says Tenzin Palmo, "but many come out of prisons and labor camps just radiant, as if they've been in retreat. They say how grateful they were to their tormentors, who allowed them to really practice the *dharma* by loving their enemies and turning them into spiritual helpers."

When she teaches and lectures in the West, Tenzin Palmo finds plenty of negative emotions right in the *dharma* centers where she's invariably asked to talk about compassion. "They'll say, 'We have the wisdom aspect, but we lack kindness,'" she says. "*Dharma* centers should be nests of love and consideration, but there's too much bookishness, which makes overly analytical minds worse. Often, people aren't even kind to each other. Something's not filtering down." Western Buddhism stresses individual meditation, "but the *dharma* is more than quiet seated meditation—a lot more," says Tenzin Palmo. "One can do an enormous amount of practice that remains an ego activity. Very few are motivated by their hunger for the unconditioned and by the misery around them."

One of Tenzin Palmo's major themes as a teacher is the importance of the right motivation for religious practice. Most people begin to meditate because they want something for themselves—the ability to reduce stress, for example. That's all well and good, she says, "but being more comfortable in *samsara* has nothing to do with the spiritual path." At the next level of motivation, the practitioner wants to escape the cycle of birth and death and enter nirvana. When I say that sounds all right to me, Tenzin Palmo laughs and shakes her head no. At the highest level of motivation, the Buddhist responds like a *bodhisattva,* by relinquishing personal reward until all other beings have overcome their limitations and freed their minds. "You don't have to be enlightened to have that feeling," she says pointedly. "Right from the start, it can permeate everything you do."

Spending twelve years alone in a cave may sound antisocial, but Tenzin Palmo's fundamental reason for retreat is her *bodhisattva* vow. To that end, she looks forward to the day within the next several years when she can return to the cave's age-appropriate equivalent. The usual *bodhisattva* analogy, she says, is to the person who escapes a burning house or quicksand, leaving family and friends behind: "You're saved, but so what? First we set our own house in order, then through eternity we benefit others." She gives me the blue look. "That's what we're here for, because that's all that matters."

. : . : . : .

Tenzin Palmo has business in Dharamsala, and some members of the nunnery team hitch a ride in the Indian taxi hired for the two-and-a-half-hour trip. Everyone is excited to be going to the big city, as it were, and a holiday atmosphere obtains in the crowded car. Even Tenzin Palmo is moved to reminisce about a Bob Dylan tape that her mother sent to India in the early 1960s. Several movie stars interested in Tibetan Buddhism have recently been in the environs, and Pierce Brosnan and Richard Gere occasion some girl talk. Tenzin Palmo recalls first seeing Gere many years ago and finding his then-girlfriend Cindy Crawford more glamorous. Pierce gets high marks for quietly buying a costly little Buddha statue in a shop and giving it to an *ani* whom he had overheard admiring it. Pierce also trumps Richard in the perennial who-would-you-rather-be-shipwrecked-with-on-a-desert-island contest. Tenzin Palmo says she would prefer the Dalai Lama, "so I could get teachings." When we rib her for high-mindedness, she laughs and switches her choice to a *togden,* "because one wouldn't have to take care of him!"

We're not really going to Dharamsala but to McLeod Ganj, a throbbing village a few miles above the Indian town. Since 1959 this New Age capital, which sprang up at the foot of the Dalai Lama's pleasant, no-frills "palace," has come to mix the earthly and the sublime in equal measures. Western seekers and dopers in every mode of dress mingle with throngs of Buddhist monks, older Tibetans in traditional garb, and younger Tibetans in jeans and T-shirts. The narrow clay streets are getting their first layer of asphalt, which adds to the pandemonium created by Jeeps, vendors, cows, and soapbox orators. Shops and stalls offer sheep carcasses and custom tailoring, *chai* and jewelry. Monkeys swing from telephone lines that support McLeod's numerous Internet outlets. Despite the prayer wheels and incense, monks and nuns, McLeod's hustle and bustle, juxtaposed against snowy peaks, suggest a frontier boomtown during the Gold Rush.

Before we head off in separate directions, Tenzin Palmo shows us where we're to meet up with our Indian driver later on. Surveying the hordes of people, I say that I hope he'll recognize us. Giving me the mother superior treatment, Tenzin Palmo says, "Will *you* recognize *him*?"

After a shamefully worldly orgy of snacking and shopping, I join the others for our ride back to Tashi Jong. En route we stop to have tea with Didi Contractor. This larger-than-life New Mexican expatriate has also lived in India for forty years, raising a family, studying with Hindu teachers, and working on housing issues. Indeed, she has built several homes, including her own very charming one. While the others dally in Didi's pretty garden, she talks with me about her old friend Ani-la.

When the two women met back in the sixties, Didi says, she was immediately impressed that Tenzin Palmo could speak Tibetan: "She wasn't just another Western flake. She had little formal higher education but has become as learned as a Ph.D. And Ani is the most serious Western practitioner I know. What you see in her eyes—that elevated mode of awareness—is natural to her."

When Tenzin Palmo took on her long, unbroken retreat, Didi says, her health, never robust, was frail. Didi was so worried that she sold some prized possessions so she could afford to escort her friend to her austere new home and help her settle in, even spending two nights there. "It was south-facing, so that the light poured in, and meticulously organized," she says. "It was a cave of great bliss."

Three years later, when the long retreat was over, Didi watched Tenzin Palmo get off the bus in Tashi Jong. Others have remarked that during this period the nun was nearly incandescent. "Ani was always 'glowing,' before and after the retreat," says Didi. "The cave didn't make her a different person, but it spurred a tremendous natural growth. She was still warm and lovely, but more self-assured. At her first *dharma* talk afterwards, people were expecting this angelic, la-di-da creature, but she was direct, forthright, and perfectly aware of what was going on in the world. She's a mystic, but she's humble and practical. Ani's a Hobbit!"

When I tell Didi that, notwithstanding different robes, Tenzin Palmo is every inch the formidable mother superior, she says, "Yes!" Despite that steely strength, she says, "I worry about Ani. She just thinks about building her realm of goodness, but I see the evil powers in the world as well—the cheapening and commodification and globalization of everything. I worry about the gems like Ani. She's sacrificing herself to build the nunnery, but she's delicate. I hope she can remain who she is and be useful without being used. Such a rare person becomes a website?"

The others return with a pile of Didi's well-thumbed books, including mysteries. We have more tea and some sweet and savory snacks made by Didi's houseman, with whom she speaks rapid Hindi. When I admire her proficiency, she cheerfully describes her Hindi as "terrible." Tenzin Palmo says her spoken Tibetan is no great shakes either, although her reading isn't bad. As we take our leave of Didi, Tenzin Palmo gives my shoulder a little pat, and I feel as absurdly pleased as when Sister Teresa Joseph told me that I could wash the blackboard.

As we ride back to Tashi Jong, Didi's recollections about the cave give me the nerve to ask Tenzin Palmo about this very private time in her life. "I went to the cave because I thought it would be a quieter and more pleasant place to practice," she says. "It wasn't a penance. I couldn't think of any place nicer to be." She goes on to describe a regimen as strictly structured as any monk's in a monastery. Her daily schedule revolved around four sessions of four hours each that were devoted to meditation, the recitation of mantras, prostrations, and other practices. Her goal was to have strong realizations: insights into the nature of mind that aren't just intellectual but deeply rooted, gut-level perceptions of ultimate reality that reveal the conventional sort as little more than an illusion. "For three years," she says happily, "I lived the same day, and the years seemed like three months." At the end her practice was more "fascinating" than it had been at first, "because a retreat is like being cooked by a slow, steady heat," she says. "You *become* the practice as it moves from head to heart, transforming you in a slow cooker. It takes time and can't be forced."

That many Westerners can't understand the utility of the contemplative life just offers more proof to Tenzin Palmo of how badly society needs contemplatives. "We've never had more to give," she says. "Contemplatives are the yeast in the dough. Mind has great power, and its nature is the same for all beings. So, at a very deep level, one person's enlightenment is enlightenment for all." Then too, she says, contemplatives' prayer and meditation "fill the universe with powerful forces of light and love, which has a very strong effect. There are hermits transforming themselves into Buddhas and sending out that tremendous love, power, and wisdom to raise the consciousness of all beings. Considering the darkness in the world, if these people weren't there meditating, we would be overtaken by disasters."

As to the retreat's personal rewards, Tenzin Palmo first mentions self-sufficiency: "You're there with your own mind, and that's it—no distractions. You learn how your mind works and how to deal with it." She allows that solitude is "demanding." For one thing, one's identity is largely created by one's relationships, but she was completely alone in the cave for years at a time. "By yourself, what role will you play?" she says. "You go through all those identifications to which we cling. 'This is who I am!' As you keep peeling the onion, however, even the idea of being female becomes irrelevant. When all the roles drop away, who are you?" Then too, with so little external stimulation—her only books were religious ones in Tibetan—it's easy to "fill the mental vacuum with a lot of garbage," she says. "In solitude the mind can either get completely sucked into daydreams, memories, and emotional stuff that comes up or become very grounded and present in the moment."

From the start, says Tenzin Palmo, her spiritual development has been a gradual evolution rather than a series of dramatic epiphanies. "It has just gone along, with one thing leading to another," she says. "A growth—a just keeping going. There have been times when I felt more cheerful or depressed. But I'm not the sort of person who has great peaks and pits."

The cave brought tests of physical as well as psychological mettle. Tenzin Palmo was unperturbed by howling wolves and *yeti* tracks, but, particularly for someone with chronic joint problems, sleeping seated in a wooden "meditation box" instead of a bed couldn't have been easy. Inevitably in a cold, damp cave, there were spells of sickness. With a striking detachment Tenzin Palmo says, "If one could cure oneself, one would, but if one couldn't, so what? It really doesn't matter that much. My body was sick, but my mind wasn't. Tibetan Buddhists have a saying: 'If you're sick, you're sick, and if you die, you die.' They talk a lot about death and impermanence, not to be depressing but to help you realize the preciousness of this moment, which you shouldn't lose."

During her retreat Tenzin Palmo had at least two close brushes with death. Once, while carrying a heavy load of firewood on her back, she stumbled and would have fallen off the mountain had she not been caught by brambles. On another occasion she was immured in the cave by a colossal snowstorm that killed many villagers below. "The first thing that surprised me was that I didn't care," she says. "I didn't panic. I was perfectly cheerful at the prospect of dying soon. The second surprise was that the only thing that could help was Khamtrul Rinpoche. The lama's mind is omniscient and always in your heart, so I prayed to Rinpoche to be there and guide me through the *bardo*"—the Tibetan term for an important transition, such as death. "Then I heard this voice saying, 'Tsk! Stop all this *bardo* stuff, you idiot. Tunnel out!'"

Despite the rigors, the cave brought Tenzin Palmo the sense of infinite time and space that's her greatest joy. Whatever private experiences she had there will remain private. Ever since, however, she says simply, "I don't feel involved in feelings and things that

arise. Whatever happens, I have an inner peace I didn't have before."

The Dalai Lama first met Tenzin Palmo when she was still
Diane Perry in her civvies. Nonetheless, to her astonishment, he
greeted her as Ani-la. Many years later, he affirmed her desire to
live in retreat. "His Holiness said, 'That's the way you're really
going to help people,'" she says. "In this life, the way I can benefit
others is to practice in solitude, which will strengthen the realizations." I know better than to inquire further. As Tenzin Palmo has
already told me, "No one who has realizations will claim to. The
more you realize, the more you realize there's nothing to realize."

Halfway between Dharamsala and Tashi Jong, the driver
proudly points out the local zoo. "Don't look!" says Tenzin Palmo,
wincing at the thought of the incarcerated sentient beings. "Shut
your eyes! It's awful." We stop in a small town to pick up some
fresh vegetables and a newspaper. Tenzin Palmo reads her Cancer-
ian horoscope aloud. It's simply spectacular, mentioning "visitors
from abroad" and "media attention" and heralding a new stage of
life glorious in every particular. There's much riotous laughter,
then the conversation turns to books. Tenzin Palmo describes one
of her childhood favorites, illustrated in the Beardsley style, that
told the story of a certain king who went out for a ride, only to
have the sky fall down. His Majesty's response puts me in mind of
what his countrywoman Tenzin Palmo might say in the same
situation: "How unprecedented!"

· : · : · : ·

When I first began hiking near my summer cottage in upstate
New York, I wasn't sure I'd be able to distinguish a rattlesnake
from one of the area's harmless species. "Don't worry," said a veteran woodsman. "You'll just know." So it is with a *togden*. When I
glimpse for a moment an unfamiliar figure just outside the
Khamtrul's house one morning, I immediately understand that
the monk with a warrior's striking physical grace and sangfroid is
a *togden*.

The yogi-monk Achö really must be described as beautiful.

Chronologically, he's an old man, but he's lithe and straight-backed. His huge bun of braided hair is jet black, and his skin is smooth and glowing. His features suggest a Hollywood Cochise, perhaps, or Genghis Khan. Instantly I grasp that he knows whatever is really worth knowing. This impression is confirmed later in the day, when thunder rolls across the Kangra valley and an *ani* says, "Achö must be shaking his blanket."

Achö's status partly derives from his position as viceroy to the young Khamtrul, whom he helped raise. An old photo shows the *togden* bent solicitously over the little rinpoche, seated with his books at a table, like Arthur being tutored by Merlin. A timelier analogy would be Luke Skywalker and Obi-Wan Kenobi. Like Jedi knights, the *togden*s are said to live in a reality that the rest of us can only imagine, in which the laws of classical physics don't necessarily apply. In one often-told story, the Tashi Jong monks were doing *puja*s—prayers—all night long in the *gompa* when the electricity went out. A *togden* snapped his fingers, and the lights went on; the same sequence of events occurred again, but when the lights went out a third time, the *togden* made a disgusted gesture and everyone continued praying in the dark.

On an everyday basis the *togden*s are distinguished less by what they do than by how they do it. Their training replaces ego and attachment with selflessness and spontaneity. When Tashi Jong was being built, the eighth Khamtrul set the elite *togden*s to road building and other rough work, knowing that they regarded it as no better or worse than the fine crafts in which they also excel. The effect of their example on the rest of the community could not have been far from the Khamtrul's mind either.

One morning I join the steady stream of visitors seeking blessings and counsel at the home of Togden Amtrin. His house is set high up on the mountainside, just beneath the roped-off terrain of the *togden*s in training. Amtrin, who's eighty, sits cross-legged on a divan, wearing a gold Adidas tank shirt. His beard is gray, but his huge topknot is still black. Like the Buddha, he has big ears, and of the same shape. Tenzin Palmo describes his looks as Semitic, and, with his long aquiline nose and calm, clear gaze, he might indeed be a Hebrew prophet of the more benign, eremitical sort. Certainly he would have no difficulty living in the desert. While the young Amtrin was training he went on a long retreat, and his brother sometimes forgot to leave food for him. In one famous story the starving *togden* had wrested the remains of a kill from a leopard, only to realize how attached he was to food. He dropped the bones and returned to his cave.

For the duration of the audience, Amtrin's fingers tell his prayer beads, and his expression remains that of someone just about to smile. There is something about him that makes one want to look and look, and every eye in the room is focused on him like a laser.

When introduced I bow and give an offering in a zipper-lock plastic bag, at which he cocks an eye. I say, "America," and he laughs. Through his translator I add that it's easier to see the Dalai Lama there than in Dharamsala, and he nods and laughs again.

When the time comes for questions, a Westerner asks Amtrin if he's happy. He chuckles good-naturedly at this absurd query and says, "Yes, are you?" She says she finds it hard to quiet her mind and asks what she should do. "Don't do anything," he says. "Don't try."

When I ask Amtrin about Tenzin Palmo, he is a master of diplomacy. Everyone at Tashi Jong, he says, hopes to achieve enlightenment in one lifetime. Some people go off to practice in a cave, but everyone follows different paths to the same goal.

*Togden*s are great yogis, and I try to wheedle a teaching to improve my yoga practice. Amtrin says that here even preliminary yoga teachings take a long time, so a student must come to study with commitment. No sound bites from celebrity gurus in Tashi Jong!

Finally Amtrin blesses me, placing his prayer beads on my head, throat, and chest to purify the body, speech, and mind. The core of the visit, however, isn't what he says or does but his simple presence. Seeing him is like seeing a snow leopard. Just knowing that he's there makes one feel that maybe things are all right after all.

Tenzin Palmo has always gravitated toward the *togden*s. When she first joined the eighth Khamtrul, they accepted her more readily than the other monks did, and in time shared some practices and teachings with her. Historically, the Khamtrul's community had included *togdenmas* as well as *togdens,* but the former tradition died out.

When we meet later in the day, Tenzin Palmo says that when she told the eighth Khamtrul that she wished to become a *togdenma,* he was very pleased. The *togdens* were, too, and agreed to train her further. Other monks, however, objected strongly. "The *togdens* are extremely precious," she says. "For some monks this monastery's importance is that it upholds the *togdens.* There were objections that having a female associated with them could bring disrepute." With a detachment that must have eluded her at the time, she says, " 'Why would a woman—a Western one, too—be with the *togdens?*' It's understandable."

Thirty years later Tenzin Palmo will offer some young nuns yet another opportunity she was denied: to train formally as a *togdenma.* "In my heart, I want to do that for Rinpoche and for women," she says. "The lineage of these practices is very precious, and once it dies out, that's it." Already the novices meet with one of the *togdens* and the lamas, and some, says Tenzin Palmo, "take to practice like a fish to water." When their preliminary studies are completed, the young women with the right potential and desire will begin to work with the *togdens.* In time, she says, "they can teach other women quick ways to become realized—and the world needs realized women!"

· : · : · ·

Living in close proximity to the Olympians of meditation makes plain who is in the Pee Wee League. One hot afternoon I confess to Tenzin Palmo that I can't think of anything more difficult than trying not to think. "Tibetans don't ever try not to think," she says blithely. "They regard the mind's thoughts as being as natural as the ocean's waves. They'll just arise and go if we understand that we're not our thoughts and don't cling to them. Then we get into some contact with that naked awareness, which isn't judging but just knowing. A knowing that doesn't talk because it's not conceptual."

In the beginning of meditation, says Tenzin Palmo, "the important thing is just to be present in a very relaxed manner. Nothing in the world matters but becoming one with your breathing—just flowing with it and letting the thoughts come and go without taking notice." Focusing on something simple, such as one's breath, reduces the sensory, emotional, and cognitive static that usually swamps pure awareness, allowing it to emerge. The point, she says, is not to concentrate on anything—breath included—but rather to "relax the mind into a spacious awareness that's the foundation of all our consciousness."

In Tibetan Buddhism, however, this tranquil attentiveness is the beginning, not the end, of meditation. "Once you can get your mind one-pointed, then you turn its searchlight back on itself," says Tenzin Palmo. "What at this moment is going on there? Who is thinking? What is a thought? Is it the same as mind? Where does it come from and go to? What does it look like? How about emotions? 'I feel so angry!' What is anger? Who is angry?"

Practicing this *vipassana,* or insight, meditation helps the mind "split" in order to observe itself and the habitual mental constructs— "I'm a such-and-such kind of person," say, or "Life is always such-and-such a way"—that we confuse with true reality. In time the practitioner is forced to question the assumption that he or she *is* this familiar grab bag of thoughts and emotions—and especially problems. As a person escapes from the confines of this rigid, ego-centric worldview, life becomes more relaxed. "We begin to respond to situations afresh," says Tenzin Palmo, "as we did as children, when the days were long and full of interest."

In her travels to the West, Tenzin Palmo sees a tendency to keep meditation "all in the head," she says, "as if the meditator and the meditation are almost facing each other." She describes a Tibetan Buddhist exercise in which the practitioner surveys the body, looking for the mind: "Is it in your hand? Stomach, heart, liver? The one place that's not suggested is the brain." Tapping her breast, she says, "Tibetans regard the head as a computer that's driven by the heart, which is where they really think from."

Tenzin Palmo, who's in fact a natural intellectual herself, repeatedly stresses the primacy of heart over head with such fervor that one suspects this principle is one of the realizations she gained in the cave. After all, she says, "When we say, 'Who, me? Do you mean me?' we point to our hearts, not our heads. The only way to bring head and heart together is to let go. The practice isn't to try to stop thoughts, which aren't the enemy or the problem. If one relaxes and allows the mind to become very easy and open, it will center itself—down in the middle of the chest, not up in the head. As long as we battle with our thoughts, it's all going on up here in the brain, not the heart center."

Once the meditator has become adept, Tibetan Buddhism offers any number of sophisticated practices. Advanced persons may even sleep in seated meditation posture and pay particular attention to the moment that psychologists call hypnagogia and the rest of us just call "falling asleep." For an instant, says Tenzin Palmo, "the mind's clear-light nature appears. Normally, we don't recognize it and just go to sleep. Certain meditations and visualizations help you modulate enough to be relaxed yet aware. It's tricky, because if you're too aware, you don't fall asleep."

At the time of death, Tibetan Buddhists believe, the clear-light mind appears more powerfully for a moment; again, most people don't recognize it. As a result, they fall into the sleep of the limbo-like "intermediate state." Those who, like *togdens*, are trained to recognize clear-light awareness, however, can sustain it even while dreaming. At the time of their deaths, Tenzin Palmo says, "there's an instant recognition, and instead of swooning they become one with the clear light."

These infinitely subtle forms of meditation are just part of what Tenzin Palmo calls the *togdens*' "perfection of a very profound practice that creates a very quick way to have realizations. They can put out lots of fuel for the spaceship. It's not just that they live in caves or other remote places but that they've really fine-honed these inner yogas that came from India." Eventually, she says, a *togden* doesn't even have to practice anymore: "In a stage called *mi-gom*, one is undistracted without meditation—present without trying to be. But that's the result of many years of practice."

At death, *togdens* and great lamas stay in a state of what's called *tukdam,* or mind practice, for days or weeks. Tenzin Palmo, who has witnessed it several times, says that, although the brain registers as dead, "the heart center is slightly warm. Instead of going into rigor mortis, the body shrinks, often becoming very youthful-looking and giving off a beautiful perfume. All the conceptual thinking has gone, and the only thing left is the clear-light nature of the mind. It's a very powerful presence to be in. It's said you should meditate and pray in front of that mind because it has no limits."

When I say that she makes meditation sound exciting and, well, fun, Tenzin Palmo says, "I tell people all the time to enjoy the *dharma.* If you decide to read a book or watch a movie or listen to music, nobody has to force you to do it. Practice has to be like that—like that of a musician who loves his instrument."

· : · : · : ·

One evening I'm permitted to sit outside a row of large windows while the Dongyu Gatsal Ling Nunnery's novices sing their *pujas.* During my visit they're on a two-month-long retreat, by the end of which they will have done 100,000 full prostrations and recited 100,000 mantras. I glimpse a few of the appealing, rosy-cheeked girls, whose bloom is only accentuated by their shaved heads and simple robes. Their chanting has a lovely, silvery quality, very different from the more familiar Tibetan monks' sound, that brings unexpected tears.

From women's perspective, few things in the world of religion are more important than access to the kind of rigorous education these young women are beginning to receive. As we walk away from the *pujas,* Tenzin Palmo says that despite her desire to be a hermit, "the nunnery needs to be done, and if I don't do it for these girls, no one else will." She doesn't identify herself as a feminist and loves to point out that one never knows what gender one will have in the next life. There's nothing strident or politically correct about her, and she clearly enjoys male company. Indeed, she's quite voluble in insisting that one of celibacy's great rewards is the ability to have true friendships with the opposite sex. Even when she describes her gender-based frustrations as a young nun, she's temperate: "There I was, surrounded by all these exemplars of the *dharma*—a great banquet!—and I was getting just little crumbs. It wasn't anyone's fault. I was a woman, so I just couldn't live in a monastery."

Equanimity notwithstanding, when I tease her about becoming the first female Buddha, Tenzin Palmo makes a wry face and says, "Well, why *can't* women follow the path in the female form, you know? If you have very clear aspirations, they're likely to be fulfilled, because you plant seeds in your mental continuum." She asks, however, that I not "go on" about her and the first-female-Buddha business, which she feels has been made too much of: "I think that in the past as many women as men have attained enlightenment, but they just weren't recognized by male-dominated society."

In an all-too-familiar catch-22, Buddhism maintains that it's not that women *can't* become enlightened, they just face many "obstacles." The eighth Khamtrul told Tenzin Palmo that there were many more auspicious signs at his sister's birth than at his own, but when the baby turned out to be a girl, "people said, 'Whoops, there's been a mistake,'" she says. "A boy born under those auspices would have been specially cared for and trained. And she was just one of many such girls! Their society wasn't geared for them, and, as a result, their ability to benefit many beings was limited." As she talks about these Tibetan girls, I think of how hard this self-taught English one has worked to attain not just wisdom but knowledge. "Without education, even a realized person can't teach or write," she says. "It's the key to so much."

It is not surprising that religious Tibetan Buddhist women have traditionally prayed to be reborn as males. "Better a male rabbit than a female human, apparently!" says Tenzin Palmo. "One very high lama who's the head of a tradition—I'm not saying who—assured me that up to the last millisecond before enlightenment, you could be female, but then you had to have a male body. Why a penis is essential, who knows?"

Far from being poorly equipped for the path to enlightenment, Tenzin Palmo thinks that women have certain advantages. For one thing, because women "wash dishes and care for kids," she says, "they tend to be less theoretical and more practical about using the *dharma* in life as it is." Then, too, many spiritual masters have told her that on the whole women have a greater affinity for meditation than men. "Men like to analyze and go one step at a time," she says. "Women are generally more at home with the intuitive. They are more able to let go and feel unchallenged by the infinity and spaciousness of the nonconceptual. It's that 'different way of knowing.' Their minds are often quite undisciplined and emotional, and that energy usually gets dissipated or creates problems. But if they can harness it, they can use it to propel themselves higher, faster."

Showing her British mettle, Tenzin Palmo says that the obstacles and pressures women confront on the spiritual path are "all the more reason to be born in that form! You can't abandon people because of their difficulties. That would be lacking in compassion. Why should I go over to the other side?" She pauses for a moment, then says, "My prayer is that whatever form is most beneficial to all beings, may I be reborn in that form." But her eyes flash blue steel.

Even in this lifetime Tenzin Palmo is encouraged by signs of progress. She points to a framed copy of the Dalai Lama's personal endorsement for the Dongyu Gatsal Ling Nunnery, which makes a special point of referring to Tenzin Palmo not just as *ani* or "venerable" but as both *gelongma* and *bhikshuni*. Outside of China most Buddhist traditions don't give women this monastic distinction, on the grounds that, to be valid, the line of such ordination has to be unbroken back to the time of Buddha. Years ago Tenzin Palmo had to travel to Hong Kong for the ceremony, but now the ordination is given in India, and in the future the DGL novices will receive it.

Beyond Tashi Jong, too, women's status in Tibetan Buddhism is improving. For the first time in history a group of nuns recently debated philosophy in front of the Dalai Lama. Soon women may be eligible for a *geshe* degree, which is equivalent to a doctorate in divinity. A well-regarded young female lama named Khandro Rinpoche is already traveling abroad for teaching tours. And then there's Tenzin Palmo. She might be talking about herself when she says, "If some woman will just do these things, the walls crumble, because there's no real opposition. Then it's a fait accompli."

·　:　·　:　·　:　·

The natural, integrated way in which Tibetans live their Buddhism is one reason why this tiny population has captured the world's heart. Tenzin Palmo isn't given to sentimental generalities and insists that the average Tibetan is "no better or worse than anyone else," yet even she allows that they're "generally easy to get on with and ready to laugh."

The tea shop of Tsering Dolma quickly becomes my favorite hangout. From its outside table on what passes for Tashi Jong's main drag, one can sip tea and watch the monastery world go by. Tibetans have no traditional expressions for hello and goodbye, so they use the salutation given on their all-purpose national and personal new-year holiday, greeting all comers with "*Tashi Delek!*"—Good Fortune!

In her small house's low-ceilinged front room, Tsering Dolma serves omelettes and chapattis cooked on a hot plate, homemade yogurt, tea, and other simple fare to monks, including her strapping third son, and visitors seated around a trestle table. It's nearly impossible to eat a dollar's worth of food. Tsering Dolma also sells incense and toothpaste, soap and bottled water; anything she doesn't have must come from miles away. For me much of Tibetans' charm lies in their directness, of which Tsering Dolma is an exemplar. She's all business during the monks' rush hours and has little patience for tourists wanting special orders: "I'm busy now! Can't you come back later?" But in the evening she'll sit outside the shop to chat and enjoy her geraniums, which, "thank God," the wandering Hindu cows won't eat.

One dusk, to my surprise, the tea shop's door is bolted. I wait a bit, exchanging "Tashi Delek"s with the circumambulators, till Tsering Dolma comes hurrying up the hill. Brandishing a pair of underpants, she says that last night someone snatched her drawers—"black ones and white ones too!"—right off her clothesline. Fortunately, she says, she was able to borrow a pair from her auntie in the village. She hurries inside, presumably to gird her loins, and returns with little glasses of sweet, milky tea to enjoy the *passeggiata*.

After spending forty years among Tibetans, Tenzin Palmo has her own trickle-down theory about the origin of their special joie de vivre. She believes their culture is permeated by its emphasis on the attainment of enlightenment in a single lifetime. As a result religion is woven into nearly every aspect of daily life. Moreover, this small population has produced a phenomenal number of enlightened people as leaders, "even one of whom would be a treasure," she says. "A genuine lama is . . . something else. Intellect, heart, and spirit are all developed—that's what makes them so extraordinary. From an early age they lead very special lives, yet they're so approachable—even old, very traditional ones."

The most familiar lama, of course, is the Dalai Lama. He's often described as a god-king but is actually the *bodhisattva* of compassion, the incarnation of the deity called Chenrezig by Tibetans, Avalokiteshvara by Indians, and Kwan Yin by the Chinese. "He was raised by old monks, speaking a special language just for him, yet he's so accessible!" says Tenzin Palmo. "He's the same with presidents as with simple farmers. There are levels, of course, but Tibetan lamas can be so . . . cool! If you meet one of the greatest, you can't help but think this being is what we're all trying to evolve toward."

Being a lama in a culture in which the first person to consult in a health crisis isn't a doctor but a spiritual master is a weighty responsibility. Earlier I had heard about a recent incident in which the desperate parents of a comatose child took the boy, hanging limp in his father's arms, to their rinpoche. The lama withdrew into himself and seemed to become larger, so that his eyes bulged in his head. Then he spat in the boy's face. The child sat up and began talking. My informant attributed this cure to the lama's power over that matter-energy business.

The lama's most important public role, however, is that of teacher. Tenzin Palmo's first one was Dugu Choegyal Rinpoche, chosen for her by the eighth Khamtrul himself. An artist as well as a spiritual master, he and Dorzong Rinpoche, a highly regarded scholar who often acts as a delegate of the Dalai Lama, are the Khamtrul's two most important lamas and Tashi Jong royalty. Choegyal Rinpoche, who's regarded as the eighth incarnation of a great lama, is also very involved with his community back in Tibet and with an educational center and arts workshop in Kathmandu. One afternoon Tenzin Palmo takes me up the steep hill to his house, introduces a small man with a friendly, open, interested manner and good English, and leaves us to talk in his garden.

Making short work of the *kata* ritual, Choegyal Rinpoche invites me to sit on a carpet mat. Gently brushing away an ant, he thoughtfully offers another mat to cushion Western ankles. He's in his mid-fifties and has withstood harrowing travails since a terrifying escape from his homeland at thirteen, but the smiling rinpoche looks ten years younger. More impressively, he engages in what most busy people would regard as an interruption in a demanding schedule with every appearance of delight.

Choegyal Rinpoche has known Tenzin Palmo since she was twenty-one and he was just nineteen. "Ani-la is not ordinary—no," he says, laughing. "And that's good!" Growing serious, he continues, "She's a genuine *dharma* practitioner—sincere, devoted, and determined. She's not polluted by worldly motivations. Her nature was deeply understood by the eighth Khamtrul, who could with one glance read a person like a book. He had a lot of trust in her, which gives us a lot of confidence in Ani-la."

That's not to say that in the beginning the student-teacher relationship between the working-class British female novice and the rarefied lama was an easy one. Tenzin Palmo often refers to her distress at being barred by gender from a standard monastic education and has said that Choegyal Rinpoche, albeit brilliant, was a "frustrating" teacher. The rinpoche, however, casts another light on their lessons. "My way of teaching is not traditional," he says. "In my opinion, it's not good to force practice. I just helped Ani-la have glimpses of things, then she developed herself. She's smart, pure, and very determined regarding her goals."

The rinpoche's freewheeling teaching style emerges as we discuss the dynamic nature of religion in the fast-paced twenty-first century. Just as Tibetans' way of thinking changed when they first journeyed to India, Choegyal Rinpoche's perspective has been changed by his travels, including six trips to America. Rather than feeling threatened by challenges to his tradition, he finds an encouraging precedent in the way Tibetan culture grappled with the new philosophy of Buddhism. "As we kept practicing the *dharma*, we had to struggle with its contradictions to our old Tibetan animism," he says. Sounding what will emerge as his theme, he says, "The most basic Buddhist belief is to stop the mind from clinging to things—even to religion!"

Much of Buddhism's appeal to educated Westerners lies in its apparent freedom from dogma. But, says the rinpoche, "Even though many people think Tibetan Buddhists don't believe in God, for many of us, Buddha is like God. We also have heaven and spirits, because we put solid, clinging descriptions onto such things. We say 'empty mind,' but mind makes Buddha! We cling to Buddha, but he always says, 'Don't cling to me!'" The rinpoche laughs delightedly at the very thought. "Buddhist practice deletes Buddhism!"

Just as the West has been influenced by Tibetan Buddhism, the rinpoche makes clear that the religion is being influenced by its encounters with a new culture. "In Tibet, I just lived and felt like a Tibetan Buddhist," he says. "Then I moved about in the world and saw different ways of life that call for different religions. They are all good for the mind. I also saw that, in the East and West, the mind is the same. Now I don't feel Tibetan, Buddhist, or any such thing." He points to his robes. "These don't make us special— they're just clothes. Now I feel that we're all sentient beings, and the other stuff is not important." In the end, he says, with more laughter, "after all the practices and views, I have no view!"

Like the Dalai Lama and the Vietnamese Buddhist Thich Nhat Hanh, the rinpoche sees no necessity for people of one culture to convert to another culture's religion. "I feel that all religious people are one family," he says. In my many years of reporting, the rinpoche is one of few people I've interviewed who would rather ask questions than talk about himself. He's particularly interested in other religions and notes several titles of books that come up in our conversation, including ones on Sufism and Kabbalah. "We Tibetans think there's an infinity of planets with beings," he says. "Buddha was an Indian on earth but will be something else on some other planet, which will need other teachings."

Choegyal Rinpoche's religious tolerance notwithstanding, he's a master of a tradition whose layers of teaching he describes as "public, semiprivate, and very private." He compares the complexity of Tibetan Buddhism to Indian food: "There are many dishes, eating styles, and flavors." *Yidam* practice, for example, is a "spicy food."

When I ask how one chooses a personal deity, the rinpoche says that, although one's mind is ineffable, "when it manifests your best qualities—projects them outward—that's your *yidam*." Although many people venerate popular gods such as Chenrezig and Tara, he says, "You can practice with whatever deity your mind can make, which means *yidams* are often more interesting than the serene Buddha. Some are fantastic creatures with horse heads or necklaces made of galaxies. Even if you practice being God, perhaps, or the Buddha, that's okay, just so there's not you and the deity, but you *as* the deity." Turning to body language, the rinpoche says, "*Yidam* practice makes me not"—he slumps over and scrunches up—"but"—he straightens up and looks expansive.

Resounding his theme, the rinpoche says, "You can bring Jesus, Allah, God, or Buddha into your self, but then you must break out and not cling to your *yidam,* because that makes another boundary. Any practice should make the mind loose, not clinging, no matter how nice it seems, because clinging strains the mind. There should be no striving to accomplish. The thing is not to feel 'I'm great' but just to *be* great!" He laughs. "That's what we call en-lightened."

Before I leave the rinpoche deftly underscores the teaching he has given me. "Some of the people who come here to see me want to cling to my advice," he says, "but there's nothing to cling to."

Later, when I think back on the hour or so spent with the rin-poche, what I cling to is not so much his advice about not clinging as his brainy, merry, shimmering presence, which expressed what I can only unimaginatively call the incredible lightness of being.

· : · · : ·

Perhaps by design, conversation at the nunnery staff's lunch is on the light side. Books and films are popular topics, and even the odd bit of gossip about a movie star's divorce may be entertained. The celebrity of the moment, however, is the fifteen-year-old Karmapa Rinpoche, the spiritual leader of the Kargyu tradition, who re-cently escaped from Chinese control and found asylum outside Dharamsala. He has just given his first press conference, which was a great success, and his photo is all over the newspapers. The hunky lama in his shades looks like he'd be at home on a big Harley. The nuns, who have visited him, describe his powerful presence and piercing gaze.

At first lamas and lineages, deities and rituals, can intimidate Westerners interested in Tibetan Buddhism. After lunch Tenzin Palmo quotes the eighth Khamtrul, who told her, "You can drop the Tibetan culture, just don't drop the *dharma*. The *dharma* speaks straight to our hearts, so we know it's true."

Despite the challenges, Tenzin Palmo believes that a new "Western Buddhism" is already emerging and finds a parallel in Tibetan Buddhism's own evolution. At first, she says, Tibetans in search of teaching had to bribe Indian instructors and translators, whose attitude was " 'We can't give the *dharma* to these barbarians! It's much too subtle and profound. They'll just mess it up. They'll never understand it!' " Several hundred years later, when Muslim invaders had razed the Buddhist monasteries and slaughtered their monks, she says, "The Indians said, 'What about those barbarians?'

They saw the *dharma* being destroyed in their own land and decided the barbarians ought to have it, just so that someone did."

Now Tenzin Palmo sees this historical drama repeating itself with different characters in the principal roles. "The Tibetans look at us Westerners and think, They'll never understand this *dharma*. Those barbarians will just mess it up. That's their underlying assumption, but they see it being destroyed in their own country— and the increasing indifference of many of their own people now in India. So they think, Maybe something good will happen if we hand it over."

Despite the bumps in the road, Tenzin Palmo says that "more and more, you see Buddhism merging into a basic *dharma* in the West. Things are moving very fast. In a generation, it will be there." Many elements of this new form of Buddhism come from the Zen, Theravadan, Tibetan, Korean, and other traditions, each with its strengths and weaknesses. Extraneous beliefs and practices that suit only other societies are dropping away, and new things that are meaningful to Westerners, such as insights from psychology and increased roles for women, are being added. Tenzin Palmo already sees evidence of "a more active Buddhism, in that it's not enough to sit on your cushion. You must show compassion in action."

Tenzin Palmo is no believer in tradition for its own sake. She sees no reason why Europeans and Americans shouldn't have a vibrant, resilient form of Buddhism that suits them, just as the Japanese, Koreans, Thais, and Tibetans have theirs. This new Western Buddhism will "go back to the fundamental teachings of the *dharma,*" she says, "which has nothing to do with culture, but concerns your mind and how to deal with its problems." Bringing up an obvious example, she says, "Buddha didn't speak Tibetan, which isn't a sacred language. It's wonderful to read Milarepa in the original, but translations of the main texts are getting better and better, and for most people, they're enough."

The two things Western Buddhism most needs, according to Tenzin Palmo, are "great scholars, which we have, and enough realized beings, which we don't have. We need people who have digested the *dharma* and can give it back to Westerners in the right form for them." She would demur, but Tenzin Palmo herself seems to be one such, and her earliest Tibetan mentor was another. When she met the legendary Chögyam Trungpa Rinpoche, the lama was an unknown, friendless student at Oxford; soon he was visiting the young Englishwoman and her mother almost every weekend. Of this meteoric, controversial figure, known for his womanizing and hard drinking as well as for his brilliant teaching and writing, Tenzin Palmo says, "Trungpa wasn't ordinary. He was already realized back then, I'm sure. But he was very emotional and . . ." To this seemly nun, the lama was one of those rare persons to whom the usual rules just don't apply. "There was something indefinable about him that other, proper lamas didn't have," she says. "He wasn't acting at all as I thought a monk or lama should. Yet I felt, This is the real thing, the genuine article. The normal paradigms of behavior just didn't encompass his way of being. And certainly he benefited many, many people."

Beginning in the late sixties, the kind of openness and charisma exerted by Trungpa, who advised Westerners to embrace their own culture, helped Tibetan Buddhism shed its reputation as a minor, superstitious folk religion. "Till then, people hadn't met any lamas," says Tenzin Palmo, "and as they did they saw the lamas were extraordinary beings—the proof of the pudding. People would say, 'I don't know what you believe, but whatever it is, I want to have some, too.'" Suggesting that the free-spirited Trungpa, who was a master of putting religion into psychological language, was the perfect Johnny Appleseed for Tibetan Buddhism in the wild and woolly West, she says, "He had an ability to transmit the *dharma* in a way that was suitable for the people he had to transmit it to. People who won't come to the *dharma* by a direct path, but who are drawn in without understanding what's happening to them." She grins mischievously. "Then, as they get more into it, we put the screws on, and they end up like our nuns, doing a hundred thousand belly flops!"

India in general and places like Dharamsala in particular are full of Westerners trying to be more Eastern than the Asians. But Tenzin Palmo says, "I don't want to be a Tibetan. Because most of the Westerners the lamas meet are asking them for advice, not talking about where they come from, the Tibetans get a distorted view that we're all rootless, have no culture, and are just good at making cars and Coca-Cola. They assume that, when it comes to spiritual things, only the Tibetans know anything about anything. After twenty-four years in India, I felt that I had to go back and rediscover what my own culture had to say about spiritual experience, art, and music."

Tenzin Palmo chose Italy because she had friends there and loves its medieval and Early Renaissance art—and great saints. "Assisi, with Francis and Clare and its strong spiritual sense, was a great place to be," she says. "For six years I found it extremely fascinating, inspiring, and nurturing to come back to being Western again." Nor does she rule out returning to the West, particularly for a long retreat: "Electricity is not a hindrance to enlightenment."

In Italy, Tenzin Palmo got some firsthand experience of Buddhism's increasing attractiveness to many spiritually minded Westerners. She was invited to several conferences on contemplative spirituality sponsored by the Benedictines, she says, "and all they wanted to talk about was how to incorporate Buddhist-type meditation into their traditions! One morning I got up early to go to mass, and the others were all in a different room doing *zazen!*" Tenzin Palmo traces the Christian monastics' interest in meditation to their desire not only to revitalize their own practice but also to win back the young people who've moved away from the church.

What Tibetan Buddhism offers disillusioned Westerners, according to Tenzin Palmo, is an unsurpassed range of meditative practices that, by showing a person his or her true nature, can solve two pressing problems. The first is what she sees as Westerners' chronically low, guilt-ridden self-image. Earlier she had provided an example of the positive view of the self inherent to Buddhism. She had been describing an inner voice that she periodically hears. "I argue with it continually," she said, "but it's always right. I don't think of it as being the voice of something very high, like God, but of a spirit guide. It's a definite voice—a male voice—that says things like 'Get up and do this now.' Or 'Don't worry, it's okay, go to sleep.' Then, the next day, the thing that seemed unsolvable the night before has solved itself." When I asked if such a voice would talk to "just anyone," she said sharply, "Why shouldn't it? We all have Buddha nature."

Along with reminding Westerners of the beauty and goodness of their true nature, Tenzin Palmo feels that Tibetan meditation can open their hearts. Sounding a favorite theme, she says, "Westerners live in our heads, but if religion stays in the head without transforming the heart, it's just another ego enhancement. 'I've done this many retreats,' and 'This lama said such and such to me,' and so on. Nothing changes and the person has the same problems." (I've noticed that this aspiring hermit and reluctant mother superior always makes time for people who seek her guidance and has many correspondents, including a number of prisoners.)

For Westerners who want to study Tibetan Buddhism, it's the best of times and occasionally the worst. Many illustrious lamas now teach abroad, but, understandably, their primary motivation is to raise money to keep their religion—and whole culture—alive in India, Nepal, and Tibet. They return home, often leaving behind inadequately trained students, *dharma* centers delegated to lesser teachers, and monks and nuns ordained after as little as a few weeks' training. Calling the plight of these fledgling clergy "a tragedy," Tenzin Palmo says, "They're just thrown out of the nest. If they fly, they fly, and if they fall—splotch! They're not laypeople anymore, nor are they part of a *sangha* [Buddhist community]. They get very discouraged, because there's no financial or psychological support. Their fellow Westerners adore the Tibetan monks and lamas but say things to them like 'What's your problem? Can't you face up to relationships? What are you escaping from?' They don't talk like that to the Tibetans!"

At the end of our talk, with an amused look, Tenzin Palmo points out that there's nothing new about the process of an Eastern religion establishing itself in the West. "Remember that Judaism, Christianity, and Islam came from the very different culture of the Middle East," she says. "There were a lot of adjustments, rearrangements, and rejections in the beginning for them, too."

If Tenzin Palmo could share a single teaching with Westerners, whether Buddhists or not, it would be to "use 'worldly' activity as a method to achieve genuine clarity and understanding and to open the heart," she says. "Otherwise there's no hope. People no longer spend twelve years in a cave or practice as they used to, so the only option is to make their daily life their practice."

· : · : · : ·

On a hot Saturday I have lunch with Sarla Korla, a Hindu lady whose sprawling house, complete with verandas, roses, and small yapping dogs, might appear in a movie about the Raj. "Good to see you!" says her husband, a towering, mustachioed retired major general in the Indian Army. "Hope you can stay the night!" Over the past twenty years Tenzin Palmo has often stayed here. "She used to stop off on her way from the cave to prepare to visit her lama," says Sarla-ji. "My husband would tease her, saying, 'Oh, there you are! Have you had your bath yet?' "

Sarla-ji's beautiful gray *salwar kameez*—a long, flowing shirt and trousers—embroidered in brown "chicken-scratch" needlework, highlights her silver hair and brown eyes. A few moments with her is long enough to see why her grandchildren all over the globe have forced her to learn e-mail. She humorously prefaces her remarks about Tenzin Palmo with an old Indian saying: " 'It's always dark right under the lamp'—that means you don't see the holiness of people you're close to."

Sarla-ji describes her relationship with Tenzin Palmo as "close, affectionate. We don't talk about religion, but Hinduism recognizes that there are many paths to God. Ani-la is a *saddhu*—a person who's the same in sorrow and gladness and to all people. She has led a difficult life and faced many obstacles, including painful health problems, but she's always accepting. Even though she wishes she could do her solitary practice, for example, she is work ing on the nunnery project. She has a very good aura and attracts very good people to her." Defining one effect of spiritual genius, she says, "If your thoughts become elevated in someone's presence, that person is a *saddhu*."

Hinduism not only acknowledges the validity of other religions but also has a genius for incorporating their ideas into its capacious self. This kind of syncretism, called "cafeteria religion" by critics and "blending" by enthusiasts, is becoming a characteristic of postmodern Western religion as well. One day, this new, multilayered spirituality comes up in a discussion with Tenzin Palmo. When she describes infinite awareness, I say, "That's what I call God." "And that's what we're all trying to get for ourselves," she says. "Religion is based on form and dogma, but genuine spirituality goes beyond all that to the unconditioned. True practitioners in all religions are very similar in their experience of ultimate reality, whatever they call it—and also the basics of being a good person and not harming. It's the bit in the middle, the religion part, that makes the problems."

Tenzin Palmo converted to Tibetan Buddhism, but she sees no reason why other Westerners who are content in their religious lives should do likewise. Nor does she object to practitioners of the great religions who borrow "skillful means" from each other. "If Westerners of different faiths can take the right things from Buddhism, that's fine," she says. "Your label doesn't matter. Buddha himself said the *dharma* was just a raft across the ocean of *samsara*. Once on the other side, you don't carry it on your back but let go of it. The important thing is the moon, not the finger pointing at it. We need the finger as a guide, but it's only a finger."

· : · : · ·

Not long before leaving Tashi Jong, I nervously set off to visit Achö. Tenzin Palmo has known the most imposing of the *togden*s since their youth. During her six years near Assisi, she became an admirer of St. Francis and his platonic soul mate, St. Clare, who founded the Poor Clares and whose picture hangs above her bed. If the Buddhist nun has such a friendship, it might well be with

Achö. An *ani* says that once, during an all-night *puja,* Tenzin Palmo was about to take a seat in the back of the *gompa.* Achö led her up front and seated her on his tiger skin. When the night grew cold, he let down his long hair to cover her and keep her warm.

Fortunately, I'm accompanied on the visit by Phuntsok, the nunnery's lissome young Tibetan office assistant, who will translate. She explains that whenever the Tibetan villagers face an important decision, they visit the *togden*s for a divination, called a *moh.* The people also consult the *togden*s for advice on health problems, she says, and, "of course, we ask them to stop the rain." The *togden*s, particularly Achö, are revered, she says, and even a little feared.

The second we ring the Khamtrul's bell, the door swings open. Achö indicates some mats on the floor and sinks into lotus pose as gracefully as a young ballet dancer. Along with his red-trimmed white robes and red shirt, he wears a watch, pen, and shades. He has to be the coolest person on the planet.

When I ask how he thinks of his old friend Tenzin Palmo, Achö readily answers in a pleasant, resonant voice, saying considerably more than Phuntsok translates. His first remark reflects an Eastern, more formal way of assessing a person that's less concerned with individual traits and quirks: "Ani-la is a disciple of the eighth Khamtrul and was ordained by him," he says. "She came to help him, her guru, which she does from the heart. She is *gelongma.* She went to the cave. She has been very good in all endeavors. All here feel that she's an extraordinary achiever."

Thinking of the painting of the blue-eyed lama back in Tibet, I ask if a venerable Tibetan monk can reappear as an Englishwoman. Achö smiles. "Maybe in a previous life," he says, "she and the rinpoche had a relationship. In a previous life, maybe she did very good things, which is why she came here. A person doesn't have to have been Tibetan to end up here!" The normally impassive *togden* seems much amused by this line of questioning. "If people do lots of good deeds, they have a better chance of a better next life. But all people who do *puja*s can't just decide what will happen in their next life. Even *togden*s don't know where or when that will be." I ask if a *togden* could surface in America. "Yes!" says Achö, laughing and shaking his head as if at the funniest thing he'd ever heard.

Toward the end of the visit I ask this great yogi, who allegedly can leap high in the air and land seated in lotus, for a teaching to use in yoga. With an appraising glance, he asks again how long I've been practicing and nods his head the slightest fraction. With a kindly look, however, he says, "I teach no one."

Screwing up my courage, I ask the question that has been in my mind almost since I arrived at Tashi Jong: "Is Tenzin Palmo a *togdenma*?" "This is not an official title with us," says Achö, "but you could call her that, yes."

· : · : · ·

In our last conversation Tenzin Palmo talks about the future of the contemplative vocation. Secular society's allure notwithstanding, she sees the peculiar services of those who dedicate themselves to a life of solitude and religious practice as a growth industry. In a confused, fast-paced world, contemplatives are "living examples of sanity," she says. "A true exemplar of the spiritual path is like a light in all the craziness. Society tells us that more is better—more stuff, activities, sensory indulgence—but monastic life says the opposite. It says that true happiness lies in shedding, in letting go, in simplicity and purity. In not rushing or worrying about what you eat or wear. In being present and having an open heart. In really caring about others yet having that still center. In spending your life developing your understanding and compassion! People need this example."

At the end of our talk, I tell Tenzin Palmo that Achö said she could be called a *togdenma*. For the only time in the many hours I've spent with her, she becomes flustered. "What?" she exclaims, her face bright pink. I repeat the remark. "It's hard to believe," she says, quickly adding, "Anyway, it would be such a blessing to the world if there were more realized women."

· : · : · ·

Long after I leave Tashi Jong, I think of a characteristically profound, succinct teaching about our true nature that its *togdenma* offered one hot afternoon in "Tibet," sitting beneath her little icon of St. Clare. "If I tell you to visualize yourself as Tara," said Tenzin Palmo, giving me the blue look, "you think, I'm Winifred, pretending to be Tara. But the truth is that you are really Tara, pretending to be Winifred."

4. ACTIVIST

· : ·

With thousands of other Americans, I first encounter Riffat Hassan, a pioneering scholar of Islamic feminist theology, as a guest on television's *Nightline*. The brainy news program is examining a horrific crime against women wrought in religion's name. Each year thousands of Muslims are the victims of "honor killings," murdered by male relatives for behavior alleged to jeopardize their families' reputation. Such offenses range from adultery and elopement to being seen with a man or gossiped about.

This dismal statistic assumes human faces when *Nightline* shows clips from a BBC documentary called *Murder in Purdah*. A distraught mother explains that her young daughter was hacked to death with axes for talking to a male childhood friend while fetching water. A mutilated woman who managed to take her abusive husband to court weeps as she recounts that the judge declared she was insane. A sixteen-year-old Pakistani girl, who was accused of infidelity by her husband's family, doused with kerosene, and set aflame, moans and tosses on her hospital bed; a voice-over says that she died the next day.

Right away Dr. Hassan's traditional Pakistani *salwar kameez* distinguishes her from the talking heads usually recruited to discuss the news. Then, too, her flashing eyes and the posh British accent of her upper-class background present a very different image of Muslim womanhood from the familiar anonymous figure shrouded in a *chador.* She may be a professor of religious studies, but she soon makes plain that, for her, neither scholarship nor religion is just an abstract pursuit; they are matters of life and death.

First, Dr. Hassan goes straight for the stereotype lodged in the Western viewer's mind. Any abuse of women is utterly unjustified by the Qur'an, she says: "In a society constructed on the true basis of Islam, men and women would be equal, as they are in the sight of God." The religion's real teachings about women have been perverted by those who believe that "male honor is priceless and irreplaceable and women are not."

It's impossible to determine exactly how many thousands of women are murdered each year in honor killings, because most of their deaths are never reported. When they are, the killers are rarely prosecuted and often become local heroes. In the BBC documentary a grinning man in a group of admiring villagers explains that women are weak-minded and immature. If they were allowed to venture beyond the bounds of *purdah,* he says, immorality and chaos would result. A proud father who killed his daughter because she eloped says with a smile, "There is no greater honor anywhere!"

What's striking about Dr. Hassan's brief remarks about honor killing isn't so much her assertion that Islam doesn't advocate the oppression of women but her declaration that it can actually stop such injustice. It's soon clear that this aristocratic scholar who fights for the uneducated poor is also an ardent feminist who's a devout Muslim. "Women need to be educated about their rights under Islam," she says. Already young women pursuing this inquiry are discovering "a different kind of Islam," which, she tartly adds, "the Western media don't see."

Even the grim documentary offers glimpses of Dr. Hassan's "different kind of Islam." In one arresting sequence sixteen women who've been sentenced to be hanged for killing abusive or murderous husbands go about their routines in jail. Such women often like prison, says the narrator, because it provides not only protection and the physical necessities but also education. In another shot a poor woman holds up her maimed hands and explains that she doesn't blame God for her burns and missing fingers. "It's the men who have done this," she says.

Intrigued, I do some research on Dr. Hassan's kind of Islam and find that it's a profound challenge to the misogynistic sort promulgated by "Islamization." This rapidly spreading political movement seeks to establish governments that rule by "Islamic law," which in reality imposes not just religion but patriarchal culture. The paradoxically modern phenomenon's two legislative hallmarks are harsh criminal punishments, such as stoning and amputation, and rules that control women. For example, Islamizers distort the custom of *purdah,* or the separation of women from male society, until all public space essentially becomes a male preserve. Women can rarely venture beyond the home, and when they do they must be heavily veiled and segregated. Those who disobey can be beaten, mutilated, burned, or even murdered.

The "Islam" that deprives the average Muslim woman—who's a poor, illiterate villager in the developing world—of basic human rights is based on male theologians' traditional readings of certain sections of the Qur'an. As one of the first feminist Muslim theologians, Dr. Hassan has spent years meticulously analyzing the text, and she disputes these long-entrenched interpretations. Chapter 4, verse 34, for example, has long been regarded as the Qur'an's definitive verse about women. This passage describes men's relationship to women with the Arabic word *qawwamun,* which is usually translated as "rulers," "masters," or "custodians." Dr. Hassan's interpretation is "those who provide support or livelihood," or what we might call breadwinners for childbearing women.

It's hard to overstate the immensity of Dr. Hassan's goal of persuading the Muslim world to read the Qur'an in a new way. After a hundred years of scholarly analysis of the Bible, most main-stream Jews and Christians no longer subscribe to scriptural in-errancy, or the view that its every word is literally true; moreover, they actively strive to make the ancient text relevant to their post-modern lives. In contrast, most Muslims consider the Qur'an to be the literal words of God as spoken to the prophet Mohammad. Its canonical text has not changed since it was established in 651–652 C.E., and it has not been subjected to modern Islamic scholarship. A "historical Qur'an" may be inevitable, but it's still a highly controversial idea within the vast, volatile Islamic world. In much of it, Dr. Hassan's seemingly unexceptionable assertions that the same word can have different interpretations, and that a proper understanding of the Qur'an requires "looking at the whole picture, rather than lifting out one line of Arabic text," are dangerous heresy.

Despite the risks, women's plight in her native Pakistan has turned this American scholar, who has been a professor in the University of Louisville's religious studies program for twenty-five years and formerly taught at Harvard and the University of Pennsylvania, into an activist. Her major tool is the International Network for the Rights of Female Victims of Violence in Pakistan, which she founded to marshal international political pressure and financial support on behalf of endangered women throughout the Muslim world. There are signs of progress. In 2000, Dr. Hassan met privately, in Lahore, with General Pervez Musharraf, the president of Pakistan, who has proclaimed official opposition to honor killings and promised to improve medical care for female burn victims. At the same time, however, the crisis is spreading. *Honor killing* has a medieval ring, but, according to Amnesty International, the number of such crimes in Muslim countries— including Jordan, Turkey, Syria, Egypt, and Morocco—is "on the rise as the perception of what constitutes honor . . . widens."

· : · : · :

Riffat Hassan invites me to attend a program called "The Many Voices of Women in Islam," convened by Auburn Seminary at Manhattan's Central Synagogue. As soon as she begins to speak, I pity those who share the stage. This diva grips the audience by its collective lapels with her small, expressive hands and, in an urgent voice, bombards us with facts and theories, anecdotes and arguments that illustrate the disastrous effects of conflating religion and patriarchal politics.

Offering an example, Riffat says that Islamic courts require four witnesses to a crime, but in Pakistan this law has been reinterpreted to mean four *male* witnesses. Thus, even a woman who has been assaulted can't testify on her own behalf. As her listeners trade startled looks, she describes a nearly blind servant who was raped and impregnated by her master. The victim's own testimony counted for nothing, and the court went so far as to blame her for the crime. Even Pakistan's beleaguered women were so outraged by the sentence of a hundred lashes and ten years in prison—regarded by the judges as a merciful alternative to death by stoning—that they dared to protest. The servant was freed, but the law remains.

Just warming up, Riffat asserts that oppressing women in the name of Islam is particularly heinous because the Qur'an and the Prophet accorded women not just the basic human rights but special ones meant to protect them from abuses tolerated in pre-Islamic Arab society, such as female infanticide. "The way I interpret the Qur'an," says Riffat, "there's no discrimination at all against women. If anything, they're favored! How can Islam, which teaches that man and woman are equal in the eyes of God without distinction of color, creed, and language, be biased? The answer is in the Qur'an, if one reads with open, unprejudiced eyes, but some clerics just want us to memorize it without understanding the meaning! We need a radical revision of how the Qur'an is interpreted!"

Next, Riffat really shakes up her liberal audience by challenging their moral complacency. Ultraconservative Muslim men are not the only group that doesn't understand and respect mainstream Muslim women, she says. Neither do secular human rights activists and feminists who "insist that Islam and human rights are incompatible." These good liberals fail to appreciate that the core of the average Muslim woman's life is "a very deep faith in God and the goodness of God," says Riffat. "Whatever happens to such a woman, she's able to survive, because her faith keeps her going from day to day. What she doesn't know about is the empowering vision of the Qur'an—that God has given a woman the right to be educated, work, have justice, be her own person." The typical Muslim woman's "Islamic" understanding of her role is actually a cultural one, which asserts that women are secondary, derivative, and subordinate, says Riffat, so that even though religion keeps her going, it doesn't transform her life. "But if she can be made aware that she has religious rights—say, to be educated—then she has a weapon, a tool of liberation!"

Like Mohandas Gandhi and Martin Luther King, Jr., Riffat insists that religion can free people, not just control them. She finds a powerful precedent for her nonviolent revolution in Christian liberation theology, which has used the Gospels' theme of social justice to break up Latin America's feudal structure and create a middle class. "How do you reach the average Muslim woman?" she says. "Ask her if she believes in God. She does. Then ask her if she believes that God wants her to be abused and beaten. You can see the light go on in her eyes when she understands that she has power within herself and that her religion can help free her from society."

Riffat has seriously exceeded the time apportioned to each panelist. In response to the moderator's alarmed looks, she smiles, sighs, and ends on a life-or-death note. She points to the progress of the international effort to outlaw the practice of female genital mutilation, then urges her listeners to support the International Network for the Rights of Female Victims of Violence in Pakistan. Its worldwide membership, like those of many other human rights movements, posts news and conducts much of its business via the Internet. "Women are being killed each year by the thousands," says Riffat, nodding to the agitated moderator, "and so much remains to done!"

After resounding applause, the audience releases a collective sigh and sits back in their chairs. The male editor of a prestigious religious journal shakes his head wonderingly and says, "She could have been the whole show!"

· : · : · :

Riffat Hassan travels a lot. When she's not teaching, she takes her crusade for Muslim women's rights on the road, giving lectures, lobbying at national and international conferences, and making extended working visits to Pakistan. On a cold winter day in Manhattan, she arrives for an interview wearing a barn jacket over her *salwar kameez* and pulling a wheeled suitcase stuffed with information about violence against women. She has just come from the United Nations, which she hopes will make honor killing an international issue.

After seating herself on a couch and fielding a few phone calls, Riffat sighs deeply. "I'm so tired—really brain-dead," she says, "but that's fine, that's okay. On the way here, this cabdriver said to me, 'You know, the problem in this country is these white women. They have manipulated the Caucasian men. They're just so awful! They sleep around and have no morals. The courts favor them. The man has no chance. Muslim men are good, because they know how to keep their women in check.' It's that stereotype of Muslims as barbarous, backward, antimodern, antiwomen!"

If Americans could once afford to ignore seemingly foreign Islam, they can no longer, since it's now the country's fastest-growing religion. There are already more Muslims in the United States than Jews or Episcopalians. Nonetheless, says Riffat, a "legacy of misunderstanding still exists at every level." Her work makes her especially concerned about one common form of Islam bashing: sweeping generalizations about oppression of women based on the worst offenders. To her, honor killings are part of a global spectrum of violence against women that includes the battered-wife syndrome only recently acknowledged in the West. When their men are singled out as abusive, she says, "Muslims react defensively, which makes the real problems more difficult to uncover and address."

After a glass of ice water, Riffat settles down to discuss her evolution as a feminist Muslim theologian. She says that this unusual career was jump-started by several unavoidable realizations. "I became angry for two reasons," she tells me. "One was the gap between what the Qur'an says about women and what actually happens to them in Muslim society. The other was what had happened to me."

Nothing would have been easier than for the brilliant daughter of a wealthy Lahore family of distinguished Muslim lineage to distance herself from the hard life of most of her countrywomen. A stormy childhood, however, made Riffat sympathetic to underdogs. Her proper, traditional father "thought girls should be married by sixteen to someone picked out by their relatives," she says. "He was a very good man trying to do the best thing, but I saw him then as an authoritarian who wanted to sacrifice me at the altar of convention." Her fiery, difficult mother was a radical nonconformist who refused to be submissive to men and insisted on her four daughters' education. Relations between this odd couple were such that "the one roof under which we all lived could not be called a home," Riffat says, "if one defines this term as a place of love, warmth, and security."

Seeking refuge, Riffat spent much of her childhood alone with her books and "the Creator and Preserver, who at all times seemed very close," she says. "I often asked God to reveal to me the purpose of my life and help me to fulfill it." Watching her older sisters married off at sixteen, however, eventually galvanized the dreamy, reclusive girl into rebellion. "I realized that the drama would be repeated again, and that I had to fight," says Riffat. "Whatever my father said, I said no, because once I said yes, that would be it."

With the support of her mother, who nicknamed Riffat the "leader of the opposition," she escaped an early arranged marriage, stayed in her British coeducational school, and, at sixteen, ranked first among her province's 24,000 students. At seventeen she had published two volumes of poems and stories. A relative helped her gain admittance to the University of Durham. On the day she departed for England, her father spoke to her for the first time in five years, conferring an unexpected blessing on the daughter who made him both ashamed and proud. Still a schoolgirl, Riffat was already a veteran of the struggle between devout Muslim women determined to be free and a patriarchal culture, buttressed by religious language, that was equally determined to constrain them.

The tumultuous 1970s meant social revolution in the West, political revolution in much of the Islamic world, and personal transformation for Riffat. By the age of twenty-four, she had her Ph.D. in literature—her doctoral thesis was on the poet-philosopher Muhammad Iqbal—and "there was nothing else to study," she says. "I left England, went back to Pakistan, and got married to a man I chose." Riffat had dreamed of a writer's life in her homeland, surrounded by beloved siblings and friends. Rampant political corruption, however, soon motivated the young couple to seek their fortune in the United States.

Describing the mind-boggling transition from Pakistan to America, Riffat recalls that, when she and her husband first arrived, they lived with relatives who got her a job—as a cashier in a supermarket. "I had a Ph.D.," she says. "I didn't even last one day!" America was still deep in the throes of cultural upheaval, from civil rights to the sexual revolution, that began in the sixties. Riffat was particularly interested in feminism, which she defines as "believing that women have the same rights as men to develop their potential, which has nothing to do with anti-men or -children or -marriage!"

Just as Riffat was discovering such new political movements, Americans, stunned by the oil embargo and the Iranian revolution, were discovering the Muslim world. All of a sudden, she says, "everyone wanted to talk about Islam. And a Muslim woman who was also a feminist—that was a real rarity!" Before long the young academic was not only a professor of Islamic studies but an early participant in the new forum of "interfaith dialogue." With characteristic candor Riffat remembers wondering, "If I had stayed in Pakistan, who would be interested in my opinion? Here, everyone wants to know what I think!"

Riffat's real debut as a feminist Muslim theologian took place in the unlikely venue of the University of Oklahoma. When she was hired as a professor of Islamic studies there, she automatically became the faculty adviser to the Muslim students' organization. Most members of the entirely male group came from ultraconservative Islamic oil nations, such as Kuwait and Saudi Arabia. "The students believed that my presence was *haram*—dangerous to their souls," she says. Nevertheless, the men had to accept her as their adviser and listen to her deliver an annual address. "They assumed that I was capable of speaking only about women and Islam," she says. "They wanted me to talk about being a good wife!" Spurred by her students' unquestioning acceptance of patriarchal interpretations of Islam, Riffat decided to make a systematic study of what the Qur'an actually says about women. "That's how it started with me!" she says.

Riffat's rapid intellectual and professional growth exacted a toll on her private life. Her traditionalist husband couldn't cope with his wife's higher status and earnings in their new culture; after five years and the birth of a beloved daughter, the couple divorced. Again unlucky in love—"I had to make my own mistakes"—Riffat next had a brief marriage with a domineering older Muslim activist; the legal and emotional aftereffects of their hostile divorce dragged on for years. Somehow the young woman who had once dreamed of being a happily married writer in Pakistan had become a twice-divorced single mother and professor in America.

From the ashes of Riffat's personal life, however, rose a profound understanding of how culture can combine with religion to shape women's lives. "My experiences of being a Muslim female— with my father, husbands, and so on—all began to fall into place," she says. "Before, I had just lived through things without analyzing them. Now, I began to see that what I experienced was not just something that some man did to me but something systematic that involved a whole society."

Most people who arrive at such conclusions, whether in a political movement or in a therapist's office, simply try to protect themselves and their dear ones from future injustice. Riffat took on a much larger challenge. "I come from a family and society in which there's tremendous discrimination in terms of status and roles," she says. "But I had always been for the underdog. That's part of who I am. Sometimes God says, 'There are certain things that I intend for you.' So I just got into this thing."

If Riffat's unusual "thing" makes her stick out among Muslims as a feminist, it also makes her stick out among secular rights activists and feminists as a devout Muslim. "I don't have any problem with them, because they want to do some good," she says. "But they have a huge problem with what I'm doing. They're in denial about the life of faith of simple people. Religion isn't the 'opiate of the masses,' because an opiate drugs you. Millions of people who go to bed hungry and suffer hardship and oppression need to know that religion can empower them instead of just sustaining them. If they become aware of what rights they actually have through religion, they can start analyzing their lives. It's just a short step—and one that seems so central to me—but it's so hard to establish with secular groups, from the UN on down, because they're so hostile to religion."

Hostility to religion can spring from surprising sources, including major divinity schools. Riffat recalls a year spent at one such institution. "At first, the women scholars there saw me as a deviant from the Islamic tradition, so they supported me," she says. "But once they understood that I was very religious, they became extremely negative. Everything I believed in was challenged in such a brutal way, because they were so clever and mostly antireligious. I came out of this ordeal by fire knowing exactly who I am and what I want to do, and if they don't like it, fine. My experience is that these women are very small in number."

If Riffat faces some opposition to her brand of religious feminism from both the left and the right, she also enjoys much support. For twenty-five years she has belonged to a group of Jews, Christians, and Muslims who work for interreligious understanding and human rights. Her commitment began in the 1970s, when the American Jewish Committee invited her to speak about the relationship between Islam and Judaism, past, present, and future. "With such a subject," she says, "you're going to annoy someone! They had never had a Muslim speaker before, and I don't know how they found me, but that was the beginning."

Where sexism is concerned, Riffat sees more similarity than difference among the monotheistic cousins. "The Jewish, Christian,
Arabic Bedouin, and Hellenic biases against women all fell into
Islam's basket, because it's the youngest of the three faiths," she
says. "There are some distinctions, but the basic problems are very
much alike. They've all treated women terribly—as misbegotten
males."

Making a powerful statement about postmodern religion, Riffat
says that she regards her interreligious group as her "community
of faith—the only one I've ever had. Some members have become
lifelong friends who've supported me in a way my own birth community hasn't." During dark moments, she says, "I know I'm not
alone in the wilderness, because there are people in the world who
understand my calling."

· ⋮ · ⋮ · ⋮ ·

Many of my contacts with Riffat take place through the modern
globe-trotting activist's most powerful weapon: the Internet. Her
frequent e-mails alert INRFVVP members about abused women
who need help, protests to be lodged with government officials,
news about women's rights in general and Muslim women's in
particular, and, not infrequently, a bit of personal news.

One classic e-mail of ten pages begins with Riffat's assurance
that she has weathered a recent health crisis—"by the grace of
God, I feel stronger"—and ends with a report of a private interview with General Musharraf, who she feels is well-disposed
toward the cause. In between, she covers a lot of ground.

Touching on ideology, Riffat laments that, just as ultraconservative Muslims have "hijacked the discourse on Islam," "equally
zealous" antireligious social activists have co-opted the discussion
of human rights. Rather than importing their secular code, writes
Riffat, Muslims should realize that "the strong affirmation of
human rights found in the Qur'an and the life of the Prophet
(peace be upon him) can be made the basis for building a just society in which the rights of every woman, child, and man are honored."

Next Riffat reports on a recent visit to a clinic for poor mothers and children outside Lahore. Even the center's twenty female staffers at first denied any personal knowledge of violence against women, she writes. After much reassurance, however, they all eventually admitted that they had been beaten by husbands or other relatives. One woman had seen a man strangle his sister because she stood in a doorway to peer at a shop across the street.

Riffat is nearly as upset by the women's reaction to the men's behavior as by the brutality itself. Many women said it was "normal" for men to beat their wives, who must have done something to "deserve" it. Nor did they feel sorry for these victims or wish to help them. Perhaps saddest of all, they felt that it was their daughters' "destiny" to be beaten, too. "The road to the uplifting and empowerment of these human beings who do not understand what it is to have human rights is a long and arduous one," Riffat writes. This realization, however, should only increase the "indomitable determination" that no girls or women should regard being beaten as their destiny.

One afternoon, when Riffat is passing through New York on her way to a large women's rights conference in Baltimore, she makes some time to talk about her experiences in Pakistan since emigrating to the United States. Scholars are often accused of dwelling in ivory towers, in a state of lofty ignorance about real life. Riffat's continuing work in her struggling homeland grounds both her politics and religion in hard reality. She credits the two years she spent in Pakistan while the country was in the throes of Islamization for helping her realize the transformative power of religious activism. "The nation's whole public discourse had suddenly become Islamic," she says. "To take part, you had to be able to talk about the religion knowledgeably."

Islamization appears to be all about religion, but it's mostly about the idea that "modernity doesn't offer a better life, but only more colonizing from the West," says Riffat. In response to this perceived threat, governments try to uphold and impose anti-Western cultural mores in the name of Islam. If Islamizers are suspicious of modernity, they see the West as downright demonic, particularly where women are concerned. "When a boy and girl return home after studying in the United States," she says, "the boy is 'modernized,' but the girl is 'Westernized.'"

When women are murdered in the name of Islam, it's easy to overlook subtler yet more pervasive consequences of religious sexism. One such problem is many Muslim women's seeming tolerance of injustice. In 1995 in Beijing, at the fourth UN World Conference on Women, a large group of black-robed women, backed by conservative Muslim men, staged a protest against human rights activism on their behalf. "Those women in Beijing insisted that Islam is great for them, that they're treated as queens, and that the UN and lesbian feminists should stay out of their business," says Riffat. "But most Muslim women aren't queens. They're poor and uneducated."

Riffat gained insight into such women's apathy, even hostility, regarding their human rights from research on a community health problem conducted at Pakistan's top medical university. The hospital, which treats its community's poor regardless of their ability to pay, couldn't understand why 97 percent of eligible women didn't even seek care; the few who did came only when they were dying. A study revealed that the women simply didn't believe their lives were worth the effort. This stark report stunned Riffat. "For the first time," she says, "I became aware of how cultural stereotypes were killing women. They had internalized these ideas to the point that they put no value on their lives. That was a turning point!"

Much of the oppression wrought on women in Islam's name is economic. Riffat offers an experience with the medical center's school of nursing as an example. The Canadian administrators consulted her about possible religious reasons for their students' improbably low self-esteem and puzzlingly high dropout rate. First, she explained that the Qur'an doesn't say anything about nursing per se, but that caring for men violates Muslim norms of female modesty. From this perspective, she said, "no girls want to become nurses, because they must touch and clean male patients in intimate ways."

Next, Riffat offered the administrators a feminist Qur'anic perspective on nursing: its departure from the code of modesty is more than justified by a higher duty approved by the Prophet himself. "If you read it in a comprehensive way, you see that because the Qur'an puts a lot of emphasis on learning, service, and healing, it has a very *positive* view of nursing," says Riffat. "Mohammad's wives used to go to the battlefield and pick up the wounded, give them medicines, and bandage them." Until such interpretations of the Qur'an circulate widely, however, Pakistan will be deprived of badly needed services and its women of badly needed careers.

The emphasis on a certain aspect of tradition, such as female modesty, over its larger, more philosophical vision is characteristic of religious fundamentalists, whether Christian, Jewish, or Muslim. Among the other traits they share are a distrust of outsiders, the conviction that they own the Truth, and the defense of their narrow views with a rigid, literal interpretation of selected scripture. This practice of removing religious text from its context has had particularly disastrous effects on women. For example, Jesus was just plain nice to women and had important female disciples. Nonetheless, for nearly two thousand years the church used a few words from Paul's First Letter to the Corinthians—"Let your women keep silence in the churches. . . . If they will learn anything, let them ask their husbands at home" (14:34–35)—to legitimize treating women as second-class Christians. Developments such as female ordination became possible only when the first generation of Christian feminist theologians emerged in the 1970s to reinterpret scripture and reassert its larger value of human equality.

Thanks to the Taliban, Westerners are becoming more aware of how Islam can be distorted for secular purposes. The Afghani extremists cite the Islamic principle of *purdah* in order to force women into the all-enveloping *burqa* and out of schools and jobs. Riffat's analysis of the Qur'an's Chapter 24, verses 31–32, which is usually invoked to defend *purdah,* reveals a prescription of modest behavior for both sexes. Women are merely asked to "draw their veils over their bosoms and not display their beauty" when they're outside the home. Similarly, in Chapter 33, verse 59, the Qur'an says that when "believing women" go out in public, they should "cast outer garments over their persons" so that they will be recognized as righteous and not bothered.

Muslim women around the world follow the rule of modest dress in culturally appropriate ways, from a headscarf to a caftan to a *salwar kameez*. The Qur'an never suggests that there's anything objectionable about such customary clothing, says Riffat, yet in its name women are punished or even killed for allowing their faces or ankles to show. "Why the big fuss?" she asks. "Because when women appear in public, as Augustine of Hippo said, 'They cause erections even in holy men.' It's always female, not male, sexuality that's the problem."

Riffat's scholarly probe of the creation story as recounted by the monotheistic faiths reveals how insidiously cultural bias creeps into and subverts religion. In contrast to the Bible's male-oriented "Adam's rib" version, the Qur'an portrays the first woman in an egalitarian light. Humanity's creation from a single source is described in both male and female language; subsequently, man and woman make a simultaneous appearance. Despite their own religion's account, however, "most Muslims have picked up the idea that Eve is secondary to Adam," says Riffat. "She was created not just from but for him, yet is somehow also responsible for their fall!"

Despite such obstacles, there are signs that women in the developing world are making progress in achieving equality. In this regard the UN International Conference on Population and Development at Cairo in 1994 was "a real step forward," says Riffat. "Men have always been seen as both spirits and bodies. Women were just bodies and weren't even the owners of them. At that conference, women said they owned their bodies." Where Muslim women in particular are concerned, Riffat points to Iran. "The country has a hundred percent literacy rate because women there insisted that education was their Islamic right," she says. "Human rights aren't given. They must be taken."

· : · : · ·

One afternoon, between speaking engagements at Sarah Lawrence College and Columbia University, Riffat talks a little about her personal spiritual life. First, however, she remarks once more on the negativity toward religion that often prevails in such elite academic communities. To Riffat, this attitude reflects "what happens when you see religion only as institution, dogmas, language, gender issues—things that have nothing to do with the spiritual experience." She shrugs. "The Sufis have the idea that you can't get faith through reason or effort. It's a gift. You have it or you don't."

As a professor, Riffat defines religion as a worldview whose six dimensions—ritual, mythological, doctrinal, ethical, social, and experiential—are meant to help people understand the meaning of life. As a private individual, she sees religion as "a profound relationship with God. The way I read the biblical and Qur'anic texts, it's very clear that God is involved with us. The Bible even uses metaphors like 'suffers' and 'rejoices.' I don't think of God as a person with a capital P but as God appears in the Qur'an, described with metaphors, like light, life, consciousness. Religion is a relationship between this ultimacy and the believer." This bond imposes a certain relationship among God's creatures as well. "In my own life," says Riffat, "I understand God in terms of love, compassion, justice. The Qur'an says everything in the world has been created for a just purpose, and all of the so-called prophetic religions are very justice-centered. As I see it, Islam's mandate is to create a better world."

Even within Riffat's own family, not everyone agrees with her view of Islam. Her brother, who's a brilliant Oxford-educated barrister, joined a Muslim organization that insists that this world doesn't matter; only the hereafter is significant. "It's all he can talk about," says Riffat wonderingly. "He doesn't read, study, think. He just wants to memorize the Qur'an. In his view, my life is all wrong. Why would I bother talking to Jews and Christians? He prays all the time and goes on missions for this group, but that's not fixing the world. You pray, and that's it? He has very little to do with his siblings now." She sighs again. "It's hugely depressing."

Many years after finishing her doctoral dissertation on Muhammad Iqbal, Riffat remains deeply stirred by the poet-philosopher's contention that the purpose of the whole universe was the creation of humanity. "Iqbal believed that God cares very much that each individual should realize his or her potential, which he called self-hood," she says. "We're made in God's image, and if God is your limit . . . That kind of vision."

That kind of vision has supported Riffat throughout what she calls "a very difficult life in many respects. Yet I've never lost that belief that there's a purpose to life and to my life. I believe very strongly in what Judaism calls the principle of election—that you are chosen for certain tasks." She stops to laugh over Jonah, one of her favorite Bible characters, "who runs in the direction opposite from what God asks!" Shaking her head, she says, "Things don't 'just happen.' I was born a Muslim, which was intended. It's not just simply something that's to be accepted rationally but something that permeates every aspect of my life. There's a certain paradox, because the Qur'an says that there's a direction in which God turns a person, and also says that one is free to choose. I think the freedom is that one can say no to God, or choose to submit."

Islam means "to submit to God." Riffat once described her faith as "Sufi-oriented, in the sense that it's very personal and not tied up with institutions and rituals, or even a community." Her remarks inspired me to learn a little more about Sufism, as Islamic mysticism is called.

Sufi derives from the Arabic word for wool, which refers to the plain garments that distinguished early Sufis from Muslims who had diverged from Islam's original simplicity. Muslims esteem science as the study of God's creation, and Sufis are the scientists of the soul, which they regard as a copy of the universe; indeed, Sufis believe that whoever masters his or her soul masters the whole world. In Islam, "There is no God but Allah," but in Sufism, "There is nothing but Allah."

Sufism is not a conventional religion. According to its "new school," popularized in the West by the writings of Idries Shah, one needn't be a Muslim, or even religious, to be a practitioner. A

Sufi I consulted said, "We believe we're all born with the truth. God told Mohammad to 'remind' people of what they know. Those who get initiated always know." To him, Sufism is just a deep "inquiry into the truth. It's another way of seeing things, of crossing into another dimension. You lift a veil, you see something. You can't explain it to others, but afterwards, what they say about the world doesn't matter anymore." Comparing the individual's quest to the Qur'anic model for the attainment of mystical knowledge—the Prophet's night journey through the seven heavens to God—he said, "It's always inside, in you. You're already there, but you can't see it. A teacher just helps you know what you already know."

When there's nothing but Allah, reality is, according to one Sufi metaphor, simply the divine raiment. Even individual existence is a "sin," because it implies separation from, or something that isn't, God. The Sufi remedy is the spiritual practice of *fana,* or extinction; like *satori, samadhi,* and other experiences of mystical enlightenment, it eliminates self-consciousness and empties the person of everything but the divine.

Sufis rarely identify themselves as such and are circumspect about their mystical practices, which can include chanting, dancing, and study with a spiritual master. From its beginnings, in fact, Sufism has been surrounded by secrecy. One reason is that its openness to inquiry and its universalist perspective, which are endemic to mysticism, upset mainstream Muslims, who are strong doctrinal believers. Then, too, without study and preparation, most people simply can't grasp assertions such as "There's nothing but Allah." As my Sufi adviser put it, "If you start with the truth, no one will believe you."

After I tell Riffat about this impressive man, she describes a Sufi in Pakistan who's "a wonderful person and very good friend. He's the one living person I've met who . . . when you're in his presence, you know he's a very holy person. That radiance. If I'm in Pakistan for only two days, I go and see him because it gives me a lot of spiritual comfort." Unlike Sufis, however, she's uncomfortable with the idea of surrender to a spiritual master. "He's right and he's beautiful, but he's not God. My life and struggle are mine! He understands that."

Despite her respect for Sufism, Riffat prefers what she calls Qur'anic mysticism. She grabs a piece of paper, sketches a diagram that shows "the sought," "the way," "the seeker," and "the goal," and explains that different mystical traditions vary in how they fill in these blanks. For Islamic seekers, "the sought" is always God, and "the way" is always love, but there are two different goals. Sufis strive for a merger between the lover and the beloved. "When that happens," she says, "the identity of one of them is lost—in human relationships, usually the woman's! When you merge with God, the goal is *fana*—extinction. Your own personality is annihilated, extinguished. It's very much the same in Hinduism, with its image of the drop of water falling into the ocean."

Tapping her sketch, Riffat points out that in the Qur'anic mysticism she shares with Rumi and Iqbal, the goal is "to get to God's presence, as when Moses stood before the burning bush, but not to merge with God, because then one ceases to be. The dialogue isn't 'We love each other and become one, and I'm really the one.'" Instead, it's 'We love each other because I am I and you are you, and for our love to be preserved, you need to be you and I need to be me.' After you've been in God's presence, you're transformed, and you must come back and change the world, like Moses."

Effortlessly segueing from the Qur'an to the Bible to Plato's *Republic*, Riffat says, "Let me refresh your mind about the allegory of the cave." She sketches the famous tale of prisoners whose only glimpse of the world comes from shadows cast on the cave's wall. One person breaks his chains and escapes. His first impulse is to be thankful that he's free and to run away. "But then he thinks about all the others, so he comes back and liberates them," says Riffat. "Having been freed by the presence of God, you must come back and help. This is very much how I understand Islam."

Without intending to, Riffat has neatly described her own genius. Because of individuals like her, more people now live in freedom than ever in history.

It has been another long day for Riffat, and she gives one of her operatic sighs. "It must be so easy to be in a monastery or temple or whatever and not have to deal with the real world," she says. "Maybe it's a certain calling—"

The doorbell rings. A pretty Columbia sophomore, whose typical student garb is set off with a headscarf, has arrived to escort Riffat Hassan to her next mission of liberation.

5. GODDESS

Perhaps a pilgrimage to a living goddess *shouldn't* be easy. Travel is generally hard in India, but the trip to Amrithpuri, a fishing village on a thread of sand woven into Kerala's backwater region, is especially complicated. From Cochin, a port on the Arabian Sea that's an Indo-Portuguese improvisation on Venice, one drives to Alleppey, a gay market town of desultory canals that's famed for its bad water. From there it's five hours by boat to the ashram of Mata Amritanandamayi, popularly known as India's hugging saint.

To her devotees, however, Mata Amritanandamayi is not merely a saint but an *avatar,* or incarnation of a deity; not just holy but holiness. The Bhagavad Gita, a sacred Hindu text, promises that, throughout history, the divine will periodically manifest itself in these special persons, who will help keep things on the right track. Mata Amritanandamayi is regarded as an incarnation of Devi, the Mother Goddess of the Universe. As her nickname Ammachi, "dearest mother," suggests, the *avatar* of Amrithpuri personifies goodness as well as holiness. Her large network of charities includes an orphanage, a home for the aged, a hospice, schools, training institutes, and various food, housing, medical, and pension programs.

The unique ministry of this up-close-and-personal goddess is as simple and earthy as it is profound. Over the past twenty-five years Ammachi has spent from five to fifteen hours a day embracing all comers—so far, some 20 million—so that each person has a chance to feel divine love in the most literal sense. For some the hug is a cataclysmic event that jump-starts a new spiritual life. For others it's a gentle affirmation of something that they already know but often forget. Still others get what one genial Canadian wanderer calls "a great hug from a really nice lady." Particularly for educated, analytical Westerners, the hug's least common denominator is Ammachi's stunning ability to bypass the mind and go straight for the heart. The historian Peter Brown has underscored the philosopher David Hume's connection of religion's swings between monotheism and polytheism, including permutations such as the veneration of saints, to shifts in the stability and rationality of historical eras.[1] In an anxious, unstable age such as ours, it seems, many people look past the abstract God of theology toward living spiritual geniuses, whose personal actions speak louder than dogma and whose personal stories inspire trust.

When I get to Alleppey, it's stunningly hot. Nearby Kottyam reports seventy-five cases of cholera. I buy some bottled water and a gauzy, short-sleeved *salwar kameez,* stuff some essentials in a backpack, and head to the pier for the trip through the backwaters.

On schedule the boat glides off into the shimmering, narcotic air, past cantilevered fishing nets, rice barges, sea eagles, and countless tiny islands improbably supporting thatched huts and even masonry cottages. I try to relax and enjoy the trip but feel uneasy about ashrams and *avatar*s. I'd just visited the sprawling headquarters of a famous guru, which struck me as a mix of fundamentalist Bible camp and Graceland. Life seemed centered less on spiritual practice than on the guru's personality cult and getting a good seat at the daily *darshan*—audience—in the hope of seeing a *siddhi*, or miracle. I left after one night.

In the late afternoon the skipper breezes by Amrithpuri just long enough for me to jump to the sandy shore, then heads back to the channel and Kollam, the backwaters' southern portal. It's so hot on the narrow tropical island that what looks like a crumbling Soviet version of a Holiday Inn complex might be a hallucination. Beyond this vast pink pile and several uncompleted construction projects lies a palmy clearing that's dominated by a temple apparently designed by Walt Disney. People wearing every sort of national dress, including lots of small, extroverted children, swarm around this large pink, blue, and yellow building festooned with prancing horses, elephants, and deities. Life at the ashram revolves around its queen, and her temple buzzes like a beehive.

Inside the temple's business precinct, newcomers line up at the office to trade their passports for padlocks to no-frills berths in the pink tower. Work crews fold pamphlets and wrap up pinches of *vibhuti*, sacred ash, which are given to pilgrims as souvenirs. People browse among religious books and secondhand saris in an impromptu flea market.

In the temple's sanctuary Ammachi's daily *darshan* is under way. People sit in rows on the floor, praying, meditating, and chanting rounds of *bhajans*, or devotional songs. That many are men adds to the jolt the very idea of a goddess gives to the Western mind. (Some scholars claim that the prominence Hinduism accords to female deities suggests that Indian women enjoyed much higher status in antiquity.) The diverse crowd, which includes simple Indian farmers worried about failing crops and educated Europeans and Americans worried about finding happiness, share the same desire: a dose of Ammachi's *shakti*, or spiritual energy, regarded as feminine in nature. A few conversations suggest that even Westerners who have come out of curiosity and don't really believe in such a thing are secretly hoping for a buzz.

Along the sides of the big sanctuary, two columns of devotees have lined up for hugs. They creep toward a central stage, where Ammachi sits on a divan, giving her peculiar hands-on *darshan*. As

I queue up, I think of my reaction upon first hearing of Mata Amritanandamayi: pity for gullible folk who would stand in line for a stranger's embrace. Months later, however, and just weeks before leaving for India, I had an experience of the sort usually filed under "strange but true" and kept to oneself. I was in yoga class, doing the *asana*s, or postures, and not thinking about anything in particular. Suddenly a pretty, round, smiling Indian woman in a sari appeared in my mind's eye and for some minutes flooded me with her infectious joy. I had no idea who this lady was, but my Indian trip, which was beginning to loom as a scary solitary voyage that required a traveling pharmacy, seemed like a wonderful adventure again.

As I finalized preparations, Mata Amritanandamayi's name kept cropping up in conversations with knowledgeable people. Even some who weren't particularly interested in religion spoke highly of her charities, sterling reputation, and international stature. Each year Ammachi travels widely to make herself available to more of her devotees, who number 10 million worldwide. In 1993 she represented Hinduism at the Parliament of the World's Religions in Chicago and in 1995 spoke at the fiftieth anniversary of the United Nations.

I tried repeatedly to phone and fax Amrithpuri to arrange a visit, but communication with India, particularly its rural regions, remains a sometime thing. I arrived in Kerala with higher hopes for sightseeing than for connecting with this hard-to-reach, touchy-feely "goddess" on her remote island. Nonetheless, as I inch along in line, I have to admit that I've somehow flown, driven, and floated my way to Ammachi and one of those hugs that had seemed so pathetic only a short time ago.

When it's finally my turn, I want out. Surely I could just interview other people about getting one of these corny, scary embraces! But it's too late—and too crowded—to turn back now. It must be over a hundred degrees on the stage. An aide wipes my sweaty face with a tissue and whispers that if words become necessary, an assistant will translate between Ammachi's Malayalam and my English. She says to keep my left hand on my chest and the right on Ammachi's couch. "Don't touch her," she says. "Amma will touch you." Then she pushes me forward and onto my knees.

Suddenly I'm staring up at a chubby, smiling, dark brown lady in white robes. A jewel sparkles in her nose. She looks really, really glad to see me.

Whether from the sheer strangeness of the experience, embarrassment, or proximity to divinity, compounded by the stupefying heat, I immediately start to cry. Not the least perturbed, Ammachi grabs me and kisses my head, which disappears into her fragrant, capacious bosom. She rocks me and croons a little song—*neh-neh-neh*—as if comforting a fretful baby.

Instantly, I think, Why do I worry so much? *Neh-neh-neh,* sings Ammachi. What if there really is a God who loves like this? The experience isn't so much revelation as remembering: *Everything is all right.*

Someone asks if I have a question for Ammachi. Journalists are supposed to. I babble something about her "message." Ammachi says to read her books. Of course, the moment is the message, which is too deep for words. Only the ancient, formal, incantatory ones suggest it: *Om. La illaha illa Allah. Sh'ma Israel. Kyrie eleison.*

As suddenly as it lifted, the veil descends. Ammachi smiles and gives me souvenirs: a candy *prasad*—food blessed by a holy person—and a packet of *vibhuti*. The exact relationship between the holy of holies and this plump, motherly woman doesn't seem to matter much. When I knelt down I didn't get the *avatar* business. When I get up I do. I think, *This is what Jesus did.*

The kindly aide somehow wedges me into the crowd of seated women packed onto the floor around the dais, folded knees touching. No one pays the slightest attention as I sheepishly mop my eyes. *Genius* doesn't seem too strong a term for a person who can, as if lending a pair of binoculars, allow a stranger to glimpse the mystic's worldview.

The hundreds of heads around me strain in one direction. Hindus sensibly acknowledge four different *yogas*, or spiritual paths, to the divine. Temperament inclines some people to one or another, while many blend several approaches. Ammachi's devotees follow the emotional *bhakti* path of love for and devotion to a deity. They cultivate union with the divine through the passionate fervor of small children for their mother, who in turn treats them as her dear sons and daughters. Philosophical *jnana* yogis use the mind to "realize" the individual's union with ultimate reality. Empirical *raja* yogis take a "mind-body" approach to the divine that includes *asana*s, say, and breathing exercises. A familiar American type, action-oriented *karma* yogis selflessly social-work their way to the sacred, becoming its tools in the world.

Despite the obvious parallels to Christianity, *bhakti* devotion and *avatar*s often strike Westerners as "pagan." Hinduism is polytheistic, but there are just three principal gods (who also have feminine forms). The unfathomable Brahman resembles the mysterious "I am who I am" of the Hebrew Bible. Vishnu, the Christlike preserver and restorer, is best known in his loving human incarnation of Krishna. Fiery Shiva is often compared with the Holy Spirit. Numerous other colorful deities can be regarded as different aspects of these three gods, who themselves are thought by some to be manifestations of a single divine essence.

Hinduism's both-and rather than either-or approach to religion eliminates much of the conflict between spiritual and intellectual life that many modern Westerners experience. Sankara (788–838 C.E.), the prototypical Hindu saint, was a brilliant *jnana* yogi who pursued not only an ultimate reality beyond gods and goddesses but also the *bhakti* way of devotion to Devi. Many of the highly educated Westerners who look East to Buddhism and Hinduism are attracted to the intellectual *jnana* path of philosophy and meditation. Ammachi believes, however, that Westerners are overly analytical and should pursue the *bhakti* path of the heart.

There's certainly nothing cerebral about Ammachi's hugs or, for that matter, her theology, whose anthem might be the Beatles' "All You Need Is Love." Perhaps exercising a divine prerogative, she's remarkably undogmatic. To her, all religions are equally valid means to the same end: awakening the selfless, unconditional love that isn't the usual tit-for-tat kind but is unreservedly given to all without expectations. She doesn't actually discourage traditional religious study but teaches that too much intellectualization "dries out the heart."

In the cheap paperbacks, even comics, that offer her teachings, Ammachi is winningly breezy about divinity, including her own. Such *avatars* appear in all religions as "tips of icebergs in the Ocean of Brahman," she writes. "The whole of God's power cannot be confined to a human body five or six feet tall, but God can work at will through this small body. This is the unique quality of divine incarnations." She doesn't ask that anyone believe in her, or even in a God in heaven. "It is enough that you believe in yourself," she writes. "Everything is within you."

The catch is that in Hinduism *self* isn't the ego but *atman,* or the spiritual essence that people share with Brahman: ultimate reality, which is characterized by infinite being, awareness, and bliss. From this perspective, not only spiritual geniuses but even *avatars* are explained by quantity, not quality. Like countless masters before her, Ammachi teaches that once a person truly awakens to the hidden holiness that underlies and unifies creation, his or her inevitable behavioral response is goodness, or treating others as the "self" that all share. She holds her advanced disciples, who are *sannyasins*—orange-robed ascetics—to this high standard of awareness and action, but she has a pragmatic understanding of the average person's religious life: "It's no use telling a worldly man, 'You are not the body, you are Brahman. The world is unreal,'" she writes. "Instead, he should be given practical advice that he can apply to his daily life."

The *darshan* has been going on for hours and shows no signs of waning. As Ammachi greets her visitors, who range from passionate devotees through desperate petitioners to the merely curious, their tears and smiles show plainly enough how people react to her. The truly amazing element of the *darshan* is her response to them. She greets each person as if she had been waiting all her life for that particular face to appear. Again and again I watch her deliver the deep with stunning simplicity and directness to fisherman and Ph.D. alike. It's hard to imagine how anyone could do this—or even fake it—for an hour or two upon occasion, much less for long periods every day for twenty-five years.

Something strange is going on here, but what? Perhaps the real question isn't What? but Who?

"Spiritual genius" is a safe answer. Some people conclude that Ammachi is so holy and good that she must be divine. Others regard her as a saint—an extraordinary human. Many of my friends back home would assume she suffers from a psychiatric disorder that compels her to go around loving everyone and being worshiped. In the end, decisions about Ammachi's identity are subjective. As her nickname suggests, however, there's an objective prototype for what she does.

In his intricate explorations of the mother-baby relationship, the child psychiatrist Daniel Stern has found that infants depend on their mothers not just for survival or even love but for their identity and orientation to the world.[2] When the pair is separated, the baby doesn't just "miss" his mother but loses his own sense of self. Without her defining presence, a vast emptiness threatens to annihilate him. Upon their reunion the baby, like all primates, "pulls himself together" by establishing so-called ventral contact: with his chest to hers, his head to her shoulder or neck, "all's right with the world" once more. This interaction is so essential that babies deprived of it, such as orphans reared in crowded, understaffed institutions, can fail to develop normally.

The powerful emotional reactions of many of Ammachi's "children" to her ventral embrace certainly suggest a religious version of our earliest bonding experience. In fact, psychoanalysts think the capacity for faith derives from the bond between child and parent. Because your seemingly all-powerful parent loved and cared for you, this reasoning goes, you can imagine or experience a cosmic equivalent. From the same viewpoint, mystical experience, which always includes a sense of oneness with the sacred, would be regarded as a re-creation of the nursing infant's blissful fusion with the mother.

Like a mother's embrace of a small child, Ammachi's hug reminds the person of who he or she really is—a beloved son or daughter—and how things really are—all right. Like a mother's verbal and sensory messages to her child, or a skilled therapist's to a patient, Ammachi's cues are "internalized" by her devotees in a way that influences their identity and worldview.

Because of the crowds, the senior staff members have told ashram residents to forgo their hugs today. Feeling that everything is all right is addictive, however; that's why people take drugs. A sari-clad Westerner in line shrilly argues with one of Ammachi's assistants: "There are some days when you just *have* to!"

· : · : · :

Dusk descends on Amrithpuri's beautiful, feces-flecked beach, whose black sands serve as the local fishermen's toilet. To Western eyes, an Indian village like this one—with its ambling animals, huts clustered around wells, barefoot people in drapery, and the odd prophetic-looking *saddhu*—has a peculiarly biblical quality. As in that scriptural world, religion here is not an option but is woven into every part of life. Much as Americans look upon health, Indians regard sanctity as something to be cultivated. Posters on walls and photos in food stalls and autorickshaws are likelier to show *avatar*s, gurus, and *rishi*s, or saintly sages (flexible terms that often overlap), than sports or pop stars.

Back in 1953, when the baby girl called Sudhamani was born here into a fisherman's family, no one could have imagined that one day this remote island would be crowded with her devotees. Yet she was different from the start. At birth her skin had a dark bluish cast later likened to that of the god Krishna. At the time, however, a doctor attributed her strange hue to disease, which made the child into a pariah. Her own family treated her as a kind of domestic slave, but cruelty only seemed to increase Sudhamani's sweetness. She composed and sang love songs to Krishna, then to the Divine Mother. The raptures, trances, and blissful dances of the local "crazy girl" attracted increasing ridicule until, when she was seventeen, her family drove her from home.

Gender notwithstanding, young Sudhamani adopted the path

of a *saddhu* and lived in the open, devoting herself to prayer and song. When she experienced *samadhi,* the mystical state of realization of the unity of human and divine consciousness, she merged with Devi, the mother goddess, and then with the ultimate reality, called Brahman. At that point, Ammachi writes, she understood that "nothing is different from my own formless Self, in which the entire Universe exists as a tiny bubble."

Young Sudhamani's story vividly illustrates some cultural gaps between India and the West, where religious intensity can be interpreted as a symptom of mental illness. To modern psychology, the girl's retreat into the world of the gods looks like a dissociative defense against her abusive childhood, just as her theology of unconditional love seems like a denial of her brutal experience of ridicule and rejection. To Hindus, however, the girl's extreme, precocious spirituality, particularly in the face of trials and hardship, is an augur of special sanctity.

Deciding whether someone is an *avatar*—even a genius—or a potential mental patient can be complicated. A former president of the American Psychiatric Association once told me that the major difference between Thomas Edison and a schizophrenic was that Edison could effectively communicate his insights to others. Like some famous televangelists, some "saints" are troubled people who don't feel like "good enough" human beings and so try to be godlike. In turn, some devotees are insecure people who infantilize themselves in a relationship with a powerful parent figure. The combination of flawed leader and vulnerable follower invites abuse, such as the financial and sexual scandals that periodically rock ashrams and churches alike, and even tragedies like the Jonestown and Heaven's Gate mass suicides. To my great relief, although Ammachi has her share of hysterical devotees, neither she nor her ashram has the cultlike, authoritarian quality that surrounds some other gurus and centers.

To be credible, a spiritual genius must meet Freud's basic criterion of mental health: the ability to love and work. As the Bible puts it, "By their works you shall know them." Ammachi's good reputation and tireless efforts on behalf of others' spiritual and material well-being over many years seem to render psychiatric diagnoses academic.

When the sun slips into the Arabian Sea, it's time for supper. The dining hall is the ashram's second busiest place, yet the main path to it is partly obstructed by an adjacent building's overhang. This preposterous architectural blunder is redeemed by the sign plastered on it: MIND YOUR HEAD. Over a comfortingly bland vegetarian dinner in the Western canteen, Europeans and North Americans on the guru circuit trade gossip and horror stories about the side effects of a leading antimalarial drug.

After dinner a young staff member and erstwhile Finnish rock star kindly shows me to my digs. The stairs in the pink tower are crumbling, but as we climb he explains that the building is only three years old. "Nothing works here, but it doesn't matter," he says, laughing. "We have Amma." Finally we reach the right floor, and he shoves open the door of what might be a concrete prison cell. The only furnishings are some gritty plastic-covered foam pads on the floor and a few bare lightbulbs. A woman passing by in the hallway suddenly stops. As if discussing a suite at the Ritz, she irritably addresses my guide: "Is she getting the *whole place*?" The young man grins and says good night. He's right—none of it matters when bells and *bhajans* ring in the dense, moonlit tropical air.

· : · : · :

Protocol prevents an interview with Mata Amritanandamayi herself, but her two highest-ranking staff members agree to talk about their experiences of her. Swamiji Amritaswarupananda, a former Brahmin banker, has been her senior aide for twenty years (*swami* is a title given to a respected *sannyasin; ji* means "honored"). That the ashram elite bend down to touch his feet suggests that suave, handsome Swamiji, clad in deep orange, is a personage in his own right.

Asked what life with an *avatar* is "really like," Swamiji smiles. He says that the most difficult aspect of life for her *sannyasins*, who relinquish their egos to their spiritual master, is coping with her energy level—particularly if people are waiting to see her or there's some service to perform. She's rarely tired, and closes her eyes for only an hour or two each day. Even an *avatar* is burdened with a body, and Ammachi occasionally feels grumpy or out of sorts, he says, but she recovers almost instantly. She's considerate of her staff in many ways. She doesn't need social conventions, for example, but understands that they do, so she chats with them to help them feel comfortable; for the same reason, she avoids discussing the past or future. The degree to which she "manifests divinity" varies, says Swamiji. On Sundays and holidays, when she may receive three thousand visitors, Ammachi "reveals more radiance."

In India a guru's or saint's reputation is often embellished with reports of *siddhis*—demonstrations of supernatural powers, such as levitation, materialization of objects, or healings. In one much publicized incident, observers reported watching Ammachi cure a leper by licking his sores. As *Paradise Lost* suggests, however, supernatural powers aren't necessarily the prerogative of the virtuous. Like most thoughtful religious people, Swamiji downplays *siddhis*, which "can be used for good or ill." He has spent two decades with her and I just a few days, but we agree about what seems miraculous about Ammachi. Day in and day out, she embraces anyone and everyone who comes to see her—skeptics and devotees, babies and grandparents, tycoons and paupers—and, as Swamiji says, "each one is like the first."

Swamiji Shubamrita Chaitanya, a slender, outgoing man who's Ammachi's younger chief aide, has spent a dozen years with her, but he still sounds surprised when he describes their initial encounter. Then a skeptical college student majoring in science, he agreed to attend a *darshan* in order to humor some relatives. He recalls that Ammachi took his hand and, to his astonishment, said, "Where have you been for so long?" Afterward, he says, "her form was always in my mind." By the time he finished college, at Ammachi's insistence, the young microbiologist had changed into a monk.

Swamiji C. regards Ammachi not merely as a *jivamukti,* or advanced soul, but as a divine incarnation who "feels one with the supreme consciousness—with Jesus, Devi, Krishna, or any divine form." Where daily life is concerned, however, he too describes a down-to-earth *avatar,* who regards people's intense reactions to her as signs that they've glimpsed their own true Self. When asked who she is, says Swamiji C., Ammachi often laughs and says, "I'm a crazy woman—the servant of servants." She delights in telling the story of a man from her village who was exclaiming with great pleasure over a beautiful song on the radio. His wife said, "It's just that crazy girl from next door singing." "Oh!" said the man. "It's not so great."

To Swamiji C., the smiling Indian lady from my yoga class is just an "expression of Amma's omniscience and omnipresence. She's not confined to her body." She describes such events as "tuning in" a particular person, he says, as one might a radio station. He too, however, downplays the importance of *siddhi*s in comparison with a spiritual master's holiness and goodness or, as he says, "purity and actions that benefit others. Amma cares least about herself. Her love and service just go on and on, which no normal person can do. You aren't even allowed to touch other masters' feet, but Amma greets the worst sinner as her darling child."

The cultural chasm that widens at the thought of, say, prostrating before Swamiji C., as many here do, yawns wider when he says, "Amma is my god, guru, mother, father. My life is in her service and humanity's." To most Westerners, such talk sounds crazy. Yet, like Swamiji A., this thoughtful, well-educated man, trained as scientist, seems a model of sanity and good humor. When he describes the generic hug response, which he's seen hundreds of thousands of times, I recognize my own. "You feel that a divine mother loves you, so you have nothing to fear," he says. "Even to the poor villager worried about his livelihood, Amma's concern and solace give confidence. Every person has a burden. Amma says that the only thing that heals old wounds is selfless love. For a few seconds with her, at least, one is free."

A pilgrimage is meant to be not an isolated experience but a step on the path to lasting change. Far from Amrithpuri, says Swamiji C., "you can recollect those few moments in Amma's arms, her words, and the peace you felt. If you are sincere and keep your heart open, her grace is always there for you. Slowly, she works on people and makes them more expansive, so they can love and help others and enjoy empathy, peace, and happiness. Those are the things you feel near a true master, and they remain when you leave the master's presence."

· : · : · : ·

On the day I leave Amrithpuri, I line up for another hug. Amma beams and enfolds me. This time she doesn't sing the wordless lullaby but repeats, "Daughter, daughter, daughter." Her voice is very different from her normal musical one: strangely guttural, neither male nor female, as the Delphic oracle's has been described.

In this age of information rather than wisdom, Mata Amritanandamayi has a peculiar genius for helping people, one on one, to experience their own perhaps unsuspected depths, then allowing them to take it from there. As I sit near her again, she greets a hundred more men and women like long-lost children. The feelings she elicits in them must reflect something of what it's like to be her. How in the world, I wonder, am I going to describe this without sounding like a Hare Krishna? From somewhere in the crowd, a voice cries out, "Amma! Give me back my innocent heart!"

· : · : · : ·

Paying Mata Amritanandamayi the supreme compliment, Swamiji Amritaswarupananda said, "Like Ramana Maharshi, she sees only the divine." This sage, who lived between 1879 and 1950, was India's greatest guru of living memory and the gold standard for contemporary mystic masters. He epitomized the *advaita vedanta* tradition, which teaches that pure consciousness, called the universal Self, is all that exists.

All religions have forms of mysticism, which emphasizes direct awareness of and communion with the sacred. Hindu *samadhi* and Zen *satori,* Jewish *devekut* and Christian *unio mystico,* all describe an intense consciousness of ultimate reality's underlying unity and goodness. To express this cosmic oneness, mystics often use romantic imagery, as when Kabbalists swoon over the Torah as seductress and bride. Remarking on the "sexually colored"[3] tone of many mystics' religious experiences, Dr. Auke Tellegen, an eminent personality psychologist at the University of Minnesota, cautions against facile assumptions about the connection: "Just as the Freudians probably account for mystical rapture as a barely disguised substitute for true sexuality, so the Jungians might be happy to recognize instances of the reverse—sexual experience as a variety or precursor of mystical experience. Depending on one's theoretical leanings and on the case, one perspective may be more believable than the other."

Teresa of Ávila wrote that during one of her transports, God said that "from here on in you are my wife. Until now you didn't deserve to be." Such accounts prompt Tellegen to wonder if "the sexuality-mysticism connection" might be largely a "female phenomenon." In any case, he says, "Perhaps it is infatuation that especially matters here," rather than sex per se. Possibly to enhance strong bonding, even animals seem to fall into the "altered state" that Tellegen describes as that "worshipful, boundary-dissolving getting lost in someone else." In a person inclined toward transcendent states—a trait he calls absorption—infatuation is likely to be an "especially mind-altering and near-mystical experience." For someone whose love object is the transcendent, he says, infatuation may actually be "the psychobiological foundation for, and first step toward, the *unio mystico.*"

To delve deeper into mysticism in general and the Hindu sort in particular, I joined the many pilgrims who have made their way to Ramana Maharshi's former home. (Maharshi is a rare honorific reserved for persons of the greatest sanctity.) The so-called Ramanashram lies at the foot of Mount Arunachala, sacred to Shiva, just outside the bustling town of Tiruvannamalai, a few hours from Madras. A half century after his death, thousands visit each year to pursue peace, enlightenment, and the presence of Ramana himself.

As a youth Ramana hadn't been particularly religious. One day in 1895, when he was just sixteen, he underwent a kind of near-death experience. He was in good health but suddenly became terrified that he was going to die. In a desperate effort to conquer his fear, Ramana decided to simulate death as nearly as possible. Mimicking a corpse, he lay still, holding his breath until he felt his body "die." In a flash he comprehended what was left: the changeless Self.

Ramana rose from the floor and shed all possessions and personal attachments. He spent seventeen years as a hermit on Mount Arunachala, then moved down to the ashram built by his devotees at the mountain's base. Until his death he lived in a single large room that was open day and night to the public—a radical lack of self-consciousness that, like youthful *samadhi,* Hindus regard as a sign of true sanctity.

Ramana's teaching was deceptively simple. He advised those seeking enlightenment to meditate continually on a single question: Who am I? This inquiry would inevitably lead, he believed, to the ultimate mystical revelation: All is One. Ramana mostly remained in silence, using his presence as his major teaching tool. "In truth," he wrote, "God and the Guru are not different."

The Ramanashram's Zen-like atmosphere bespeaks its serious, silent saint. Beyond its gates trucks, cars, buses, and autorickshaws indulge in an orgy of Indian horn honking. Inside, however, the holy mountain seems to cast a mantle of quietness over the ashram precincts. Sleeping quarters are simple but comfortable, and the vegetarian fare in the dining hall, served on banana leaves on the floor and eaten with the fingers, is delicious. The center of ashram life, however, is the open, airy, marble-floored shrine adjacent to the room in which Ramana lived.

Several times a day bare-chested Brahmin priests chant and perform rituals. At any hour, however, pilgrims meditate or slowly circumambulate the altar. After I'd been there a few days, the visitors seemed to me much like a congregation at any church or temple. A few were ostentatiously "holy," fewer seemed genuinely so, and many seemed to regard their pilgrimage as both a religious and a social experience. The Westerners, most of whom affected Indian dress, tended toward a more overt piety, as if, having traveled all this way, they were determined to get a spiritual bang for their buck. The Indians, many of whom were on family junkets, seemed to take a more relaxed, Canterbury Tales approach.

The Ramanashram imposes no dogma or practices on its guests, who design their own experience, from attending *pujas* to meditation near the saint's bed or cave on sacred Mount Arunachala. Ramana is revered not only for his mysticism but also for his asceticism—the forfeit of legitimate pleasure, even the taking on of voluntary suffering. He cared nothing for food or physical comforts and owned nothing but a breechcloth. As Auke Tellegen observes, just as cultures vary in regard to "the intrinsic virtue of ecstasies and visions," they differ regarding austerity and penitential practices. Although there were masochists and anorexics among the Western saints in the past, "mortification of the flesh as a main focus and as virtuous in itself seems 'out' today, even in the eyes of the church." For thousands of years, however, all religions have taught that some degree of asceticism, from the fasting of Yom Kippur to Buddhist and Christian monastic rigors, can improve character, heighten awareness of the sacred, and increase compassion.

According to the eminent psychiatrist and personality researcher Otto Kernberg, the effort to achieve enlightenment, in the sense of being able to see reality as it is, without distortion, is the province of all healthy egos. He regards the attainment of such awareness as an "ideal state," however, which most people only experience as an "oscillating condition" that's achieved partly and from time to time. Thus, to this rigorous scientist, enlightenment is "a road, an aspiration . . . except perhaps for extremely gifted, unique individuals whom we would consider saints. And even those probably have achieved such a condition only in a transitory way."[4]

According to V. S. Ramanan, the ashram's current director, his uncle Ramana Maharshi, whom he remembers well, was one of Kernberg's saintly exceptions. This quick, delightful man treads lightly among huge metaphysical ideas and smiles as he describes Ramana's nature as "not necessarily human." How else can one explain that 80 percent of his devotees have been drawn to him after his death? Or that many still experience him here? However, Mr. Ramanan doesn't obsess over the question of whether Ramana was an *avatar,* guru, or sage. To him all such individuals understand that God is inside, not outside. "That's why all saints are the same," he says. "As Jesus said, 'I and the Father are one.'"

Haunting photographs of Ramana are displayed throughout the ashram, and Mr. Ramanan says that many visitors come here after encountering one in a book or public place. After all, he adds with a merry grin, "most people seeking the divine need a form." The striking feature of these photos of Ramana, which were taken at all ages, from adolescence to old age, is a changeless, penetrating gaze that's aware but eerily *neutral.*

"Egolessness!" says Mr. Ramanan delightedly. "Ramana Maharshi was completely indifferent to praise or abuse! He was like a three-month-old baby! If you were standing in front of him, there was a Winifred. When you went away, no Winifred! Always thoughtless! Thoughtless!" This odd compliment seems to mean "thought-free." Most people accept their perceptions as reality, but for his uncle, says Mr. Ramanan, reality lay much deeper, far beyond the reaches of senses and intellect. To him perceptions were just distractions, even illusions.

The *samadhi* state, at least as depicted in Ramana's photographs, is one of calm, impersonal, unchanging awareness. This condition of freedom from happiness and sadness, desire and fear, even good and evil, is described by Hindus as bliss. In the West, however, where more value is placed on stimulation and the expression of individuality and emotion, such a state can seem, well, boring. Accordingly, Western descriptions of mystical states often have a personal, romantic, and ecstatic cast. Such differences between East and West seem eminently "cultural" but, like human behavior generally, may reflect nature as well as nurture. In one intriguing study on temperament, or personality's more biological, heritable aspect, researchers contrasted the behavior of Chinese and American children; the former were in some metabolic respects more inclined to introversion and, by extension, to a more inner-directed spirituality.[5]

Despite long walks on the sacred mountain and meditations at various recommended holy hot spots, my only inner reward from this visit was a new appreciation of how similar, despite cultural differences, are the deepest perceptions and longings of human hearts. The genius of such a one as Ramana Maharshi lies in the ability to represent this depth without words and across social barriers. As I take my leave of Mr. Ramanan, I complain that an "oscillating" sense that "all is one" is one thing, and living accordingly quite another. Blithe Mr. Ramanan concedes this gap between insight and action, but with a jovial wave of his hand he assures me, "In time, that will come!" He does not specify how many lifetimes.

· : · · : ·

It's fitting that the headquarters of Sri Vijayeswari Devi, known as Karunamayi, or the "compassionate one," is in India's booming computer capital. Bangalore is a kind of improvisation on Los Angeles, complete with cyber-cafés, vertical malls, ethnic restaurants—including a KFC—and, especially, traffic jams and pollution. Karunamayi's devotees regard her as the incarnation of the Divine Mother, in a graceful, elegant form identified with intellect. And, in fact, her genius lies in her ability to be a new kind of Ivy League *avatar*, able to communicate with modern, educated people across cultural boundaries in language they can relate to. In a sweet but no-nonsense way she discourages "blind faith" and urges her devotees to worship not their guru's form but the divinity in it.

Karunamayi is a guru with a college education. Just short of graduation she withdrew to a remote forest, now the site of her rural ashram, and spent ten years in solitary rigorous spiritual practice. Much as Zen seems to Westerners more accessible than other forms of Buddhism, Karunamayi's spare, intellectual religious philosophy has greater appeal to the postmodern taste than more complex forms of Hinduism. She urges her followers to prepare for meditation by "praying from your heart with tears," but she really belongs to the austere, cerebral tradition of *advaita vedanta* masters.

Like Ramana, Karunamayi believes that life's ultimate goal is the "realization" of the supreme Self and nothing but. She teaches a straightforward, roll-up-your-sleeves approach to attaining *samadhi*—and the lesser rewards of energy, tranquillity, and compassion—by adopting a strict regimen of meditation. In cultlike ashrams, *darshan*s resemble hysterical Elvis concerts and *siddhi*s seem more important than spiritual practice. Karunamayi would rather meditate with people than have them venerate her.

Considering the psychopharmacological effects of driving in Bangalore, it seems prudent that most of Karunamayi's visiting disciples stay in a hotel that's within walking distance of her townhouse ashram. Each day at 6:00 P.M. the three-hour ritual of *bhajan*s, *puja*s, and *darshan* takes place in its small temple, formerly a large parlor. This sanctuary appealingly mixes ghee lamps and fluorescents, colorful statues of deities and abstract symbols. A television just to the left of a Hindu altar silently screens a Karunamayi video. Over the din of traffic, about seventy-five people chant the thousand names of the Divine Mother. Indians and women outnumber Westerners and men, but not overwhelmingly so. Not surprisingly considering the air quality, the temple rings with what sounds like smoker's cough.

The small, lovely forty-two-year-old woman swaddled in a voluminous orange sari who sits on a thronelike chair certainly looks as a goddess should. Hinduism doesn't rule out the possibility of more than one Devi living at the same time. Both Karunamayi and Mata Amritanandamayi are intensely feminine and are called Amma—mother—by their disciples. If the atmosphere at Amrithpuri burns with *bhakti* heat, however, the Bangalore ashram radiates a cooler *jnana* light.

When the *bhaja*s are over, Karunamayi leans slightly forward in her chair and begins teaching in a musical voice. Although she speaks good English, she uses the Telegu language spoken by her local devotees. Her manner is sweet but so earnest that even her smiles seem serious. When she finishes, Swamiji Vijayeswarananda, who's her cousin and chief aide, summarizes her remarks in English, periodically punctuating his translation with a "Mother was saying. . . ."

The gist of Karunamayi's lesson tonight is that meditation is the surest route to freedom from *karma,* or one's destiny, which is predetermined by behavior in past lives. Every thought we have is rooted in *karma,* says Swamiji, so "purifying our minds of them is one way to free ourselves from the shackles of *karma* and the chain of death and rebirth. Amma was saying that her thoughts go silent when she recites the Om mantra, because she becomes Om." Stressing the *advaita vedanta* premise, he says, "This is the highest level of consciousness—realizing that there's no difference between your universal Self and God."

Karunamayi recognizes, however, that most people can't get there from here. At first, Swamiji translates, one may need a mantra to help focus and then reduce one's thoughts, until they eventually drop away. Karunamayi's special mantra, which honors Saraswati, the goddess of knowledge, is not a mere bunch of words, he says, but a powerful "shield" whose "seed letters have power and energy in them." Because it targets the heart, "if one is always repeating this mantra, one will be filled with love. It can be also sung or listened to, even while driving, so that it's always with us. That's Amma's blessing to us today—to let us sing the mantra."

No lesson from a reputable spiritual teacher is complete without a reminder to look outward as well as inward. "We have trouble loving beyond ourselves," says Swamiji. "Mother was saying that we meditate not just for ourselves but for others. We must serve others, especially the needy and abandoned." Karunamayi practices what she preaches by sponsoring charities for tribal people, the elderly, and orphans, as well as meeting each day with individuals seeking her help.

Next, Swamiji presides over a stirring prayer ritual involving lots of ghee lamps and rousing chants to Shiva. Karunamayi prays with eyes closed, sometimes shaking her head from side to side in the seemingly paradoxical South Indian gesture of affirmation. Then, at what's clearly the high point of the evening, the staff sets up ropes of the sort used for theater queues, and the devotees fall into line.

Karunamayi stands up and comes forward. She smilingly greets each person and responds to brief requests and questions. When it's my turn, she calls me Baby in a charmingly quaint manner. This *darshan* is personal, but there's none of the roiling emotion that prevails at, say, Amrithpuri. Rather than hugging her visitors, Karunamayi pours some springwater that has been blessed and infused with herbs and flowers into their cupped hands; they drink it as a benediction. Despite her robes and exotic setting, her demeanor is remarkably like that of a modern career woman. In her unusual profession, Karunamayi has a very auspicious credential. None other than Ramana Maharshi told her pregnant mother, who was his disciple, that she would give birth to "the Mother."

· : · · : ·

One evening in Bangalore, Swamiji Vijayeswarananda agrees to speak with me about his experiences with her. He, too, has an academic air and, but for his orange robes, might be a bespectacled professor. Indeed, he says, until he experienced Karunamayi's *shakti,* he hadn't been drawn to the religious life: "I thought I'd be in business."

Swamiji's career plans changed suddenly one day shortly after Karunamayi emerged from her long retreat. As soon as they met, he says, "I saw that she was entirely different. The room was dark, but a glow and a divine fragrance came from her. When she put her hand on my shoulder, it was like an electric shock." Confused, the young man went home and puzzled over this pretty cousin who suddenly seemed like the Divine Mother herself. He soon found that he was no longer interested in worldly affairs. He began to meditate, according to her instructions, and a year and a half later took monastic vows. He considers his life to be joined platonically to Karunamayi's for good.

To Swamiji, Karunamayi is much more than a spiritual teacher.

"Amma is part of the Devi tradition," he says. "She isn't just a guru, but a Mother. Her mission is to supply love to the whole world and free us from the bondage of *karma* that shackles us to the cycle of death and rebirth." Terms like Devi and *karma* open the culture gap between East and West. When Swamiji talks about the compassion linked with great holiness, however, he describes a phenomenon that transcends such boundaries. "When we listen to the sixth person's problems and questions, we're fed up," he says, "but not Amma. She says people need to share the unseen injuries in their hearts, and sometimes they can only tell her. She takes on all their troubles without fatigue. She's the same with the first person who comes as with the last. When we urge her to rest, she says, 'They may feel they have no one to listen, so these are golden moments for them.'"

In this hip ashram, even a passionate devotee such as Swamiji is relatively low-key, at least when conversing with a Western newcomer. "Amma says that she's just a mother who's checking on our progress," he says. "Inspiring us to continue on the path." Although cures have been attributed to her and *vibhuti* sometimes appears at her feet, Swamiji says that her true *siddhis* are "other things that one doesn't often see—unconditional love and the personal transformations of people."

Guru gossip has it that, like Karunamayi herself, her devotees tend to be the brainy type and are increasingly Western. Swamiji, however, denies that she attracts a particular kind of person. "All people are her children," he says. "To her, different cultures and countries are just different rooms." Nonetheless, he mentions a quality that's particularly attractive to postmodern Westerners. "Many people like her openness," he says, "and her refusal to insist that she be their sole guru."

In his years with Karunamayi, Swamiji has watched her closely and also watched thousands of people respond to her. When I ask him what she does that's so special, he gives as good a description of the feeling produced by the presence of spiritual geniuses as I've heard. "The effect of her power is like that of intense yoga practice," he says. "When we encounter a realized person who glances at us, we instantly gain an energy that would take us hours of our own work to acquire. Some people just fall silent. Some see a glow of light. Many say they feel they've had mountains lifted from their shoulders. That's the divine grace—that relief of pain. Some people are so moved by unconditional love that they weep, and she wipes their tears."

· : · · : ·

One evening I shower, put on a freshly laundered white *kurta pajama*—the ashram equivalent of black tie—and travel through eye-watering pollution to a private audience with Karunamayi. One indication of her modernity is her willingness to be interviewed; I even have permission to take notes. I wait in a hallway at the ashram until a crippled woman hobbles down the stairs from the reception room and an aide signals that I'm next.

Karunamayi rises, comes forward, and again calls me Baby. When she hugs me I reflexively hug back, which probably isn't the right thing to do. She feels fragile under her voluminous orange drapery. Her demeanor seems just right for a twenty-first-century goddess or guru: a nice mix of dignity and benignity. When she sits down in a chair near Swamiji, I settle onto a mat at her feet, take out a notebook, and ask what she'd like Westerners to understand.

Karunamayi responds by offering a very contemporary spiritual fitness regimen. "Westerners are running toward spirituality now," she says. "They are real seekers. They have all this *stuff*, but they can't have peace. There's too much 'I' and 'me.' The problem is how to get beyond the body and mind to the supreme Self. What they need is meditation—thirty to sixty minutes each day. People need inner strength from divine energy, which is different from the human sort. It comes from meditation's silence, which improves your capabilities and quiets your mind."

Karunamayi seems much more interested in promoting meditation's power than in pushing her own. It's easy for Westerners to get bogged down in the notion of an *avatar*, but Indian culture tolerates a broad, undogmatic spectrum of spiritual identities. Karunamayi doesn't seem particularly concerned about others' assessment of her nature. When I screw up my courage and ask her who she is, she smiles and says only, "Not this body, not this mind. I and my daughter are the same." Implicitly referring to certain celebrity gurus who cultivate reputations of divine status through demonstrations of magic, she shakes her head and says, "Miracles are meaningless. Religion is nothing but strong love."

The motto of Karunamayi's teaching might be borrowed from E. M. Forster: "Only connect." "Everything you need for spiritual beauty is inside you already," she says. "Righteousness, love, vision, selflessness, peace, wisdom. If you meditate, you'll experience them in the supreme Self. The highest consciousness of Brahman! All the radiance that belongs to you."

Regarding religious expression, Indians blithely go where reticent Westerners fear to tread. Bending forward earnestly, Karunamayi says, "You *are* your supreme Self—attributeless and indestructible. When you experience that, you're calm. You have no tiredness. You feel like you have thousands of hands. There's only oneness. You are time past, present, and future. With this divine wisdom, flowers, mountains, birds—all the same! Good and bad, the same! There's no need for criticism, because everything belongs to you. All religions and gurus are yours. Your Self is supreme truth and absolute peace."

Her selfless way of life proves that Karunamayi not only talks the talk but walks the walk. "My responsibility is to comfort people and share their pain," she says. Shaking her head fondly, she adds, "People are so sweet. Very divine! Sometimes they make mistakes, but as a mother I never see them."

When I ask if this is how God loves, her face becomes radiant. "God loves us a billion times more than a mother!" she says. "Far beyond anything we can experience in our minds and intellects!"

It happens to be the birthday of a loved one who has been through a lot. From time immemorial people have told gurus and goddesses their troubles, and it turns out that I'm no exception. Karunamayi wipes away my tears with a fold of her robe. "Don't worry about him," she says. "He's my son. I will send blessings."

When a *darshan* is over, you just know it. Karunamayi gives me souvenirs of *vibhuti* and a special *prasad* of honey-dipped pastries. I give her my last zipper-lock plastic bags—indescribably handy items in India. She smooths my hair. I pat her foot. She says that I'm "sweet" and reminds me that I need only to meditate in order to connect to the One.

As the autorickshaw speeds across town through the starry night, I realize that, once again, I've experienced just what many others have in the same situation. As Swamiji described, I feel as if I've just returned from a yoga retreat, full of calm energy. A dose of what I'm happy to call *shakti* or unconditional love or any other term still brings tears to my eyes. I cannot say exactly who Karunamayi is or what she does, but for a few moments in her presence, the clouds parted, and I could see that all is well.

· : · · : ·

If mystics are correct, the old song that goes "It's all right/ To have a good time/ 'Cause it's all right" is a profound philosophy. Ramana Maharshi put it this way: "We know that the train carries all loads, so after getting in, why should we carry our small luggage on our heads to our discomfort, instead of putting it down in the train and feeling at ease?" At my final *darshan* in Bangalore, Karunamayi rephrases this mystical worldview and its perspective on life's vicissitudes.

"Mother was saying," Swamiji begins, "our life span on earth is very short and has many sorrows and problems. But remember, we're just in a play, in which we characters must play our parts. Nothing is in our hands. Until this play is done, we're just instruments of God. We just experience the happy and the sad as it comes." Reiterating the importance of meditation, he says, "Mother was saying that to keep harmony and balance, use the mantra. Because this evening is the first day of the full moon, it will be a very powerful time to meditate, and we should do so between twelve and three A.M. Mother was saying, Don't waste time."

Like Ramana Maharshi, Karunamayi has a genius for finding ways for very different cultures to share each other's riches without losing their own identities—one of the twenty-first century's great challenges—and upholding values that transcend such boundaries. When I approach to get my scented water and say good-bye, she says very intently, "Don't worry about your dear one. Nothing will happen to him." I stop worrying.

6. PREACHER

Driving around the slums of Camden and Philadelphia with the Reverend Dr. Tony Campolo is like traveling with a hybrid of Mr. Toad and Francis of Assisi. This minister, professor, author, and orator, anointed by *Newsweek* as one of America's best preachers, has long been well-known among Evangelicals, or fervent, theologically conservative, "born-again" Protestants. During the impeachment crisis he became more widely recognized as one of then President Bill Clinton's spiritual advisers. Prominence notwithstanding, the man everyone calls Tony exults in a certain resemblance to Homer Simpson. He delights in antics like paying the bridge toll for a stranger in the car behind his. The more incredulous the reaction—Who *is* that guy?—the better Tony likes it.

Tony is a merry man on a serious mission. Like a Zen master, this Baptist preacher plays with people's heads in order to get them to question the status quo, from notions such as the permanent underclass to Christianity's image as the don't-rock-the-boat religion of the middle-American establishment. "To be a Christian is by definition to be countercultural," says Tony. "In an America suffering from 'affluenza,' *countercultural* means responding to the poor, which is the only criterion for judgment that Jesus gives."

Tony's reputation as a character doesn't derive just from his tendency to lead spontaneous sing-alongs in crowded elevators. He's an unusual figure in the ministry. For one thing, Tony has all the talents of a successful entrepreneur. Many a Fortune 500 CEO would envy the salesmanship, creativity, and sheer moxie he deploys in serving the poor. Then too, he's a secular scholar with a doctorate in sociology, a subject he taught at the University of Pennsylvania and now teaches at Eastern College, a Christian school in St. Davids, Pennsylvania. Last, but far from least, Tony eschews born-again hellfire talk for something close to a thinking person's stand-up comedy.

Fire-and-brimstone debates in Evangelical circles about who is "saved" often center on homosexuals and pro-choice advocates. However, Tony points out that Jesus himself gave other criteria for being right with God, beginning with "When I was hungry, did you feed me?" Because Americans constitute 6 percent of the world's population and consume 40 percent of its resources, Tony insists that the nation's Christians have a particular moral obligation to emulate Jesus' clearly preferential attitude toward the poor. "As the Bible says, 'From everyone to whom much has been given, much will be expected,'" he says. "If we're going to be a loving people, we must share. That's the choice." Moreover, Tony says that for Christians, serving the poor and helpless is not just "the right thing to do" but a deeply spiritual act: "For me, the most important passage in Scripture is from Matthew 25, when Jesus says that whatever we do to the least of the brothers and sisters, we do unto him. Not *like* doing it, but doing it to him."

Tony serves the least of his brothers and sisters through the Evangelical Association for the Promotion of Education (EAPE), which he founded in 1972 and continues to direct. From its roots in two American inner cities, its far-flung "congregation" of impoverished youth now extends into parts of Latin America and

Africa. The association focuses primarily on education, but its programs include everything from promoting cottage industries to caring for children orphaned by AIDS.

The caricature of an Evangelical portrays a reactionary, judgmental proselytizer who makes the poor sit through a sermon before getting the hot meal or warm coat. But contemporary Evangelicals are an increasingly mainstream group that differs internally along both theological and political lines. Some are fundamentalists who take scripture literally, but others, particularly among spirit-filled Pentecostals, take a more nuanced approach to the Bible. Two-thirds are, like President George W. Bush, conservative Republicans. A third, however, including former Presidents Jimmy Carter and Bill Clinton as well as Tony, are socially progressive Democrats. Like the three presidents, Tony undermines the hoary stereotype of the born-again Christian as a dour, dim, uneducated hick.

Thirty years before George W. Bush publicized "faith-based" social service organizations, Tony had concluded that such groups are more efficient than government for two reasons. First, he says, "we can communicate *spiritual* motivations for addressing problems, from dropping out to drug abuse to violence. That makes us more effective, because the poor may not all be churchgoers but they're spiritual—if only in thinking in terms of lucky and unlucky. We're not dealing with middle-class secularists here." Religious organizations' other great asset is volunteerism. The staff of EAPE is not only highly motivated but mostly—about 75 percent, including Tony—unpaid. Many are college students recruited by Tony or his son Bart as foot soldiers in EAPE's benign conspiracy to change the world; they serve in a program called Mission Year, which Bart directs. With the support of such volunteers, says Tony, "we can deliver more services and cost less."

One day I meet Tony at 9:00 A.M. in Camden, New Jersey, at the headquarters of UrbanPromise, one of EAPE's largest youth programs. The U.S. economy is currently enjoying an unprecedented boom, but Walt Whitman's hometown could be located in a war-torn Third World country. The city actually looks as if it has been heavily bombed. Whole blocks of rubble alternate with dilapidated housing, stalked by pushers.

Running late, Tony bursts into the UrbanPromise headquarters with his coattails flying. He has just presided at the funeral of his forty-three-year-old nephew, who died suddenly of a stroke. Moreover, he says, "I've had a traffic accident, and I think I also lost my wallet." Cheer up, I say. At least you get to spend all day with a journalist. He grins, and we're off and running nonstop for the next twelve hours.

First we tour the UrbanPromise building. The brick church, which was abandoned during the city's "white flight," now also houses a gym, a community center, teen employment and "street leaders" programs, and two Christian schools, one of which "home-schools" teenage dropouts and those headed in that direction. Tony deftly shifts the focus to the Reverend Bruce Main, UrbanPromise's young director, whom he recruited as a college sophomore. Bruce is now the father of three young children and a doctoral candidate at Princeton, but he still drives the UrbanPromise bus in a pinch. He quietly shows off the uniformed African American kindergarteners of Camden Forward, the elementary school, and the teens enrolled in the home-school program. Some 70 percent of Camden's youth fail to graduate from high school, Bruce says, adding that he got some insight into why when his staff tested ten dropouts. The adolescents were working at second- and third-grade levels. Here they get much more rigorous instruction, and their attendance is "almost perfect," he says. "We just added ten more kids."

Bruce hardly looks at Camden through rose-colored glasses. Because of drugs and violence, in his decade here, he says, "I've seen a generation of boys disappear—vanish. There has been lots of tragedy. You despair over the individuals." Nonetheless, in that same time UrbanPromise's annual budget has grown to $1.2 million, which enables a thousand young Camdenites each day to find educational, recreational, and spiritual support here and at the program's five other satellites. Bruce's quiet charisma is such that it doesn't sound corny when he calls UrbanPromise "this joyful ministry, committed to Jesus and faith." Borrowing one of Tony's favorite words, Bruce says that the "fun" of his work is "being with people who are searching for real-life answers, which happens here on a daily basis with the kids."

As we leave, Tony stops to hug Monique, a former truant who graduated from the home school and has just started college. Like other older students, Monique has "paid back" UrbanPromise by working as a teacher's aide and homework tutor for younger children. "Two of the program's best volunteers are retarded," says Tony. "Elsewhere they might be seen as requiring caretaking, but here, they work!"

Monique attributes her achievement to a combination of "in-depth" study with involved teachers—"Here, if you don't come to school, someone misses you"—and "getting saved." In Camden the traditional religious values that UrbanPromise promotes, from self-control to faith, aren't just virtues, but survival strategies. Discussing premarital chastity, Monique says, "So many girls think if they have a guy's baby, like some toy, he'll stay around. But he won't." Describing the depression rampant among Camden's youth, she wishes that they, too, could find "some hope."

To Tony, Monique and Bruce personify social services provided by religious organizations. They look at life and its problems from a spiritual as well as a material perspective and are motivated more by spiritual than by material reward. Tony considers his efforts to recruit and support such young people in a religious and social ministry to the poor to be his most important work. To that end he's on the road at least five days a week, addressing church, community, and corporate groups. These speaking engagements attract 95 percent of EAPE's resources, typically in individual donations of twenty-five dollars per month, given by people who have just experienced an epiphany à la Campolo.

Like most people, I first encountered Tony as a speaker. Looking out at a large audience of well-off, well-educated, mostly liberal professionals, he surely figured that many, if not most, were skeptical about religion in general and Bible-thumping Christianity in particular. Tony told them a funny story about the way God works anyway. In moments I had already laughed several times and correctly suspected that before long I'd cry, too.

One day, said Tony, he attended a meeting of local Pentecostal ministers. Before the group disbanded they prayed for their community. Their supplications extended to a certain Charley Stoltzfus, who had just told his wife that he planned to leave her with their children in their trailer and go off with another woman. Driving home, Tony picked up a hitchhiker, as he often does. The two men introduced themselves. Then Tony said, "You're thinking of leaving your family, aren't you?" Mr. Stoltzfus turned pale. "I'm going to drive you to your trailer," said Tony, as his passenger gasped, "and we're all going to pray together!" Not only did Mr. Stoltzfus stay with his family, Tony informed his now whooping audience, "but today he's a Pentecostal preacher in Florida!"

Then Tony told another story. This one was about three young girls in Haiti, which suffers from an 81 percent illiteracy rate. Beyond Borders, one of EAPE's projects, runs eighty-five schools there for adults and children called *restaviks*, or indentured servants who are in effect slaves. When the girls offered to go to his hotel and do anything he wanted for ten dollars, Tony paid up. Then he took them to the Holiday Inn for an orgy of a different sort: eating sundaes and watching Disney videos. By the time Tony finished speaking, I was actually hoping that someone would pass the plate.

· : · : · : ·

Tony's next appointment is in Philadelphia, just across the Delaware River from Camden. As we head for the Walt Whitman Bridge, he points out a particularly terrible block. For a consummate do-gooder, he has a remarkably unsentimental perspective on the world, from the White House to the ghetto. As we drive slowly down a street on which the only people who aren't pushers are panhandlers, the latter stir up a familiar mixture of pity, guilt, and resentment in me. I ask Tony if he ever feels exploited as a sappy preacher who's an easy touch. "All the time!" he says. "That bum on the street who says he wants money for food! Is he going to use it to buy drugs? If someone else is a jerk, that's not my responsibility. Jesus is very clear on this. If someone asks you to go a mile with him, go two!"

My response is along the lines of "Oh, please." No, really, says Tony, Jesus' approach is "great, because it frees you from the harsh arrogance of evaluating who's good or bad. With a bum or a president, I don't have to be successful, just faithful in loving him and sharing God with him. On Judgment Day, God's not going to ask, 'Couldn't you see through the veneer?' He's going to ask, 'Did you try to be faithful to what I asked you to do?' Faithfulness! Judge not! We need to get out of that judgment business!"

As Tony tears through Camden's devastated streets, zestfully detouring to show off the especially awful ones, I ask him where he gets his energy. "I wake up a half hour early," he says, "and without saying anything, just lie in bed and very much surrender to Jesus. He said that if you really want to pray, go into the closet— what the Celts called a thin place. A place where the wall between you and God is so transparent that the divine presence comes through and envelops and transforms you." Tony stops to think for a moment, then offers a classic description of Christianity's core spiritual experience and what Hinduism calls the *bhakti* path. For him, he says, prayer is "a kind of hugging Jesus and feeling him warmly embracing me. I feel him flowing into my life, cleansing me. Changing me, little by little each morning. The more I surrender, the more loving, joyful, and peaceful I am. The best way I can describe prayer is coming in out of the cold."

Tony's personal spiritual life was not always so quiet and receptive. "When I was young," he says, "I used to read off to the Almighty a list of non-negotiable demands. I kept God informed! But more and more, I realized the genius of Scripture in insisting that God knows what you need before you even ask. It's all right to make requests. My sister just lost her son, and I have to cry out to God to comfort and bless her. But a long list of things I want from God? That went a long time ago."

· : · : · : ·

Soon we're rocketing across the bridge and through run-down West Philadelphia to EAPE's Cornerstone Christian Academy.

The bustling school began ten years ago to help tutor thirty kids through a public school teachers' strike; now it serves three hundred African American students. Eclectically housed in a former orphanage and two Quonset huts, Cornerstone begins with kindergarten and runs through eighth grade.

"Christian school" can summon up images of right-wing politics and rigid fundamentalism, puritanical severity and a Luddite attitude toward modernity. In the slums of Philadelphia and Camden, however, it seems to mean a safe learning environment that stresses the students' human worth and decency. I ask Trevor, my animated eighth-grade tour guide, what's special about his school. "What's different here is that they teach that being a Christian means living the right way," he says. "They don't teach that much at the public school." Trevor is relieved that midterms are over: "Our teacher said, 'I'll *kill* you if you don't do good!'" He proudly shows off the well-equipped computer room, which evokes a vision of Tony putting the spiritual screws to some corporate fat cat. Trevor says his goal is "to get into a *good* high school—one with computers *and* football."

On the streets outside, chaos reigns, but inside Cornerstone, old-fashioned manners are the rule. Students' uniforms differ according to grade, but all the girls wear skirts and the boys white shirts and ties. In the first-grade classroom tiny children answer quite sophisticated questions about the particulars of Jesus' baptism. The second-graders are starting to learn multiplication. In fourth and fifth grade, says Trevor, boys and girls are given different curricula to compensate for cultural pressures. The girls get an extra push in math and science, while the boys enter the Simba program in African American male leadership. Experience with two sons makes me particularly impressed by the quiet rows of fifth-grade boys—usually incorrigible wigglers. Nodding toward their formidable-looking male teacher, Trevor whispers, "He's *real* strict!" When this awesome figure introduces me, the boys catapult from their seats. "Good morning, Miss Gallagher!" Many throw in radiant smiles.

With its uniforms and daily religion classes, posters of Jesus and numerous sports teams—"everything but football," says Trevor ruefully—Cornerstone much resembles an urban Catholic school. Here, too, many students come from struggling families who aren't churchgoers yet want a structured, value-laden atmosphere for their children badly enough to pay tuition. (At Cornerstone it's two thousand dollars per year; the rest of the annual operating budget of one million dollars is underwritten by EAPE.) "To get a child here, someone is making an effort," Tony says. "They know that, at least for eight years, the kids have an oasis."

In Tony's view, Cornerstone offers students three things that are in short supply in this bleak neighborhood: a safe environment, good academics, and Christian values, which include "an understanding that you must give back as well as receive. We show the kids how one person's success is built on another's. We help them figure out what life is about, and that God will help them. We help them visualize a future, because it's hard for a kid from the housing project to imagine going to college, being a businessman or doctor."

My tour ends in the principal's office. In her Nordic sweater and corduroy skirt, Valerie Black looks like the headmistress of the school she once ran back home in Wisconsin, as well as the wife of a college president, which she is. Indeed, Mrs. Black still seems a bit surprised to find herself hard at work in inner-city Philadelphia—and for a third of the salary her public-school counterpart would get. I know why she has accepted this challenge even before she explains. "Tony's love for God is . . . *serious,*" she says. "You don't say no to him, because he portrays what needs to be done in terms of a little part of the universe that you can fix. Something that's manageable."

· : · : · : ·

As one who kind of hums through parts of the creed, I wouldn't go out of my way to talk about matters of faith with an Evangelical. Over a cup of coffee with Tony, however, I say that to me a Christian is someone who experiences Jesus somehow or other as a presence, period. Creedal beliefs, I say, don't make much difference to me. "I think you're right," he says quietly. "This is the kind of statement that gets me in trouble. But I'm convinced that when we stand in front of God in judgment, we're going to be amazed by the number of people who hadn't the foggiest notion of what Jesus was all about theologically but knew him in a personal way."

To illustrate, Tony tells a story about a well-known evangelist that starts out in a way guaranteed to rile non-Evangelicals. One day during a trip to China, this preacher famed for making conversions visited a hilltop Buddhist monastery. He saw a monk deep in meditation and was overcome by the desire to "share the Christian faith." The minister walked over, opened his New Testament, and started explaining Jesus to the monk. Tears began to run down the monk's face. The evangelist asked, "Will you accept Jesus as your personal savior? Receive him into your heart?" The monk looked at him and said, "Receive him? I've always known him. As you were reading from that book, the spirit within me was saying, 'He's talking about me.' I'm so moved that you were talking about this presence I've known all my life." Later the evangelist said, "Is that man not a Christian? Whether or not I came up that hill? I'm ready to call him my Christian brother, even though he doesn't call himself a Christian." Tony, too, is an Evangelical who respects religious diversity. "God's grace is greater than we can possibly imagine," he says. "A lot of people I can't talk to theologically I can pray with."

In the secular settings where he spends considerable time, Tony talks not about God but about "what it is that makes you a human being," he says. "Howard Gardner, who studies different forms of intelligence at Harvard, says, 'It's only a matter of time before they can replicate my organs mechanically and download my brain onto a disc and create something that thinks and acts like me. But will it be me?' Is there an essential presence or dimension that transcends the mechanical and biological? In secular terms, some essence of my humanity? In my terms, God?"

When dealing with people in need, Tony's rule is "Help first, maybe talk God later." This nonproselytizing stance allows EAPE tutors, for example, to work in Philadelphia's public schools. As the city's superintendent of schools, David Hornbeck is all for separation of church and state, but he'd like more of these motivated volunteers. "I'm impressed by Tony's commitment to Philadelphia's most vulnerable young," he says. "In terms of helping children at risk, the relationship between faith communities and our schools is not nearly what it should be."

In more personal encounters Tony follows the same simple rule of talking about religion that the Buddha did. If it seems appropriate, he says, he might ask someone, "Are you satisfied with your life as it is?" If the answer is yes, he says, "then why talk about religion? Jesus said, 'I'm a physician.' The Pharisees said, 'What if we're not sick?' And Jesus said, 'Well, then I can't do anything for you, can I?' Faith is for people who, in despair, surrender to a force out there. How many times has someone told me about getting to the point of saying, 'God—if you're there—I don't know where to turn. Help me. And I felt God come.'"

As an Evangelical minister who has been an Ivy League professor in a secular discipline, Tony is well acquainted with the intelligentsia's prejudice that religion—especially Christianity, and most especially his sort—is for dummies. "Religion *is* for dummies," he says. "It's for desperate people who are weak, like me. The postmodern age is going to be very positive for religion, because people are becoming aware that science isn't as smart as it thinks it is, and that reason doesn't hold as many answers as we think it does."

Postmodern religion's hallmark is the shift in focus from theologically oriented institutions toward emotional, individualistic "spirituality." Tony points out that Friedrich Nietzsche, "the ultimate atheist," gave up on Christianity not because it wasn't Apollonian, or intellectual, but because the Enlightenment made it too much so, at the expense of its Dionysian, or emotional, quality. "The ultimate question isn't Do I understand God? or Does religion make sense?" he says, "but Can I *feel* God? and Do I love God?"

· : · : · ·

UrbanPromise and Cornerstone testify to Tony's abilities as executive and fund-raiser, but a meeting with some Mission Year interns gives a sense of his more personal ministry. Tony is nearly obsessed with attracting such young people to serve the poor. Their initial twelve months of volunteer work is the gift that keeps on giving, he says. "Mission Year's real payoff comes later, in a ripple effect of thousands of young Christian leaders all over the world."

Much of Tony's appeal—and success—springs from his conviction that building God's kingdom on earth requires not Herculean heroism but, for many people, "doing lots of little things here and there. As Jesus said, the kingdom is like leaven, which is invisible but raises the bread. It's like mustard seeds, which are tiny but yield huge shrubs." This particular group of mostly British and Irish Mission Year interns who are assigned to Cornerstone illustrates how this mustard-seed conspiracy operates.

The interns' main task is to assist the academy's African American head teachers in the classroom for fifteen hours per week. Then they spend another twenty-five hours in the local community as unpaid social workers. "They go through the neighborhood two by two, like the apostles, knocking on doors," says Tony. "They don't push but just ask permission to pray God's blessing on all who live there." If the resident assents, the interns ask if there's any particular thing the person would like to pray about. Then it all comes out, says Tony. Someone needs a job, has drug trouble, is unwed and pregnant. Later the volunteers will contact one of various interfaith agencies. The next day the Catholic teen pregnancy program, the Methodist employment agency, "whatever," he says, "gets in touch and it's 'Gee, now my daughter has prenatal care' or 'My husband got a job!' "

Sometimes the help that's needed can be offered on the spot. Recently a frail, elderly woman told some interns that she was too weak and stiff to get into her tub, so they pitched in and gave her a bath. "That's where the rubber hits the road," says Tony. "That's the Franciscan way. Over a year a pair of interns tries to visit each home eight to ten times. And people start talking about 'that church where they pray for everybody.' "

Missionary work Campolo style illustrates several principles—

"Small is beautiful," "One day at a time," "Up close and personal"—that Tony holds dear. Experience convinces him they'd work for the larger society, too. "After two years of knocking on doors," he says, "we concluded that there's no need for new social-service programs but only for better ways to connect people to them. We need more caring presences! Most people in a neighborhood have no idea who the local ministers are! The people never see them! Pastors should stop complaining and get out there! Just by going door to door, we've been so effective."

The Cornerstone interns are an attractive crew, as fashionably funky and rakish, sleep-deprived and pub-oriented as their peers on campus. Esther, who's English, says that back home urban conditions are very similar to those in American inner cities, although inequities tend to run along lines of class rather than race. America is "very different from what I expected," she says, "but great. And our kids are amazing—intelligent and funny. They're lively but not generally naughty. One boy has these angry outbursts, but we pray together about them, and that works." Like many of her colleagues, Esther is interested in a career in youth ministry. "I heard Tony speak and said, 'That's what I've got to do—put faith in action.'"

Most parent-teacher conferences are held at school, but the Mission Year interns are preparing to visit their students' homes to discuss their progress. Without the right perspective, says Tony, these encounters between the middle-class white volunteers and the inner-city black families could be awkward. "Remember that they aren't just poor but unconnected. They may have no support network—maybe no friends—and they're suspicious of outsiders, especially whites." Tony recalls an after-school program for needy kids that was closed down by some community leaders who wouldn't believe it was a religious volunteer effort. "They insisted it was a scam and demanded a twenty-five-thousand-dollar kickback," he says. "The poor know that poverty is big business, and that they can be a means to your end."

What distinguishes an EAPE program from secular social work shines through Tony's advice to the volunteers. "It's awkward for you to walk into a poor home," he says. "Lay out your whole agenda in the first ten seconds, so they know there are no gimmicks and understand what's coming. 'I'm here to talk about Johnny and to pray with you about him.' Explain that you want to do the best job you can for their child. Not just academically but spiritually! The people you're dealing with live in a spiritual world." When all is said and done, he says, the success of the interaction between them and those they serve rests on one element: "Do you see what people appear to be, or the sacred presence coming through them?"

Next, two volunteers discuss students that they're particularly worried about. One ten-year-old boy is "bright but disruptive," says a male English intern. He recently visited the child's home to show his concern. When Tony asks him to rate the child's chances, the volunteer answers, "Slim." Tony looks thoughtfully at the discouraged young man but says only, "It's so important that you went to his home. It made the kid feel special."

Another intern describes a boy who has no father—"not even a memory of one"—and a mother who's often in jail. Like many neighborhood kids, the boy lives with a grandmother. "What will happen when this generation of grandmothers dies off?" says Tony. "They're raising kids not here and there but everywhere. Drugs have done to some African American mothers what three hundred years of slavery couldn't do. Drugs are 90 percent of what's wrong with this whole city."

While Tony has been talking, I've been brooding about that bright, naughty boy who has been given only slim chances. Suddenly Tony brings him up again. "How much do we really believe in prayer?" he asks. "That it can change someone's life?" Then he tells the interns a story about some of their UrbanPromise counterparts in Camden.

One summer, says Tony, Camden's Catholic bishop put up forty Mission Year interns in a huge, nearly empty old convent. "In the face of need like Camden's," says Tony, "denomination has no meaning at all anymore. That concept belongs to another era." Two elderly nuns cooked for the young volunteers and took a great

interest in hearing about the street kids they worked with, especially the really difficult cases. "Every morning," says Tony, "the
nuns got up at four-thirty and prayed the rosary for these kids.
This seemed off the charts to these Baptist interns. It's just so different from Protestant prayer—you know, when you define a
situation for God and then tell Him what to do about it! But the
nuns just knelt there doing their beads—'Johnny Jones, Lord have
mercy. Susie Smith, Lord have mercy.' They sent up a kind of
wailing to the heavens for this child, that child. And then the interns began to report the sheer difference in the progress of the
prayed-for kids."

When Tony challenges the interns to "think about prayer in a
new way," he's really teaching them how to produce epiphanies.
"God is already very 'concerned,'" he says. "You exist to be a lens,
a channel for that. Call it telepathy or whatever you want—it's
communication without words. Let God's grace flow through you
to that person. And the communication works two ways! Suppose
God is trying to get to you through this person you're praying for?
Instead of praying *for* Johnny, pray *to* Johnny!"

Tony is excited now. It seems as if this time his collar will surely
burst. "Don't walk into someone's house just to ask God a favor,"
he cries. "Do like Jesus, like Mother Teresa, who touched people!
'Make me an instrument of your peace'—that's what St. Francis
said! Put your hands on their heads. Use a little dab of oil. When
he healed people, the Bible says that 'Jesus felt the power go out of
him.' In Romans, Paul tells us, 'The same power that was in Christ
Jesus will be in you.' Say 'Jesus, Jesus.' Concentrate Jesus on that
person. Ask God to flow through you to that other person. I want
every child in that school to experience—to *feel*—God, not just
learn about God!"

More quietly, Tony says that, like other kinds of demanding
work, one-on-one ministry requires skill and preparation. He suggests that before each visit an intern compose a prayer for the child
that's "customized and nicely handwritten." Most important,
however, is "to get charged up spiritually. The Bible says that before he ministered to people, Jesus went off by himself to pray. You

too must ask God to energize you, to let His energy flow through you, like what happens in the laying on of hands. Then, go forth in the power of the Holy Spirit!" When the visit is over, he says, "give the family the written prayer. Tell them, 'I want to become a prayer partner with you for your child.' Then be on your way. And keep visiting. You may not see any results at first, but keep trying."

When the meeting is over, I ask Tony how he gets these bright, middle-class American and European kids to put off college or career for a year to work in tough circumstances without pay. "They want to be heroes," he says, "and nobody else asks them. At the base of every young person's psyche there's an incredible attraction toward doing something for others. We forget that young people are hungry for heroism, not pleasure. Mormon kids give two years! The enormous growth of that church is due to kids. Many churches do so much *for* youth. They think that if they provide enough entertainment—barbecues and dances—they'll hold on to young people. I don't do anything for them! I ask them to do for somebody else."

Tony shares his ultimate recruiting secret: "I make the work sound incredibly hard. I tell them that they'll live in substandard dumps in slums, where they'll have to kill the rats. They'll start early in the morning and fall into bed totally exhausted. The second week, they'll hate it, say it's the worst time of their lives. By the end of the summer, they won't trade it for anything. After I tell them all this, they say to me, 'Where do I sign up?' "

If he could wave a magic wand, I ask, what one thing would Tony do for the church? "Challenge the brightest and the best young people," he says instantly. "We have a lot of losers in the pulpit, while most of the best go into law and medicine. The church has to be more active in making ministry an important calling. And to do that the church has to become spiritual again."

Relief workers are often drawn to the world's trouble spots by a spirit of humanity and transcendence that's more apparent in such horrendous places than in peaceful, comfortable capitals. "They get turned on to what Mother Teresa talked about so often, which was the incredible privilege it is to be among poor people," says

Tony. "They're sacramental—instruments of grace. You can feel God coming through the poor, flowing into you." Again citing his favorite scriptural passage, he says, "Whatever we do to the least of the brothers and sisters, we do unto Him. I want young people to experience that before they choose their professions, because what they do with their lives will be altered forever by that encounter. Half of our volunteers switch their majors to ministry or social service."

The Mission Year volunteers remind me of my least favorite Gospel story: the one where Jesus tells the rich young man who wants to take the next step on the spiritual path to "go, sell all you have, give the money to the poor, and come follow me." The interns accept this challenge, I tell Tony, but I sure don't want to. "It's okay, Winifred, you're saved by grace," he says, "but . . ."

· : · : · : ·

As far as I can tell, there's no sphere of life that doesn't strike Tony as having potential for building God's kingdom. As we whiz through Camden on our way back to UrbanPromise, where Tony has another meeting, he puts on the brakes, makes a high-speed U-turn, and pulls up in front of Schimpf's Garage, just under a sign that reads: THOU SHALT NOT PARK HERE. He hugs Lou Schimpf, the white owner, who explains to me that he decided not to move his business from Camden, despite all its inner-city aggravations, after hearing Tony preach. "My wife and I prayed on it," he says, "and we decided we had to stay."

Lou Schimpf didn't stop there. He also gave UrbanPromise a small industrial building across the street that's now the home of Camden PrintWorks. Begun with ten dollars' worth of silk-screening supplies, the company now produces its own line of handsome T-shirts and greeting cards, as well as executing custom jobs for various clients. I pony up for a handsome green shirt that says KEEP THE FAITH. Inner cities desperately need such grassroots businesses, says Tony, because they employ blue-collar workers, who in turn help keep the community's professionals, who need paying customers. He explains that, fortunately, the print shop's job turnover rate is high, because its young workers soon learn the skills that can command higher salaries in private industry. As we pull away he crows, "There's hope in Camden!"

Hurtling through the streets, Tony outlines EAPE's next big project, to be done in collaboration with his own Eastern College: a special school for North Philadelphia, the city's worst address, that will focus on preparing poor people to start and run small businesses, such as Camden PrintWorks, from local churches. This so-called microeconomics is the latest trend in promoting development in Third World countries, and Tony is among those who think the approach holds promise for America's inner cities.

As we drive Tony explains the evolution of "mission work," which originally meant sending preachers to convert "pagans." The next wave of missionaries concentrated on running agricultural, medical, and educational institutions for the poor and increasingly left the evangelizing to the indigenous people. The new breed of missionaries, however, focuses not on preaching or providing social services directly but on stimulating the community's health and growth, often by promoting small—even very small—businesses. These cottage industries create jobs and support village life, which slows emigration to overpopulated urban slums. Tony laughs as he describes one such microproject in the Dominican Republic, in which missionaries taught poor youths to harvest abandoned tires and turn them into sandals. "We paid the kids fifty cents a tire," says Tony, "and everything was great—until we started getting a lot of new tires!"

Tony likes to say, "If there were such a thing as a Protestant Franciscan, that's what I'd be." Francis has become the patron saint of environmentalism, which many Evangelicals oppose as New Age pantheism. Tony's response is a book called *How to Rescue the Earth Without Worshipping Nature*. However, his interest in Latin America's ecological problems partly reflects their economic consequences. In Haiti, for example, nearly total deforestation means both severe soil erosion and lack of lumber for building. To bring together churches and companies to work on such issues, Tony helped start the Christian Environmental Association. One of its projects, called Base Camp, buys up rain forest in Belize for a hundred dollars an acre; Pepsico matches whatever the Evangelicals raise. In the Dominican Republic, a start-up grant of ten thousand dollars earmarked for reforestation has grown into Floresta, a thriving company with three hundred employees. "In the new ministry," says Tony, "it all goes together."

The Beyond Borders literacy project in Haiti is EAPE's biggest effort in Latin America. The program was developed and is overseen by a Haitian board and is staffed by Haitian teachers assisted by Mission Year volunteers. "These kids are incredible!" says Tony. "They sold our vans and gave up their nice residence—too much time and trouble to maintain! They'd rather spend the money on the poor. They live with the people in the slums, sleeping on straw mats." One of EAPE's board members was so upset to learn that six boys and girls were bunking in a single room that he went to investigate. Once he saw their distinctly unromantic living conditions, he moved them all to the Holiday Inn for a few days of air-conditioned R & R.

The modus operandi of EAPE is to identify a need, start a program, attract good staff, then let them run it, and even spin off other projects from it. "Jesus calls us to build God's kingdom, not mine—a very important point," says Tony. "The last thing we want is some massive organization. As soon as a project works, we help it become independent. Often some of our staffers will stay, but the programs all have their own autonomous boards. Small organizations run more efficiently, deliver more services, and cost less."

Financial scandals in Evangelical organizations such as the Reverend Jim and Tammy Bakker's PTL Club have made some potential donors leery. According to Mike Johnson, regional director of Compassion International, which operates child-development programs in twenty-two countries, "When Tony starts a project, it's self-supporting and community-run as soon as possible. He wants to empower the poor, not build his own empire. The money goes to the needy, not plush offices." Mike Yaconelli, director of Youth Specialties, a training organization for 100,000 youth workers based in San Diego, agrees: "Tony gets incredible numbers of people to ask, 'What can I do?' For twenty years he has challenged both religious liberals and conservatives to walk it like they talk it."

Tony considers the concerns of potential donors about religious charities "legitimate, although the government has really clamped down on abuses. Questions *should* be asked of charities, which should be able to produce annual audits. And it's more important to give your time than your money."

· : · : · : ·

It's late afternoon when Tony finishes up at UrbanPromise, and I for one could use a drink, followed by a nice dinner and an early bedtime. If we're lucky, Tony says, we'll be able to grab a Philly cheese steak before his evening sociology lecture back at Eastern College. We tear across the bridge again, zoom through Philadelphia's posh Main Line suburbs, and finally skid into a parking spot in front of Joe's Place, a classic sandwich joint. As a legion of others have done today, Joe and the waitress hug Tony, whom they call Doc; they then escort us to a special table in the back room.

As we dig into our cheese steaks and Cokes, I ask Tony how come an Italian guy his age isn't a Catholic. In 1910, he says, his maternal grandparents and their five children arrived here from Naples, and three weeks later, his grandfather died of diphtheria. Penniless, unable to speak English, and with no vocational skills, his disconsolate grandmother decided that her family would be better off without her; then at least her children would be able to go to an orphanage rather than starve. She wrote a suicide note to be given to the police and started for the Delaware River, weeping and muttering in the Neapolitan dialect. She was overheard by a young American man who was studying at Eastern Baptist Seminary, which is affiliated with Eastern College, and who also happened to be a gifted linguist. This stranger consoled Tony's grandmother and promised that his church would help her and her family survive.

True to his word, the Baptist even found a job cleaning jewelry for the woman's nine-year-old daughter, Mary. When she reached her late teens, Mary met a young man from Sicily, who, with the same Baptist's help, had found work as a window washer. The couple married and reared their children, including Tony, in the Baptist church because it had truly brought "good news" to the poor. When their white West Philadelphia neighborhood began to turn black in the 1940s, the Campolos stayed on, worshiping in the same church.

Many decades later Tony was asked to introduce a missionary who was the guest speaker for a lecture series at Eastern College. When he and his fellow Baptist had talked a little, they discovered that the missionary was the man who had helped Tony's parents. He was so overcome that their son had joined the ministry that he wept.

Tony preaches and practices the same gospel of compassion to the poor that saved his forebears. "The church was drilled into us in a very positive way," he says. "It has always been a part of who I am. My parents' message was that to be Christian is to be different. Paul to the Romans—'Be not conformed to this world!' "

Unlike many Evangelicals, Tony had neither the struck-from-his-horse, born-again experience nor a dramatic "call" to the ministry. Instead, his life course was powerfully shaped by attendance at a weekly Bible-study youth group, which was led by an accountant. Of its forty members, one person became president of a theological seminary, another became a Bible professor, and several became missionaries. "The intensity of faith that emerged out of the group turned mere beliefs into the kind of convictions that take hold of your life and won't let you go," says Tony. "What we tried to figure out was how to show gratitude to God and express love for others in the optimum way. We were all looking for vocations that would allow us to do those two things."

At twenty, Tony served as pastor at one New Jersey church, and at twenty-one founded another, which still thrives. At twenty-five, he got into hot water with his well-off white Main Line congregation when he helped start a fair housing program to introduce black professionals into the community; he finally resigned. "It was Christianity versus property values," he says.

To complement his theological education, the young minister studied sociology and eventually got his doctorate. In time he discerned that for him, a ministry carried out in classrooms and public forums would be more productive than serving in a single church. "There are only certain things one person can do," says Tony, "and you have to focus on the things in which you're effective. My excuse for not being a pastor is that I can help scores and scores of people like our interns love other people face-to-face."

Tony seems so resolute in his faith that I almost don't bother asking if he has ever had a spiritual crisis. "A few of them," he says. "One was early in my marriage. I love my wife more today than the day I married her. In fact, I'm not sure I even understood what love was all about on the day I married her! I'm a young guy, and I'm looking around, thinking maybe I should have married her instead—or her, or her. And wondering about what *that* says about me and spirituality. That crisis was solved by finding, through faith, the real capacity to love. Before that I was romantic, which means you're in trouble. Because romantic objects change constantly. One looks good, then six months later another one. I realized that beyond romance was very much where I had to be. Then I moved to a new relationship with my wife that, other than Jesus, is the most positive thing in my life."

Partway through just one of Tony's eighteen-hour workdays, I have trouble imagining how he manages personal relationships at all. "You don't have one way of life for your entire adulthood," he says. "I never did much out in the world before I was forty, because of my family. That took priority until my kids went to college. Then I said, 'Now I'm going to do this other thing gung ho.'" Nonetheless, Peggy, Tony's wife, has veto power over requests for his time, and she often travels with him. "It isn't that she just helps me," he says. "In God's providence, she has become an advocate for the religious needs of gay and lesbian people, and she puts a lot of time into helping them know that God loves them and that they are precious."

As we finish up supper with some coffee, I ask Tony how he has changed since giving his first sermons in that little church in New

Jersey's Pine Barrens. "The older I get," he says slowly, "the fewer things I believe, but the more deeply I believe them. When you're younger, you major in minors. There used to be so many sermon topics that seemed so important. Now I think most of them are irrelevant. Jesus boiled it down to the great commandment—love God and love other people."

Joe brings over his private bag of Chips Ahoy, and Tony grabs a handful. On the way out I notice a framed photograph by the cash register. It shows Tony in full academic regalia, just after giving an important speech at Oxford University. Grinning fiendishly, he's pulling open his black gown to show the lettering on a brilliant green T-shirt, embellished with a big shamrock: JOE'S PLACE.

· : · : · : ·

In minutes we're striding across the picture-perfect Main Line campus of Eastern College, where Tony is to give his weekly two-hour lecture on urban sociology. A skinny white kid in homeboy clothes thrusts a tape recorder in front of Tony's face and asks for a promo for the school's radio station. "If you don't listen," says the professor instantly, "may all the elastic in your underwear snap!" The boy beams as if at Steve Martin.

On our way to class Tony says that by now he has spent more of his professional life on campus than in church. He likes sociology because it's about "real people," he says. For eight years he taught at both Eastern and the University of Pennsylvania, where his courses attracted 2,500 students each semester. When Penn's department chairman forced him to choose between the two schools, Tony picked Eastern because it would allow him to keep up his missionary work.

At Penn, Tony's favorite course was Existentialism and Sociologism, which challenged his Ivy League students to question "whether human beings are the results of their choices or their conditioning," he says. "It was really a religion course." After class a group of students, many of them secular Jews, he recalls, would stay to talk further. One day they discussed what various sages would say to a prostitute. "When we got to Jesus," says Tony, "this

Jewish kid said, 'He never met one.' Well, I didn't want to argue, but I had to point out that the Gospels say he met a number of them. The kid said, 'You didn't hear me. When Jesus met one of these women, do you think he saw a prostitute?' There it is! The essence of the Christian faith!"

As usual Tony makes a detour en route to our destination. He leads me to an imposing hunk of granite, erected at the behest of an Eastern College benefactor, that turns out to be a monument to . . . gravity. "Is this great, or what?" says Tony ecstatically. "Forget Surrealism! Let's hear it for gravity!"

What looks like a cross section of American youth waits in a large lecture room. Eastern is a Christian college, but if its students are particularly religious, it's not immediately apparent. After a breezy introductory prayer for "attentive" listeners and an "interesting" lecture, Tony gets down to business.

Tonight's theme is that a city isn't a monolith but a constellation of largely homogeneous urban villages. Immediately Tony makes this abstraction personal by asking students to describe their neighborhoods back home; because he makes them wear large name tags, he's able to call on them personally. He finds something of interest in each contribution and, often, the grist for a joke that has the students either giggling or rolling their eyes as they scribble in their notebooks.

The students' replies bear out Tony's hypothesis: most of their homes are surrounded by those of similar families. This isn't bad or racist per se, says Tony, as long as the homogeneity isn't imposed or enforced. To illustrate, he brings up the "white flight" housing disaster that in the 1950s plunged Philadelphia into a crisis from which it has yet to recover. The conventional explanation is that the ways of the poor rural southern blacks drawn to the northern cities in hopes of employment drove their new white neighbors away.

According to Tony, Philadelphia's problem is not so simply explained. To qualify for low-interest G.I. Bill mortgages, legions of young veterans from World War II were obliged to buy brand-new houses in "homogeneous" communities—a requirement meant to stimulate the economy with a building boom. As expected, new suburbs sprang up, populated by the middle- and working-class whites who once lived in the cities. For black home buyers, however, there were no homogeneous suburbs. They were stuck in Philadelphia, in older, costlier houses that were increasingly hard to finance.

Suddenly Tony transforms what could have been a sociology lecture at any secular college. "The knee-jerk response to the near collapse of Philadelphia became 'The blacks did it,' " he says. "But, as Paul said to the Ephesians, there are sins of the flesh—personal evil—and of the world—its 'powers and principalities.' What about economic, social, and political evil in the form of structures that create injustice? Republicans say that West Philadelphia failed because individuals were irresponsible, Democrats because of the system. Each party has half the truth, because creating God's kingdom requires both personal responsibility and social justice. Being a Christian means both ministering to individuals and working for a fair system."

Message delivered, Tony flashes a grin. "After all this Jesus stuff, what's good about political corruption?" he asks. "To keep its political power in Chicago, the Democratic machine had to create thirty thousand jobs for a newly powerful constituency—African Americans."

After class I ask Tony to elaborate on his statements about evil. In liberal religious circles the very word is often avoided as being somehow in poor taste. If it's mentioned at all, evil is usually described as simply the absence of good. "That's why we're such easy prey for darkness," says Tony. "In C. S. Lewis's *Screwtape Letters,* the devil says the best thing you can do for him is to convince people that he doesn't exist." Just warming up, Tony blames the efforts of Augustine ("a disaster for the church" and a promulgator of "sick" sexual views) to accommodate a Hebraic-based, biblical faith to Greek philosophy for "completely destroying the realities of what Christianity is about. Which is that we are engaged in a great struggle against powers of darkness—a demonic force in the universe that's *certainly* not just the absence of good. The 'good news' is not just that our sins are atoned for and we go to heaven when we die but that God comes into our lives now and enables us to stand against the powers of darkness. The church is failing right now by talking about sin and evil only in moral terms but not also in spiritual terms. The church sees the sinner doing something wrong but doesn't see the dark powers out there."

During the Clinton impeachment scandal, I suspect, Tony spent a lot of time thinking about why good people do bad things. "Is it just a flawed personality?" he asks. "Someone who needs counseling? I think there's a kind of force that can take hold of us. I can hear the apostle Paul saying, 'The things that I would do, I don't do. The things that I would not do, those I do. Oh wretched man that I am, who shall deliver me from this?' People who don't think this way have never been to a place like Haiti. After you've said all there is to say about the political and economic factors at work, you realize that there's still an evil there that's an active force. You can feel the power of darkness in the air. Feel it! That's why *Star Wars,* with its Dark Force to which Darth Vader surrenders, rings a bell with us."

· : · : · : ·

One morning I join Tony on an early Metroliner to Washington and a conference called the National Summit on Churches and Welfare Reform. The gathering is sponsored by Call to Renewal, which Tony describes as a group of nonpartisan progressive Evangelicals "who think that Head Start programs, the Department of Education, humanitarian foreign aid, and controls on assault weapons are good things that should be supported by the richest country in the world." Espousing such "liberal" social views makes Tony a maverick in the larger, more conservative born-again world. Despite his oratorical mastery and spiritual zeal, his voice is strangely absent from the huge network of Christian radio and TV stations, large and small. His books—from *Is Jesus a Republican or a Democrat?* to *How to Be Pentecostal Without Speaking in Tongues*— aren't always available in Christian bookstores. Jim Wallis, the director of Call for Renewal and of Sojourners, a Washington-based religious antipoverty organization that publishes a well-regarded magazine of the same name, puts it this way: "Although the idea that the gospel is meant to be good news for the poor is so central in the Bible, it's often painfully absent in contemporary Evangelism. Tony is an evangelist who truly cares about social justice."

Evangelicals' internecine conflicts have less to do with theology—Tony is certainly a staunch creedal Christian—than with morality, particularly the "family values" issues of abortion and homosexuality. "If you don't knee-jerk on those two things," says Tony, "it doesn't matter what else you say or believe. You're persona non grata to a large segment of the Evangelical and fundamentalist communities."

Tony is concerned about the sometimes blurry line where religious beliefs meet civil rights. Because religious fundamentalists believe that their ethics are founded in absolute truth, they're prone to try to impose their rules on others. In contrast, Tony says that although, as a theologically conservative Christian, he finds gay marriage "contrary to [his] sense of biblical morality," that doesn't mean he has the right to say that gay couples should be denied the legal rights others have. "My position," he says, "is very different than the triumphalism of 'Our morality must become the law of the land.'"

Tony's tolerance is rooted in personal experience. When Tony was in high school, Roger, a gay classmate, hanged himself after some other boys dragged him into the shower room after gym, threw him in a corner, and urinated all over him. Tony hadn't been there during this attack, he says, "but I still grapple with the fact that Jesus would have stuck up for Roger, and I hadn't." At home, too, Tony is regularly exposed to a Christian view of homosexuality that differs from his own. Wearing a pink cross in her lapel and espousing the slogan "Straight but not narrow," Peggy, his wife, actively works for homosexuals' dignity and equality within Christianity. Both Campolos are heartened by signs of greater tolerance among Evangelicals toward gays.

"It's interesting that Jesus didn't mention homosexuality or abortion—the hot issues in our culture wars," says Tony. "One of his hot issues was 'religious' people who go around persecuting those who can't defend themselves. Being a Christian means being a friend to those who have none, and when the church is picking on the friendless, we must speak up. The question is, Are the hot issues of the fundamentalist and Evangelical communities the hot issues of Jesus?"

When I wonder why he doesn't simply join a kinder, gentler branch of Christianity, Tony says, "I can't give up. I have to help demonstrate how to have Christian convictions in a pluralistic society. 'We got the truth, and you don't'—that just won't work here. And I won't give up the financial base for EAPE's work with the poor. And anyway, why should *I* leave?"

The Campolos and their ministries pay a price for their fight-not-switch principles. At Evangelical gatherings Tony has been picketed for not having his wife "in subjection," as fundamentalists put it. He can no longer attend certain large events, because if he does some right-wing pastors won't allow their young people to go. After he agreed to be one of President Clinton's three spiritual advisers in the wake of the White House sex scandal, he was deluged with criticism. Members of the EAPE staff recall several months when the usually ebullient Tony seemed near despair. "I got letter after letter from people saying that, in protest, they were cutting off their financial support of EAPE. But what do you do when someone calls and asks, 'Will you help me?' What do you say? I only help Republicans? The poor? What I had to confront in my depths was, What if the whole ministry falls apart? If I have to tell these young Mission Year kids, 'Go home, I ruined it for you, there's no support'?"

During the dark days of the impeachment crisis, however, Tony learned an important lesson about Evangelical stereotypes. "When everyone was talking about me praying with Bill Clinton, I called Jerry Falwell," he says. "Jerry said to me, 'We've had bitter public controversies, but you can be sure of one thing. You have an important responsibility, and you don't need me on your back. I'm going to pray for you every day. The President chose wisely in choosing you.' It made me wonder how many enemies I could have turned into friends had I reached out to them like I did to Jerry Falwell."

Since this experience, whenever Tony gets a nasty letter he writes a kind response. "I'm amazed by how many second letters I get saying that the person has had a change of heart and is going to support the ministry after all. I haven't been loving and gracious enough to people who come against me. I've let people get away with being my enemy too easily." When Tony says, "Looking back, I wish I had been a more caring person," I laugh.

When I ask if he feels guided about how to act in life's difficult situations, Tony says, "Never. I make lots of bad decisions, but I live with them, and I don't think they're so significant. My choices aren't always that important, but what I am is. I know what I'm supposed to be, even if I don't always know what I'm supposed to do. In Denmark, when the Nazis came to round up the Jews, the ministers came running to the bishop. He said, 'Let's stop and pray about who we are. Once we know who we are, we'll know what to do.' If someone becomes a businessman instead of a missionary, it doesn't matter, as long as there's that same commitment to live out God's will in the office. Figure out what kind of person you're supposed to be, then don't worry about what you do."

· : · : · : ·

When we arrive in Washington, Tony works the phones from the train station, then heads for the rental car desk. By the time the keys are in his hand, the previously sullen clerk is smiling like Scrooge on Christmas morning.

The crowd at the 4-H Center in Chevy Chase, where the anti-poverty conference is being held, consists of lots of black people in suits and white people in fuzzy casual clothes. Tony immediately disappears into a group of young community workers. When one asks to borrow a pen, he thrusts a fancy silver model at her: "Here, keep this. Someone gave it to me, but it's very expensive and I'll just lose it." I chat with two pretty cheerleader types from Georgia and Indiana. When I ask how they would describe their Mission Year, they smile at me indulgently. They are "totally changed," that's all.

At lunchtime we're joined by the Reverend James Forbes, the elegant, eloquent pastor of Riverside Church in New York City, said to be America's best preacher. He and Tony—the oratorical equivalents of Michael Jordan and Larry Bird—discuss some mutual friends Tony bumped into after an act of civil disobedience at a protest over welfare cuts. "That's one great thing about getting arrested," Tony says. "You end up in a room with six or more people you've been trying to get together with for ages."

After lunch we hear various speeches, including an address by Andrew Cuomo, then the U.S. Secretary of Housing and Urban Development. Then a contretemps surfaces: it seems that instead of attending the regional meetings that were scheduled for the morning, black conferees decided to meet together without whites, which has upset some people. The speaker, who is black, says that what might seem like separatism was just bad scheduling and was not meant to give offense. This assertion sets off a series of huffy statements and counterstatements, including a puzzling exchange among black conferees about the terms "black" and "people of color."

It's discouraging to see such squabbling and pettiness even among religious and political allies. I ask Tony, whose ministry largely involves black people, how he deals with the issue of race. "When I meet a black or Asian person, I may say something wrong," he says. "I'm too old to be politically correct. But I believe people are sacramental—the means by which God communicates God's nature to us. When you help someone in need, if you look into that person's eyes and have this eerie sensation that Jesus is staring back at you, when you go home, you'll ask yourself, 'Was I worthy?' The whole way you react to people is changed. Once the world comes alive with the presence of God, racism is atheism."

After the speeches are finally over, the problems of poverty and racism seem to me even greater and more complicated. I slump in the lobby, nursing a headache, while Tony happily works the crowd. A black man wearing short dreads and a clerical collar gives him a big hug, then comes over to me. "That man saved me," says the Reverend Eugene Rivers, the dynamic pastor of Boston's Azusa Christian Community, whose work with youth has been lauded in

The New Yorker and other influential journals. "Tony bailed me out of jail when I was a kid on the streets of Philadelphia."

Tony will remain at the conference for another day, but he offers to give me a lift to the station. I ask him what he does when he's burnt out and just wants to chuck it all. "I go to sleep," he says. "You remember that great scene in the Bible when Elijah is just exhausted after fighting it out with the priests of Baal? He goes into a cave and says, 'I just want to die.' What does God say? 'Go to sleep.' Also, 'Eat a good meal. We'll talk about it in the morning! Joy cometh in the morning.'"

As we speed through one of the capital's seedier neighborhoods, Tony says, "Look at those drug dealers, just waiting! Isn't this block *horrendous*?" When I ask what draws him to work in such places, he says, "There's nothing else you can do that's as much fun. There really isn't! You can go to the stock market and make lots of money. In the end, is that so much fun? I don't know why it's fun to work in a slum, but it is!"

· : · · : ·

Tony Campolo's genius lies in his ability to play diverse roles—clergyman, comedian, entrepreneur, scholar, salesman, and orator—in a one-of-a-kind ministry that delivers the most good to the most people by as many means as necessary. Most but by no means all of the beneficiaries are poor. One Sunday I invite an agnostic friend to hear Tony preach at New York's Riverside Church. Even in a minister's flowing robes, he has the sort of sheer vitality that makes it seem as if his seams are about to burst. He begins the sermon, titled "Where Do We Go from Here?," with a scene from his life as a college professor. Each year he meets with a number of students who tell him they're leaving school in order to "find themselves," he says. "And they all look in the same place—Boulder, Colorado." The kids say they have to peel away the layers of social personas that have been imposed on them and find the core of their being. "But suppose," says Tony, "after you peel away the layers, you discover you're an onion?" By Tony's lights, "The self is not an essence waiting to be discovered through introspection but waiting to be created through commitments. You are what you are committed to!"

Next Tony wants to know what American mothers say when asked what they want their children to be when they grow up. "Happy!" we chorus. "My immigrant Italian parents answered, 'Good,'" he says. "Success and happiness are positive things, but goodness takes precedence over both. It is righteousness, not happiness, that exalteth a nation!"

At least in New York City, the world's psychotherapy capital, this is radical stuff. Tony knows that many of his listeners have spent thousands of dollars looking for a true self or an inner path they never found. He explains how he discovered his. "My mother told me," he says. "She said, 'You were brought into this world to serve other people in the name of Jesus. Do you understand that?'" When he meets people who object to the fact that Mrs. Campolo also told her little boy to be a minister, Tony shrugs. "Why not?" he says. "MTV and movies and fashion designers tell your child what to do. Children will rebel—that's what they do for a living—but why not be a parent who says, like the Old Testament prophet, 'As for me and my house, we will serve the Lord'?"

A kind of electricity begins to flow through the packed, socially diverse church. People exchange grins with their neighbors. Like Italians at the opera, a few African Americans call out encouragement to the star: "Preach it!" "Now you're talking!"

Speaking of happiness, says Tony, yesterday was his wedding anniversary. "My wife said to me, 'Just think, thirty-four years of happy married life.' I said, 'But we've been married for forty years!'" Jokes aside, he goes on to blame America's high divorce rate on the notion that marriage means "happily ever after." He describes a friend who resigned the presidency of a college to take care of his wife, who has severe Alzheimer's disease. His colleagues protested at his sacrifice, saying, "She doesn't even know who you are." The husband agreed. "She doesn't know who I am," he said, *"but I know who she is."* His friend is not a happy man, says Tony, "but I want to tell you something! He is a good man."

Written accounts of great preaching are like reviews of great concerts. You had to be there. As a large African American man beside me put it, weeping: "Now, *that* is the gospel!"

Lest there be any confusion, Tony reiterates that to be good means "to bring justice, love, and hope to other people. The spirit of Jesus himself comes through each person mystically, so that you can encounter it in the here and now, waiting to be loved and embraced in those who come to you in need."

Beside me, my dazed friend shakes her head. "Well," she says, "I guess I'm born again."

7. INTELLECTUAL

On a bright spring evening at the Waldorf-Astoria, the Aleph Society, which supports the work of the renowned Israeli scholar Rabbi Adin Steinsaltz, holds its annual benefit. Before dinner, clusters of New York academics and professionals sip wine and mingle. The guest of honor, however, stands alone. The rabbi resembles a slender Santa Claus, less because of his long white beard, turned-up nose, and rosy cheeks than because of his blue eyes, which twinkle with suppressed mirth. In his tieless shirt, dark suit, and fedora, he appears to be almost the only ultra-Orthodox Jew present.

Rabbi Steinsaltz is figuratively as well as literally alone in a crowd. Scholars are Judaism's aristocrats, and this polymath is compared even with the legendary Maimonides. His major work is the first edition of the Talmud in centuries that any literate person can read like a normal book. The vast work, whose origins reach back into antiquity, includes both the rules that shape Jewish life in all its particulars and much of Judaism's classical scholarship. The rabbi began this monumental task at the age of twenty-seven, expecting to be finished in fifteen years; at sixty-three, he hopes to be done in 2006. The rabbi, however, is not only an authority on *halakah*—religious law—but also a master of Kabbalah, or Jewish mysticism.

Tonight, it's especially apparent that Adin Steinsaltz is also caught between two worlds. He was born in Jerusalem to secular, political parents and had no interest in religion as a youngster—indeed, he picked on *yeshiva* boys. When his father finally compelled him to study Talmud for cultural reasons, the teenager underwent a spiritual metamorphosis. The rabbi won't discuss this transformation, except to compare it with a physical adventure, like mountain climbing, and to say that "there came a point when this world was not enough."

Nonetheless, Adin Steinsaltz is a master of keeping one foot in it. He's a *hasid*—devout person—who insists that "by nature, I'm a skeptic." Ultra-Orthodox Jews don't pursue secular interests, and they keep to their own communities. The rabbi has a university degree in math and chemistry, however, and is a science-fiction buff, movie fan, mystery writer, and geek. He travels all over the world and has friends of many faiths and none at all. In his work, too, the rabbi performs a balancing act. He's an elite academic who works to advance Jewish education at even the most basic levels. He calls liberal and secular Jews to greater observance of *halakah* but also tries to enliven Orthodoxy's stress on the law with teachings from the long-suppressed Kabbalah.

Rabbi Steinsaltz's high-wire act illuminates vital issues not only in Judaism but in postmodern religion, which must struggle to reconcile seeming opposites: old and new, secularism and spirituality, intellect and emotion, inclusiveness and orthodoxy, idealism and pragmatism, individuality and universality. Much like Pope John Paul II, the rabbi is a university-trained intellectual who's also a custodian of an ancient religious tradition. Both leaders offer an example that says, "If I can hew to this demanding orthodoxy and discipline, so can you." Both are abundantly gifted in ways that would have made them great worldly successes in a number of fields. Perhaps most significant, both are esteemed by many people who nonetheless won't do what they say.

To Rabbi Steinsaltz, there's only one branch of Judaism: the all-encompassing way of life described in the Talmud (which means not "law" but "learning"). Indeed, Rabbi Steinsaltz asserts, the Talmud is not only the core of Judaism but the creator and creation of authentic Jewish culture. For centuries, however, the text has been inaccessible to all but scholars and rabbis trained to decipher its archaic language. Rabbi Steinsaltz's Talmud is his response to what he sees as a life-or-death crisis. If the Talmud remains closed to most "people of the book," he believes, Judaism itself will die out.

Tonight the rabbi is also set apart from the buzzing crowd by a shyness particularly charming in the recipient of honors ranging from France's Légion d'honneur to the Israel Prize, his country's highest award. He had given me some of his time earlier on this busy day, and I had resolved not to take any more of it this evening. But he looks a little lonely standing by himself, so I bring Mike, my husband, over to meet him.

That morning I had mentioned to the rabbi that Mike's paternal grandparents were Romanian Jews—a group famous for drinking. Yes, he said, "that comes with it, more than being very spiritual. Also singing." In fact, I said, my husband has a fine voice, and he's handsome, too. "That too is part of the package," said the rabbi. "Whatever else they are, Romanians created for the Jewish world the modern musical." Hastening to include a more uplifting note, I said that one of Mike's forebears had been the physician of the legendary Queen Marie of Romania. "She saved many Jews," said the rabbi. "Romania was much better for us than anywhere else because of her."

The rabbi now gives Mike his bashful sidelong glance and smile, and they're soon joking about roguish Romanians. Although he meets many people, says the rabbi, "for some reason, they don't usually discuss things like their girlfriends with me, but are more philosophical. I find very few atheists." When Mike complains good-naturedly that I nag him to study Judaism, the rabbi looks wistful. "If you became religious, you might not have so much laughter and fun," he says. "I know a young man that happened to."

· : · : · ·

On his visits to the States, the rabbi is as tightly scheduled as a pop star. He meets with many groups and individuals, from gentiles like me to Hasidim. It's said he's unable to turn away anyone who seeks his counsel. Our first quick, disjointed encounter took place at the Manhattan office of the Aleph Society. For religious reasons, ultra-Orthodox Jews, like the Amish, distance themselves from mainstream culture. Men don't customarily shake hands with women, so when the rabbi appeared, we kind of bobbed, then swooped into our chairs.

Then the rabbi began to talk. He gets tired of going on about himself, he said, and would prefer to discuss me—ancestry, education, interests, religion, the whole business. He was glad that I wasn't a Jewish journalist, because they're always *at* him. (I could imagine some of their thorny questions: What is his opinion of Reform and Conservative Judaism? What about the growing antagonism between secular and ultra-Orthodox Israelis? The stalled peace process?) Being Irish was good, too, because only Ireland had culture in the Dark Ages, which was, he said, "a very good time for us—no degradation." He reflected fondly, too, on discursive evenings with an eminent Irish man of letters: "I have a good head for drinking, possibly better than his."

Segueing from ethnicity to religion, the rabbi asked if I read the Bible. At my nod he said, "That proves you're not Jewish. You don't fit." Like Jews and Judaism, he declared, "the Irish are Catholics no matter what they believe." By way of illustration he told a story about a wealthy East European Jewish woman who goes into labor. At first her cries are in cultivated French: "Mon Dieu!" As the labor grows more intense, her supplications switch to Polish and, finally, to Yiddish. I confessed that at some point between the births of my twin daughter and son, I had amazed myself by hollering, "O Mother!"

From a professional perspective this interview was going badly. The rabbi was asking the questions, and time was short. Trying to get him to stick to an interview format, however, was like trying to keep an Olympic skier on the bunny slope. He asked if I had ever met an Adin before and explained that the name means "gentle," in the sense of "gentleman." "You won't believe it now," he said, "but I was a rather handsome child. I had lots of curly blond hair—there are photos to prove it." Only when I expressed surprise that a great Talmudist was so humorous did he grow serious.

"I'm not a tranquil person by any means," he said. "But looking at a picture from two, three, seventeen different sides makes you see things differently. If you keep trying to watch and learn, you see that even the dark spots on the sun are brighter than a hundred moons. Leibniz said our world is the best of all possible worlds. In *Candide,* Voltaire made a parody of it as the worst possible. I'm a Jewish optimist. In my formulation, we live in the worst possible world in which there is still hope!"

Margy-Ruth Davis, a dear friend of the rabbi's and the backbone of the Aleph Society, rustled tactfully in the hallway, signaling the next interlocutor. I turned off the tape recorder and prepared to leave, then decided to risk what psychotherapists call the doorknob question: the $64,000 query that a patient saves for the forty-ninth minute of a session. What is the point of life? I asked.

Life, said the rabbi, is like an experiment in which we are the mice who must run the maze. The winners are those who puzzle out that we have been created by God, who is mindful of us: "We just want to be noticed." As in a maze or a game, so in life: one participates "just for the fun of it" and the reward of figuring out the system.

But, I asked, is determining the point of life merely an intellectual endeavor? To discuss it is intellectual, said the rabbi, but truly to grasp that we're creatures of a mindful God is emotional. Talmud lies at one end of the spectrum, he said, and mysticism at the other. Either extreme alone—endless details or poetic abstraction—can make you crazy, he said, "but both can keep you sane."

After this sketchy meeting I feel strangely *encouraged.* Margy-Ruth says that, the first time she met the rabbi, she noticed "something in his eyes. He understands things." Before long I start thinking of Rabbi Steinsaltz as Rebbe and sometimes dream of him.

· : · : · : ·

Rabbi means not "priest" or "minister" but "teacher." One evening soon after our first meeting, I went to an apartment on Manhattan's Upper West Side to listen to Adin Steinsaltz teach. About thirty Jewish men and women were gathered in a large parlor. The rabbi surveyed the reverent, expectant faces, then said, "It's a shame that I have to speak, and ruin the good impression."

Traditional Jewish teaching addresses a topic not in the abstract but in reference to Torah. Perhaps inspired by the refreshments, the rabbi first observed that figs, one of the seven fruits that the Torah calls "the pride of Israel," ripen at different hours, so a tree can't be harvested in one day: "The Torah is like a fig tree. You must search over time for its sweets, but the one who tends the tree will eat the fruit."

Botany might seem peripheral to religion, but not for a Talmudist, who investigates the text's every word, whether pertaining to God or to textiles or recipes. Then too, said the rabbi, Judaism is such an earthy religion that in *halakah,* measurements are given in terms of "a finger," "to the elbow," "the size of an olive." A man raised a hand to ask how one would determine the standard olive. To someone unschooled in Talmudic discourse, talking about such minutiae with a sage might seem foolish, but not to the rabbi, who explained that the olive is purposely used as a gauge "to allow people some freedom."

After this botanical prelude, the rabbi announced that the evening's subject would be the bar mitzvah. "I never heard the expression *bar mitzvahed* until I came to America," he said, clearly delighting in such linguistic quirks. Referring again to Judaism's earthiness, he said that the bar mitzvah is rooted not in theory but in biology. "What is the measure of adulthood?" asked the rabbi. "From an intellectual or psychological view, some people may never be adults. But the Talmud says that an adult is someone who can have children. Puberty, which usually happens for boys around thirteen and girls at twelve, gives a lot of clarity that other gauges don't have."

For the same reason, other important elements of Judaism are bound to biology. "Who is a Jew?" asked the rabbi. "Someone who's born to a Jewish mother." Similarly, he said, the Jewish priests who once served at the great temple in Jerusalem were born *kohanim*—members of the clan we call Cohen. "Whether or not one agrees to be a Jew or a priest really doesn't matter."

When the rabbi first announced his topic, I wished he had chosen something less parochial. Characteristically, however, his discussion of the bar mitzvah soon ranged all the way from children's developmental issues to the question of good and evil—particularly the latter—and drew as much on behavioral science as on religion.

The rabbi's view of childhood is so unlike the cherubic American model that many of his listeners looked a bit discomfited. In Judaism, he said, "children are naïve but not good or pure. Rather the opposite. Everyone is born with the evil impulse. The good impulses come at the age of bar mitzvah. Before that we say that children are 'innocent' not because they're angelic but because they're not fully able to make decisions." Despite Freud's strong aversion to religion, he said, "Freud was a Jewish boy so, even unconsciously, he had a Jewish notion of children's purity. His theory of childhood sexuality greatly upset society."

In one of the progressions from minor to major principle that's a hallmark of Talmudic discourse, the rabbi then moved from children's nature to humanity's. First, he twitted his listeners a bit. "The Bible is a very good book. You can read it—even Jews! It says that the heart of man is evil from the very beginning. Anger, envy, and desire take us out of the world to come. Even when sexual desire diminishes, we still pursue honors—the last to go!"

While we registered the unfashionable idea that we were born with evil hearts, the rabbi elaborated, incorporating the language of psychology. "A desire isn't rational or purposeful," he said. "It has its own drive that doesn't care for anything." Some drives, like hunger and thirst, have natural limits of satiation. Others, however, notably sex, "persist even after their purpose is achieved," he said. "In this, we're different from animals. When Adam and Eve ate from the tree of knowledge, they may have cut the tie between drive and purpose."

Such an intriguing hypothesis seemed to warrant more time, but the rabbi briskly segued from the bad news to the somewhat better. "Everyone has within a little hell that has a number of devils," he said. "But when they become demanding, we have a control, which is connected to making a decision. Torah says that 'sin is crouching on your doorstep and desires you, and you shall overcome it.' Rashi's comment is, 'And you are able to overrule it.' That's human free will."

No one could accuse the rabbi of looking at human nature through rose-colored glasses. "We don't have an instinct for good," he said, "and we do have free will. That's a very dangerous combination, because the capacity to decide means you aren't an innocent and can be blamed for evil deeds."

Coming full circle back to the bar mitzvah, the rabbi said that, although we're not born good, "we can achieve it. At first, we have a lower kind of soul, but we can reach higher. We can sublimate, not just in psychoanalytical terms. Some see this as a pessimistic view of humanity, but I see it as optimistic. Rather than receding from childhood's purity, you achieve nobility and divinity as you grow older. As you grow up, you get more of your soul."

Acknowledging childhood's end with the bar mitzvah "marks that maturity isn't only something that happens to me," said the rabbi, "but something that I understand and accept. It's the beginning of a new epoch in a human life, of a heroic inner struggle that's connected to decision-making ability. One chooses to become the son or daughter of a *mitzvah*—a commandment to do something great. The bar mitzvah is about the transition between something born of human parents and a human being."

For nearly two hours the rabbi painted a very realistic picture of *Homo sapiens,* warts and all. Anyone who came to the *shiur*—lecture—in hopes of feeling ethereal must have been disappointed. Yet it was strangely comforting to hear this kind, wise man tell us that if we use our heads—with help, ideally, from a time-tested tradition—we can overcome our clay feet.

On leaving I told Rabbi Steinsaltz that, as a mother of five, I could give a hearty amen to the realistic Jewish perspective on children's morality. "You have the nice writing of Mark Twain," he said.

· : · : · : ·

Across town from the *haimish* Upper West Side, the Aleph Society dinner provides the rabbi with a venue for a different sort of teaching: that of the woe-unto-you-O-Israel prophets. Like the great majority of American Jews, most of the guests identify with Reform or Conservative Judaism. To the Orthodox, however, these more liberal branches or movements are pick-and-choose improvisations on the real thing, which requires observing the 613 *mitzvot,* or commandments, spelled out in the Talmud.

Benefit dinner notwithstanding, the rabbi lets loose some zingers in the evening's printed program regarding the dangers of secularization and assimilation. After decades of Soviet suppression, Russian Jews are in desperate need of religious education, and the rabbi spends considerable time in Russia developing schools and home-study programs. He is at pains, however, to stress that political oppression is not necessarily more threatening to religion than a materialistic, worldly culture. As usual, he frames his remarks with a reference to the Torah. It will soon be the holiday of Shavuot, when the Book of Ruth is read. The rabbi reminds his readers that this biblical heroine was descended from Lot, who was Abraham's nephew. Like many relatives of the great, poor Lot felt he simply couldn't measure up. He left the Jewish people and fathered the gentile nation of Moav, into which Ruth is born. After the death of her husband, a lapsed Jew, Ruth decides not to return to her own people but to cleave to Naomi, her Jewish mother-in-law, and join Israel. Through her second marriage, Ruth closes the broken circle and becomes the great-grandmother of King David.

Commenting on this story, the rabbi writes, "Despite the passage of time and the destructive religious environment of the nation of Moav, the spark of good in Lot persisted until it could be revealed in the purity of Ruth and the majesty of David. So, too, we see the sparks of Judaism can survive both the brutality of oppression in the former Soviet Union and the seduction of assimilation in the United States. With your help, the Aleph Society will continue to reveal and rekindle those sparks." Lest the evening's guests miss the point, he writes, "Where Russian Jewry is now, European Jewry will be in fifteen years, American Jewry in thirty years, and even possibly Israeli Jewry in fifty years."

The dozen men and women seated around one of the circular dining tables suggest the challenge the rabbi faces. They include the dean of an Ivy League university, several editors, a well-known writer, and a large, handsome native-born Israeli who looks like a commando but is actually the director of a worldwide Jewish relief agency. Not one is Orthodox. The relief administrator explains that he has just returned home to New York after a stint in war-torn Albania: "And people don't believe in hell . . ." He belongs to a Conservative synagogue and regards the Talmud as "interesting" rather than binding. As to Orthodoxy's stress on ritual observance, he says, "It's better to eat shrimp and do right in the world." He describes himself as "a friend" of the rabbi's and, like several others at the table, wonders at the price such a brilliant man must pay in choosing the restrictive ultra-Orthodox way of life.

After dinner we adjust our chairs for the evening's highlight: a dialogue about relations between religion and science, conducted by the rabbi and Dr. Larry Norton, a prominent American cancer researcher and clinician who's a religious Jew. Up on the dais the rabbi fidgets like a boy, jiggling his crossed leg and showing lots of shin. For a scholar, he has little *sitzfleisch*—sitting-still flesh. Despite suffering from Gaucher's disease, a genetic illness that threatened his life and claimed his spleen in 1980, he's a workaholic who puts in sixteen-hour days. An American rabbi who visited him in Jerusalem recently told me that he arrived about 8:30 for dessert; at midnight Mrs. Steinsaltz excused herself;

at 2:30 A.M. the exhausted visitor took leave of his still bright-eyed host.

In his introductory remarks Dr. Norton says that things have changed since the nineteenth century, when, "like all educated people, doctors were supposed to be atheists." In contrast to the rigid Newtonian determinism that then prevailed, modern physics, with its chaos theory and principle of uncertainty, now portrays reality as far more complex and unpredictable. Indeed, as science becomes more sophisticated, he says, "It's atheism that seems naïve. Strangely, people are more open to God." Medicine, too, increasingly shares this view of life as being full of surprises. Dr. Norton, for example, has noticed that "patients who recover from cancer often have a clear idea inside that they'll do well, and they will work hard for that." To him, "their irrational confidence in the future is not divorced from the idea of God and religion."

So far, so good. Science and religion are no longer at each other's etiological throats. Next, however, Dr. Norton moves into grayer areas. "What happens after death?" he says. "I don't know. We're accustomed to lose and gain consciousness, and sleep can be pleasant. So might death be." Offering a sweet metaphor, he says, "At the end of a hard day, I have confidence that I'll be able to go home to my wife, who will be waiting for me with a nice dinner. Is it unreasonable to have the same attitude about God at life's end?" Alluding to a particularly contentious subject, this cancer specialist says, "I don't try to cause death but to prevent pain. I have a hard time with the idea of prolonging life in the hope of a miracle."

Now it's the rabbi's turn. "Science and religion should be engaged not in a duel or a bullfight," he says, "but in a duet." Talmudists don't linger over pleasant generalities, however, but go for the particular. Seizing the flung gauntlet of a life's ending, the rabbi asks: "What is life worth generally? Partially?" He answers, "You can even violate the Sabbath"—a very grave matter for the Orthodox—"to save someone who will live only for five minutes."

As usual, the rabbi develops his point with stories. In Israel, he says, a certain man was diagnosed as having a fatal disease. Nonetheless, every effort was made to prolong his life. Eventually a new specialist took over and realized the man had been misdiagnosed. The patient was correctly treated and cured. To this pragmatic illustration of the value of an ethical principle, the rabbi adds a religious rationale. When his own great-grandfather, also a renowned rabbi, was consulted by a sick man who wished to die, his reply was "One day on which you can put on *tefillin* [part of a man's daily prayer ritual] is worth eighty years of suffering."

The conversation about death goes on for an hour. It's a gloomy subject for a party. Even Dr. Norton, who had clearly hoped to have more to say on more subjects, seems frustrated by the rabbi's discursiveness and polite air of certainty. At one point he waves some papers and says, "I have an hour of notes here!" The guests shift in their seats. As Americans, they like speakers to be short and sweet. As New Yorkers, they worry about being tired at work tomorrow. As human beings, many are ambivalent about prolonging an agonizing death. As a Talmudist, however, the rabbi shares none of these views. Once again, amidst a sea of admirers, the rabbi seems alone.

· : · : · :

Before my next interview with Rabbi Steinsaltz, I study up on the Talmud. This written version of the oral debates about how Jews should live was recorded by rabbinical authors who wanted to preserve their tradition in the face of the diaspora. The first of its two parts is the Mishnah, which consists of teachings about the Bible and the laws drawn from it to guide Jewish life; its authors were Palestinian sages who lived in the first two centuries of the Common Era. The Gemarah records later rabbis' teachings about and debates over portions of the Mishnah. The text was written in Aramaic and an early form of Hebrew that lacks punctuation, so even Israelis would find it very difficult to read.

To examine the Talmud for the first time is to look into a different world. A page isn't organized into the customary flowing paragraphs or measured columns but resembles a mosaic or quilt. In the center sits a piece of the ancient core text. Surrounding it are blocks of commentary from various authors through the ages, always including Rashi, the eleventh-century French sage whose explanation is considered classical.

The Steinsaltz Talmud is both traditional and innovative. The core text in its original Hebrew and Aramaic still sits in the center of each page, but it's also rendered in modern Hebrew, complete with vowels and punctuation, in an adjacent column. To the right, in the English edition, for example (Russian, French, and Spanish editions are also in progress), is a literal English translation of the core text as well as Rashi's commentary. On the left side, Rabbi Steinsaltz gives his own expanded translation and commentary, designed to help the modern reader make sense of the old texts. In the margins he offers notes on other commentators and additional amplifications of the text. In one such aside, for example, he explains that although pork is no more "unclean" than the meat of a horse or camel, it seems so, perhaps because the pig was the symbol of the oppressive Roman legions in Palestine. Sometimes drawings, too, further clarify the text. Keeping all this material straight requires as many as twelve typefaces, for which the rabbi designed special software.

In terms of subject matter, the Talmud is a combination of history and religion, knowledge and wisdom, legends and humor. It appropriates the ancient rabbis' oral question-and-answer format to clarify every detail of problems drawn from six main areas of inquiry: agriculture, holidays, women, damages, matters relating to the Jerusalem temple, and "purity," or ritual fitness. Some Talmudic questions have become academic, such as those that refer to the long-demolished temple. Many, however, concern perennial problems of the human condition, from making a living to preserving health.

In pursuit of its questions, the Talmud avoids abstraction, philosophizing, and generalities, and instead focuses on reality, facts, and particular situations. May you move your couch on *shabbat,* when work is forbidden? You may move it inside your home but not over the threshold and into the public domain. Must everyone fast on Yom Kippur? Someone whose doctor has forbidden the observance is required to eat. A peculiar logic informs even the most seemingly fanciful answer: How should a pious man observe Purim, a joyous celebration of Jewish liberation? He should foster a properly festive atmosphere by getting tipsy.

Some of the Talmud's questions seem truly bizarre. What if a rodent brings unleavened crumbs into a house at Passover? Can one fulfill the *mitzvah* of blowing the *shofar* on Rosh Hashanah if it's blown in a cistern? Such improbable dilemmas are treated seriously, however, because even a fantastical problem can shed light on other, more practical problems—in the latter case, for example, concerns about echoing in a modern synagogue's amplifying system. Then, too, certain Talmudic debates, regarding artificial insemination, say, and fetal transfer, seemed absurd for 1,500 years but are no longer so. Finally, like playing chess or teasing out the layers of iconography and nuance in a great painting, studying Talmud is its own reward—and a *mitzvah,* too.

From the point of view of ethics, the Talmud's great problem is how to achieve balance between justice and mercy. In pursuit of this goal, for example, the sages disqualified childless and aged men from courts hearing a capital offense; someone who didn't know or had forgotten "the sorrow of raising children" might be too eager to apply the letter of the law. Most of us would prefer to be the victim of a thief, who acts in stealth, rather than a robber, who acts openly. According to the Talmud, however, because he acts in plain view of God and man, the robber is more deserving of mercy than the thief, who fears man more than God.

The broad umbrella of Talmud was meant to preserve the unity of the Jewish people, partly by institutionalizing disagreement and debate. Yet differences of opinion regarding some of its teachings have caused deep divisions. Its view of women, which Conservative and Reform Jews don't uphold, is a prime example. Women can't join a *minyan* (official prayer quorum), serve as judges, or take any active administrative position in the religious community. Women are also exempted, although not banned, from religious practices such as wearing fringes. Most important, women are not required to study Torah, which is Judaism's greatest commandment. Then, too, most applicable purity laws refer to women. In *The Essential Talmud,* the rabbi's highly accessible primer, he underscores the tradition's reverence for the wife and mother but allows that "Talmudic law excludes women, in many ways, from several important spheres of life."

On the morning we're to speak about the Talmud, I'm still unsure of the drill for a private meeting with an ultra-Orthodox rabbi. I put on a heavy suit that's the closest thing I have to a *chador.* By noon the weather has turned unexpectedly warm. The subway takes longer than usual, and I have nearly to jog for several blocks in order to be on time. I arrive dripping at the hotel. The rabbi, who has just flown in from Israel, offers me a chair and settles down with his pipe. Watching me try to mop my streaming brow, he says kindly, "You can feel at home here. Would you like to wash your face? Luckily, I'm not that stiff."

While I cool off I tell the rabbi that, to my surprise, my oldest son, then a college student, knows all about Adin Steinsaltz from a television program. The rabbi, who has three children, asks, "Has your son forgiven you yet?" I laugh. He says that it's "a very sweet feeling when someone recognizes me. Once I flew to Chicago. The pilot was a woman. As I left the plane, she said, 'I'm just reading one of your books.' It wasn't something that I was expecting. For a film star, that kind of thing possibly happens more often."

I tell the rabbi that I've found *The Essential Talmud* much livelier than "the law" would suggest. "The Talmud is not a book on what to do," he says. "The law is just the material that allows asking questions. There's a joke in which someone asks a Jew, 'Why do Jews always answer one question with another?' The Jew says, 'And why shouldn't we?' In that sense the Talmud is a picture of Jewish culture."

To the rabbi, a Talmudist is just a special breed of intellectual: "Someone who can sit for an evening discussing questions that have nothing to do with his life or his work. How many Americans can do that?" The Russian intelligentsia, on the other hand . . . The rabbi fondly describes a party in Moscow that was "a little bit" in his honor and included artists, engineers, a physicist, and merchants, most of whom weren't Jewish. After very many toasts, "everyone was at least a little drunk," he says. "I have a good head for that, which gets me great respect in Russia. One of the questions we discussed was Do dogs get to heaven? No one else there was a theologian, or even especially religious. They were too drunk to be pretentious. What a discussion! Nothing in it for them but the excitement of the mind. That's what I call intellectual!"

Like other cerebral pleasures, Talmud offers the fun of "doing a higher thing just to do it," says the rabbi. "Much of mathematics has no point, other than doing it. What is the core of science? Asking all sorts of questions, some of them seemingly stupid." He describes an early experiment on electricity in which a piece of amber rubbed with flannel became charged. "What would most people do with those things? Use the amber as a paperweight and the flannel to wipe the face and that would be the end of it. But some people ask, What would happen if . . . ? If you're an intellectual, you don't even need material objects to play with. You take an idea. You look at it one way, then another."

The Talmud has no real analogue. The rabbi sees certain similarities between it and Plato's dialogues, "which are also a kind of discussion that tries to figure what is true about a point or idea, such as love," he says. "The Talmud, too, pursues truth, but Greeks and Jews go about this in very different styles. And Plato was a great writer. Most of the Talmud, which has many authors, is neither a stylized dialogue nor easy reading. It was created by—and creates—a whole culture." Indeed, even among secular Jewish superachievers, the rabbi sees the influence of Talmudic tradition's stress on both levelheadedness and the envisioning of endless possibilities.

Studying Talmud requires mastering new ways of reasoning. Modern Westerners dismiss the so-called argument from silence, but Talmudists use the fact that something is not expressly forbidden to bolster claims that it's therefore allowed or not allowed, depending on their viewpoint. Deductions are made from minor to major principles, rather than the reverse: if a man is forbidden to marry his daughter's daughter, then he's surely forbidden to marry his daughter. In the pursuit of clear definitions, the Talmudists borrowed philological methods from the Greeks, so that when a word's meaning is uncertain, they consult not a dictionary but another section of Talmud. "The more you clarify," says the rabbi, "the better off in the process you are."

We've been talking about the Talmud for some time yet have spoken little of spiritual matters in the conventional sense. When I ask if it's possible to express a religion in strictly intellectual terms, the rabbi says, "That's what the Talmud is, and that's what's so hard about it."

Only when he remarks on the sheer number of the Talmud's concerns, from hand washing to criminal trials, does the conversation take on a decidedly "religious" tone. Not especially cheerfully he says, "Judaism is a total religion, a way of life. It follows you from the moment you wake up to the moment you fall asleep. From the moment you're born till the moment you're buried. *There's no empty space.* The Torah is the blueprint of the world, so that nothing is 'secular.' Obeying the laws—for eating, tying shoes, relating to others—makes every act a ritual that links person to Creator and helps transform the world."

The "no empty space" business is sobering. Who could do all the good deeds—*mitzvot*—that could be done? I want to know. "You can do a fair amount of them," says the rabbi. "The difficulty with Judaism is that you can never be completely out of it." Surely, I blurt, not everyone is called to the same extraordinary level of observance? Without directly addressing the most contentious issue in modern Judaism, the rabbi says, "Even the most basic level is total enough. You can always enhance it. There comes a point at which it's not so much the law as . . . Let's say I just sit and don't do anything. Even that is some kind of a sin, because I *could* be studying. Doing something good with that time. There's no empty space."

The rabbi knows that many people are inclined to, as he puts it, "keep God in an old people's home and visit him once a week." The Talmud demands far more. Where observance is concerned, the rabbi compares Judaism to an army that all Jews are enlisted in at birth; some volunteer to serve in special units that work much harder for the same pay. Naturally, he says, "there are only a limited number of them. Why would anyone join such a unit? Because there are some people who, when they see a mountain, have to climb it. Like explorers who search for hidden kingdoms, they're a different kind of people."

The rabbi makes no bones about his desire to see more American Jews in the elite units of Orthodoxy. He genuinely loves America for its openness and spirituality, but whom the rabbi loveth, he chastiseth. "There's a difference between someone who's very bright and an intellectual," he says. "How few Americans really know anything—not just philosophy, but even literature—except their professional duties. It is funny, sometimes tragic, that a person who can't make a correct account of his own reality—can't even understand a simple mathematical equation—wants to understand the Almighty and judge Him." Indeed, to the rabbi, religious skepticism or indifference suggests not intelligence but a curious lack of imagination. "Maimonides writes in the beginning of his book of law a description of the world—stars and so on—like a scientist. He says that when people contemplate such things, they will understand about God. But many people today can't. Nor can they read a novel and cry, or allow a good speaker to make a symbol, a word, come to life in their minds. All these things require not relying on shortcuts. You have to work to see what's happening. Today, most people are so passive that they expect to see pictures. A movie instead of a book is a mechanical shortcut, like drugs. A movie about the Ten Commandments?"

Where American Jews in particular are concerned, the rabbi's tone ranges from that of a no-balm-in-Gilead prophet to that of the parent of a beloved but wayward child. "I say many rude things, and American Jews don't like it," he says, "but in many ways, the Jews who came here were like Europeans who settled Australia—not necessarily the community's saints and scholars. Most of what they know about Judaism is inaccurate and could be put on a fingernail and leave some space. They're speaking about

God when they don't have the faintest notion! I said to one fellow, 'That God that you don't believe in is also a God I don't believe in. That I'm not *allowed* to believe in!'"

One particular group of American Jews takes the brunt of the rabbi's tough love. "American rabbis are unspeakable!" he says. "I was unlucky enough to hear some of their sermons recently. They could have been written for any New York newspaper without changes—no religion, spirituality, life! American synagogues are horrible—Anglican churches in the dryest possible way that attempt to imitate what's around them. You come as a child into one of these places, and there's no life in it. It's made so boring you don't experience anything! You know, for many other people, going to the synagogue is some kind of fun!"

When I started to write about religion, I tell the rabbi, many friends, particularly secular Jewish ones, looked askance. "In a funny way," he says, "they're proclaiming their Jewishness by being atheists. America is the most religious country in the West, so the Jews here have established some way to be different. Perhaps there's a genetic obstinacy." Jews have been the forerunners of many revolutions, the rabbi says, and perhaps the same anti-authoritarian spirit inspires their resistance to Orthodoxy: "As Moses said to God after the episode of the golden calf, 'Because they're obstinate, forgive them. You have to wait until they're educated, then they'll stick to you.'"

As he is wont to do, the rabbi circles back to an earlier part of our discussion, when he asked if my oldest son "forgives" me yet. "Adolescence is not a happy time," he says, "but is possibly a fruitful one. Growing pains create a lot of distress, but they help you establish some identity. Then, you can reapproach your past. Many Jews here are in a childish rebellion against their ancestors, not just their fathers. To be as negative as possible is their first answer to Judaism. No, no, no, no! Maybe later, some will change their mind, but many here don't have, or take, time to rethink their tradition. Age and experience teach us something. If people lived long enough, possibly everyone would become religious. Possibly you need two hundred years for this development."

As I take my leave the rabbi remarks on the spontaneous popular mourning for a national icon: "Americans worship Joe DiMaggio, and he just played baseball. I remember when in Israel we had rebbes on baseball cards."

· : · · : ·

In the rabbi's world there are no coincidences. One day I tell him that I probably wouldn't have read *The Essential Talmud* if a blowout hadn't forced me to abandon my car and board a bus for a long trip. Oddly, his book had been stowed in my car. Suddenly we've left the intellectual territory of Talmud and entered Judaism's mystical realm, in which everything connects.

Of what might seem to be his two different worlds, the rabbi says, "*The Essential Talmud* and *The Thirteen Petalled Rose*"—his classic presentation of Kabbalah—"are different kinds of Jewish books, but they're aspects of the same thing. Now, I'm one of the few, but in the past most of our mystics were also Talmudic scholars. That someone who might seem dry and legalistic lives a kind of double life—that's no longer so common. The foremost book of *halakah* was written by a rebbe who for eighty years mostly dealt with the law. But he also had an entirely different life that was lived almost in a trance. His diary describes these dreams and visions and mystical experiences."

It's not easy to discuss mysticism with a mystic. The more he knows, the less he says. When I offer my shorthand definition of mysticism—only God—the normally loquacious rabbi looks sideways and says, "Sometimes." When I propose that such an all-encompassing worldview must be hard to live with, he says, "Yes. You want at least a corner where not everything is God."

There are no such corners in the world portrayed by Kabbalah. Its reality is very different from the one we perceive with our senses. According to its scheme, creation is, as the rabbi writes, "the transmutation of the divine reality into something defined and limited—into a world." In kabbalistic language, the universe is the "emanation" of a mysterious divine light that created it. Somehow, everything that has ever existed—including the sparks that are souls—is destined for ultimate reunion with this sacred source.

To suggest something about kabbalistic levels of reality, the rabbi returns to his favorite medium: "The Hasid says to his rebbe, 'I have now a weird experience. Wherever I go, I see letters of fire.' The teacher says, 'After learning Kabbalah, being able to not see the letters is a much higher achievement than seeing them.' " The similarity of vision that prevails among mystics of different religions is evident in this story, which calls to mind the levels of *samadhi,* as Hindus call mystical enlightenment; in the first stage, the mind stays rooted in a single thought; in the second, it becomes completely thoughtless and "lost to the world"; in the highest stage, however, the yogi functions like a normal person while maintaining constant awareness of the divine.

On a roll, the rabbi tells another story: "There was a rebbe who in two minutes could understand a great deal about a person who came to seek his counsel. He had a valet. After an hour of these interviews, the rebbe was soaked with sweat and had to change his clothes. The valet said, 'You just sit there so quietly, and you say two sentences. Why are you so sweaty?' The rebbe said, 'When someone comes to see me, I have to take off my own spiritual dress and wear his in order to understand what he is saying. Then, when I have to answer, I have to take off his dress and put on mine again. It's very tiring, all this dressing and undressing.' "

Human beings play a crucial role in this vast kabbalistic drama. Because we have free will, we can choose to behave in ways that either enhance or hinder the movement of creation toward perfect completion in the divine. To play this cosmic game, the individual must first grasp the objective, then try to "ascend" toward the light on the rungs of good deeds. Progress is so slow that most people require more than one lifetime to reach the goal.

The rabbi tells another story, this one from the Baal Shem Tov, the founder of Hasidism. A very saintly man asked his rebbe why, despite his good behavior, he led such an unlucky, miserable life. In response, the rebbe sent him to look for a certain man in another town. The righteous fellow went there and found that the man had died long before yet was still remembered as vicious. The good man returned home and told the rebbe what he had found out. As if he were a guru discussing *karma,* the spiritual master said, "You were that man, and in this life, you were punished."

Most American Jews would deny that reincarnation has a place in Judaism. The rabbi prefaces his remarks on the subject with a biblical theme, which he encapsulates as " 'You have a job to do.' We may like it or we may not, but we have to keep coming back until it's accomplished." Miming a scientist putting a mouse in a maze, he says, "If you don't get the point of life, He picks you up by the tail, and you have to run it again. Almost every person bears the legacy of previous existences. One sometimes senses this as a feeling of being in the wrong place, even body, or in pieces of a life that don't seem to fit." Although most souls are second- or even thirdhand, he says, "a few are new souls. One thing that can't be repeated is innocence."

The rabbi dismisses the matter of where the soul goes between death and rebirth as a "nonsense question, because 'where' is relevant only for a physical being. Where does a dream go after you've dreamt it? Electroencephalograms show that the fetus has a dream state. What is a fetus dreaming about? Heaven?" Accounts of near-death experiences suggest to him that "souls don't want to be reborn once they've escaped the flesh." I think of the *bodhisattva* when he says that, nonetheless, "some even 'volunteer' for tasks no one else can do." Returning to the idea of having to do your job whether you want to or not, he asks, "Does the candle want the flame? Without it, the candle has no function. With it, it will disappear."

Until the recent emergence of the Jewish "renewal" movement, mainstream American Judaism has either disparaged or ignored the religion's mystic tradition, with its talk of letters of fire, angels, and reincarnation, which had been driven underground after the Enlightenment. The rabbi remarks on the venal practitioners who gave Kabbalah a bad reputation by using debased forms for fortune-telling, as some pop Kabbalists are doing now. A true mystic master must also be a *mensch,* he says. "Someone can't be both a constant chaser of women or collector of cars and a holy person. Look at the difference between the disciples of Abraham and Balaam, who was a man with a high level of spiritual understanding but a dirty person." Observing that spiritual gifts aren't necessarily signs of sanctity, he says, "Being able to read and write is a spiritual gift—animals can't do that. Mathematics is such a gift, but I don't attach holiness to that, either."

Kabbalah has long been surrounded by secrecy and taught individually, in rough outlines, to someone who's adept enough to fill in the blanks from experience. The rabbi, however, takes what might be called the Purloined Letter approach. "If something is a secret, it can be put under a floodlight, and someone who's not prepared to see it won't."

Through its dark days Kabbalah was preserved largely by East European Hasidim, a group of ultra-Orthodox Jews who were— and still often are—ridiculed as backward or even heretical. "Our esoteric tradition has been kept alive in recent centuries by people who might seem unlikely candidates," says the rabbi. "But for three thousand years many of the people who carried it on were both scholars and mystics." His own deep ties to Hasidism go back to youth; in his twenties he even tried to start a neo-Hasidic community in the Negev. He enjoyed a close relationship with the late Menachem Schneerson, the legendary Lubavitcher rebbe.

On my way to my house upstate, I pass many Hasidic summer colonies, and I ask the rabbi about the meaning of the billboards that read: BRING MESSIAH NOW! In typical Steinsaltz fashion, he first cites Francis Fukuyama and says, "It's the end of history." Then he touches on scripture, explaining that a prophecy says that the messiah will come when people are at their best or worst. An interesting tidbit of history comes next: a heretical sect once tried the latter approach, "even exchanging women on Yom Kippur, which is triply forbidden." Perhaps because he's a "Jewish optimist," however, the rabbi sees ours as a time of positive messianic portents. For example, he says that a prophecy has it that an iron idol with feet of clay will collapse when a stone is thrown at it from out of nowhere, which the late Lubavitcher rebbe linked to the end of the USSR, history's first officially atheistic "evil empire." "So there's the collapse of evil on the one hand," says the rabbi, "and, on the other, the emergence of new things that are good, such as large-scale disarmament and the spread of human rights. The time is ripe."

Like other Jewish leaders, the rabbi is painfully aware of the many Jews who look outside their birth tradition for the spirituality that mainstream Judaism stifled for so long. India's ashrams are full of Jewish devotees, and the number attracted to Buddhism is such that they've acquired a nickname: Ju-Bu's. When I enthuse about meditation, the Talmudist says, "Can you have a useful, completely free meditation about nothing? That's a question." Before offering his answer, he throws in a bit of commentary: the practice of "contemplating the navel," or focusing on one not very interesting point to induce a trancelike state, was advocated many centuries ago by a Christian Byzantine mystic, "so this idea is not just Asian." Returning to meditation, he asks, "Is it objective or subjective? Is the point to reach deep inside yourself or beyond yourself? Sometimes a person empties himself and remains empty." Only then does he say, "In Judaism, we don't believe you can meditate about a void or that such a thing has value."

Unlike many traditional religious leaders, however, the rabbi takes people's hunger for spiritual experience very seriously. American religion has traditionally stressed good works and regarded personal spirituality as narcissistic at worst and, at best, the carrot on religion's stick. The rabbi is indignant at this notion. "Experience is not the carrot," he exclaims, "but the substance! The best religious poetry here is in the black spirituals. Why? Because they are a deeply religious people. When they sing or pray, it's real, and when it's real, it's moving, touching. Some people only have spiritual experiences when they drink, which makes them warm and close to others. But to have this experience without drinking, drugs . . ."

The mention of drugs and religious experience evokes my single experiment with LSD, way back in college, which produced generic but nonetheless ravishing spiritual visions. "Did you ever—" I begin, then say, "Sorry, no, of course you couldn't!" The rabbi, a merry prankster of a different sort, laughs, too, and protests, "I could, but I didn't!" He goes on to posit that it was belief in God that evoked my psychedelic epiphany. I don't use "believe in" anymore, I say, because what I feel is less like faith than like a sense of having been mugged by God. "Okay," says the rabbi, "that's the right way. But you can visualize things that, without a religious background, you possibly couldn't. If you see God's chariot but you don't have any knowledge of the *merkava,* it will just be a funny kind of wagon."

All religions are threatened by the spiritual illiteracy that the rabbi alludes to. As to how someone with no background can experience God he says, "Sometimes, by being hit over the head." He illustrates with a story about a friend of his father's, a very bright leftist who migrated to Palestine and then to Russia, where he rose very high in the Communist party. When the Stalinist purges came, he was arrested, interrogated under torture, and finally exiled to Siberia, because he was too well-known and important to be killed. After twenty years in a prison camp, the man, now physically broken, was released. "He returned to Palestine, which had become Israel, as an observant Jew," says the rabbi. "When I met him, he wore a black skullcap! He wrote a beautiful book about a Communist who finds Judaism in exile."

No one can accuse the rabbi of the soft sell: "So now I tell people, 'If you want a sure way to get religion, sit in solitary confinement for twenty years in Siberia!' It was an opportunity to be quiet and think about life and ideas, life and ideas, without any outside excitement, which seems to be very good medicine. You can tell your husband, if he wants to do it the hard way . . . You see what it takes!"

· : · : · ·

The next time I see the rabbi, he's on a large screen in a sleek Park Avenue corporate headquarters, where a group of his American students have gathered. Such *beit midrash* teleconferences connect him to study groups worldwide, including eighty in American universities. The rabbi is seated in his small, domed office, agreeably cluttered with academic flotsam and jetsam, in Jerusalem's Old City. When his Hasidic techie gives him the all-clear signal, he peers shyly at us and says, "I wish I were more handsome. I know it's only seven-thirty in the morning there. You're jewels to rise so early."

Today's subject is *shabbat,* or the Jewish Sabbath, which lasts from eighteen minutes before sundown each Friday to darkness on Saturday night. The day's simplest, greatest requirement, says the rabbi, is to rest, meaning "to not work." In Talmudic terms, work is making something. Thus, on *shabbat,* even study must be the reflective sort. "The prayers and meals and all the rest are just pleasant things," says the rabbi. "The real point is not doing anything—a void that's even more basic than rest."

As usual, the rabbi's topic is quite specific, yet his remarks somehow apply to people of all faiths, which also set aside times for rest and prayer, and even to secular workaholics. He doesn't cast *shabbat* in a rosy glow but presents it in terms of no pain, no gain. First comes the pain. "Humans are nervous beings who like to *do,*" he says, "as opposed to, say, cats. People once had to work almost constantly, and therefore needed to rest. We moderns have much more spare time. Psychologically, not working is okay for a few minutes, but then? Filling up leisure time is a big industry, because we can't rest without going crazy." In one of his characteristic asides, he says that couples often quarrel on weekends and holidays, "but a pair who can't just sit quietly is not in love. To demand ceaseless activity from someone is just to utilize that person." The fact is, he concludes, "for us, a day of rest means boredom and opens up a world of unpleasant things."

Now comes the gain. Whether we like it or not, says the rabbi, rest is good for us. "Even though we didn't really do anything, after a good sleep, we feel better. Our problems seem lighter, just by not thinking about them. We get a transfusion of new power." In the same way, he says, when we enter the void of *shabbat,* "some kind of inner repair goes on. For us, renewal seems to require stopping one thing and doing something else."

Just as there's poor sleep, however, there's unrestful rest. The rabbi muses on the proper *shabbes* state of mind: "How to be peaceful rather than just feeling confined and restricted?" Just as we learned as children how to change gears and go to sleep, he says, so we must learn to enter *shabbat*. The key is "totality, meaning complete abandon to rest, with no buts. Worries must cease to exist. We don't even deal with our sins—a distraction. One must say, 'Whatever happens, I'm at rest.'"

If *shabbat* means rest, it also means listening. Both states tap "the creative power of passivity," says the rabbi. "They require one to be quiet and receptive, which is easier for some than for others—for example, for women than for men. We must be receptive to enjoy music or art. In the same way, the Bible says we should 'listen to the stillness.' The joy and gift of *shabbat* begins with the ability to stop, rest, listen, receive, renew. *Shabbat* means 'I am listening, trying to receive.' It's meant to be a day of meditation, when you're renewed by forces above consciousness that you don't know."

Watching him adjusting his yarmulke, gesturing, fidgeting, it's hard to imagine that *shabbat* is easy for the hyper rabbi. At our end, here in workaholism's capital, the thought of a whole day with no phones, faxes, or e-mails sets us, too, wriggling in our chairs. "I go to sleep at one-thirty and get up at seven-thirty," a famous feminist mutters, "and I still can't get everything done." I wonder, however, if our resistance to the idea of sitting still and shutting up springs from our demanding schedules or dread of boredom as much as from the unfamiliar idea of "trying to receive" a mysterious gift.

Perhaps responding to our ambivalent faces, the rabbi says, "People have to learn how to rest. It's more than just stopping. Leisure must be learned and achieved." Historically, he says, aristocrats constituted the so-called leisure class. Like true nobility, he says, "The ability to rest is an inner achievement that may take not just a lifetime but many. Like nobility, the joy of it has been bred into the Jewish people over ten or twenty generations, yet it can be lost in one generation. Like fine glass, *shabbat* is hard to make and maintain but easy to break. As the prayer says, God didn't give it to the nations of the world, but as a special gift to our people. For those who don't work to exhaustion, however, it's a complex gift. *Shabbat shalom*—to be at peace. Okay."

The teleconference ends with a brief question period. Warily, the feminist takes exception to the notion that women might have an easier time with the *shabbat* mentality than men. Serenely, the rabbi says that "sexually and otherwise, women may be more receptive."

Once again the rebbe has taught religion for over an hour without sounding "religious." He has illuminated Talmudic prescriptions with mystical insights. He has combined ancient tradition and modern behavioral science. Indeed, much like a good therapist, he has built up to his point slowly and from different directions, so that his listeners have internalized knowledge rather than simply registered information. That the sabbath is a "day of rest" was hardly news, but now we have a subtler inside-out sense of what that means.

· : · : · : ·

Adin Steinsaltz has a genius for bridging what many educated people since the Age of Reason have perceived as a chasm between the life of the mind and the spirit. Among his most powerful tools is humor. Toward the end of our next visit, the rabbi mentions paradise. "The Muslim version is far more tempting than Jewish one," he says. "But imagine a man sitting surrounded by beautiful women. How long will it take him to become bored? It's a problem. You might imagine that Tahitians would be easygoing, but no. Sometimes it's good we are spared this kind of experience. It seems that it's hard for us to just sit in paradise." It would be like having *shabbat* all the time, I say. "Yes!" he says, delighted. "Like being doomed to everlasting *shabbat*!"

We chat for a while longer at the door. The rabbi smokes his pipe and paces as we discuss the *via negativa* of the great Spanish Catholic mystics. I quote St. John of the Cross, whose mystical credo was *"Todo es nada"*—All is nothing. The rabbi likes this. He reminds me that John's peer Teresa of Ávila, the only female "doctor of the church," had a Jewish grandfather. As the rabbi says, "She was one of ours."

Finally, I ask my doorknob question: How can I develop spiritually? "Not in church, which is relaxation," he says, "but in the kitchen, in everyday life. To see quarreling children and spilled milk as religious experiences. Judaism is a twenty-four-hour-a-day religion."

8. COMMUNITY

In a retreat center in Sierra Madre, an hour outside Los Angeles, the biannual meeting of the Association of Contemplative Sisters is off to a rousing start. A chorus line of women, mostly of a certain age, costumed as Mousekeeters, movie queens, cowgirls, and other L.A. types, belts out a spirited improvisation on "California, Here I Come." At the finale two of the singers suddenly rip off sedate civvies of the kind favored by modern nuns to reveal well-stuffed bikinis—albeit the trompe l'oeil sort painted on T-shirts. Their audience roars with delight.

The cloistered Roman Catholic nuns who founded the ACS in 1969 could not have imagined this scene in 2000. As opposed to the familiar "active" sisters, who often work as teachers and social workers, those "enclosed" nuns had withdrawn from "the world." Following guidelines established centuries before, they led deeply secluded, ascetic lives devoted to prayer—particularly the silent, meditative sort called contemplation. Thirty years later their association includes not only active nuns but also married and single women, and even a few Protestants. Moreover, this assembly's theme, "Women's Contemplative Prayer: East and West," will be explored by five teachers from the Jewish, Buddhist, Sufi, and Hindu as well as Christian faiths.

The Western contemplative tradition is rooted in the ancient Egyptian desert. In the fourth century C.E., the church began to change from beleaguered spiritual sect to state religion. In response, eremetical *abba*s and *amma*s—fathers and mothers—fled the world and its distractions for the desert, where they evolved a new Christian way of life focused on the constant awareness of God. Over time their example was developed by many spiritual geniuses, from the pioneering monastics St. Basil the Great and St. Benedict of Nursia to St. Teresa of Ávila and St. John of the Cross, the Spanish mystics who rejuvenated the Carmelite order, to which many nuns here belong.

Like the era of the desert fathers and mothers, the sisters believe, ours is a time of transition for Christian spirituality. The appeal of the traditional vocation in a sequestered monastery has greatly decreased, yet popular interest in contemplative practice itself is dramatically increasing. Much like the *amma*s of old, the members of the ACS are in the vanguard of those Christians exploring new ways to live in a state of attentiveness to the sacred that suit new times. The organization's principal function—its group genius, if you will—is to support the individual spiritual genius of each of the sisters, many of whom are designing their own contemplative lives in the postmodern world.

Despite the diversity within a group that ranges from hermits to the mothers of large families, certain themes emerge repeatedly in the sisters' conversations. They include an expanding definition of what constitutes a contemplative life, an openness to the spiritual insights of other faiths, and the increasing confluence of the mystical and activist paths. Most striking, though, is their almost prophetic conviction that humanity is on the brink of a new kind of existence in an ever evolving world, and that contemplative practice has never been more important.

222 · *Spiritual Genius*

In their different voices the sisters repeatedly evoke the mystic's vision of the unity of creation, which all the great religions have long described. They observe that physics, biology, and other sciences increasingly reveal a complementary picture of the universe as a vast web of interrelationships. To the sisters, the contemplative's posture of quiet, humble, receptive awareness of our dependence on God and each other is the ideal spiritual approach for this transformative time, as this old-new way of looking at life slowly changes society's perspective.

The diverse "sisters" may be contemplatives, but they look like an assembly of America's favorite aunts. These blithe women, whose predominant habit appears to be slacks, a jersey, and sandals, seem ready for anything from a whispered secret to a fast game of hearts. They must be the only professional women in America who bring homemade goodies to their convention. "Try one of these!" they say. "You're nothing but skin and bone!"

After a while the sisters' subtler characteristics emerge, and they bespeak an ancient way of life designed to smooth the rough edges from ornery human nature. If one adjective describes these women, it might be *refined*—not in the phony, lifted-pinkie sense but as in "pure, distilled." They're kind. They're never coarse. They're unpretentious: the least whiff of piety sets their eyes rolling. They don't complain; as one old nun explains, "We can roll with the punches." They're eager to be pleased. "Isn't she brilliant!" they exclaim of a scholar in their midst. "Isn't she lovely!" they say of a particularly shining soul. The sisters' great gift, however, is for stillness. They begin each day of their convention by meeting for thirty minutes of silence. Their brochure quotes Isaiah: "By waiting and by calm you shall be saved. In quiet and in trust your strength lies."

Of course, aunts aren't the only group of women that springs to mind at the ACS meeting. The sight of women, unsupervised by men, pursuing a reality that's more than meets the eye must summon thoughts of witches. Like them, the sisters have minds and ways of their own and have antagonized the male establishment. Indeed, the ACS's founders defied church tradition to emerge from their cloisters and meet for the first time.

The church has specific rules and regulations that define the structure of monastic life, which is intended to foster contemplative prayer. The sisters, however, speak in terms of "contemplative life," which they define in their literature simply as a "radical and risky opening of self to be changed by, and in some way into, God's own self." As "contemplative values," the ACS names "compassion, non-striving, non-judging, non-attachment, patience, acceptance, allowing and always being open to the unknown. (If many of these qualities seem "feminine" as opposed to masculine, they're also more "Eastern" than Western.) A life based on these quiet, receptive values, they continue, "causes us to see beyond our present seeing," allows "a reality beyond our own to shape us," and makes individuals "wide and broad and empty enough to hold the vast and magnificent and excruciating paradoxes of created life in the crucible of love."

· : · : · : ·

Sister Bette Edl, a Franciscan hermit, perches on a bench in the retreat center's manicured gardens, far from her rough-hewn habitat on the opposite coast. She lives in a yurt—a round tent—in Maine and supports her life of solitude, prayer, and silence by weaving. This tall, tanned, smiling woman in chinos and sneakers, her silver hair bundled into a sloppy chignon, evokes Katharine Hepburn's lanky, tomboyish grace and offhand beauty. Her quick, quirky ways add to the impression of a wild creature, ready to take off. It's hard to believe she's sixty-five.

Years of people's double takes have accustomed Sister Bette to explaining her "new" ancient vocation. She follows the ancient rule of St. Francis for hermitages, but for centuries the life it prescribes has been "more or less repressed," she says, "especially for women." She stresses that the contemporary hermit's life has many expressions—"just as many as the kinds of people called to it. There are hermits in city apartments!" Yurts and high-rises notwithstanding, some things never change. "Pretty much, what the hermit does is just pray," says Bette. "Just bring and hold that deeper awareness of God, of light, of love, to the world's heart." A Hindu or Buddhist might speak of uniting personal *atman* with universal Brahman or individual consciousness with big mind. In her Catholic language, Bette says that, as part of the mystical body of Christ, "My call—my gift—is to beat the heart of Jesus in the world. To be that living, resurrected Jesus." To that end she cultivates a contemplative state of "not knowing any more than that I am in this moment, very much just dependent on the Spirit to nudge, guide, correct."

To maintain this "waiting for the presence," Bette's day is organized around formal periods of morning, noon, and evening prayer and meditations that are usually inspired by Scripture. "Something just punches out at me that I might work with for several days," she says. "Savor it, listen to it over and over, experience waves of different meanings for it. If it nurtures me very much, I stay with it as long as I can."

As opposed to the usual praise, thanks, or "gimme this, gimme that" sorts of prayer, Bette's simply aims at eliminating barriers to the sacred. Offering an example, she says that recently she has centered on Jesus' statement in the Gospel of John "I am the light of the world." In most sermons the assertion is interpreted as equating Jesus with truth or salvation. To Bette, however, the image is "much deeper than just some symbol. 'I am the light.' The light in the world. In my body. My mind. It's so full. I can just hum it as a mantra—'Christ be my light, be for everybody.' That's my prayer for the world. I can feel it—that energy going out."

Bette's long, twisting path to her hermitage began on the Wisconsin farm where she was born, then looped down to Central America, up to Colorado, and through Canada to Maine. She grew up in a large, traditional Catholic family of Czech origin, whose children played dress-up church as well as house. By her teens, despite being "somewhat" interested in boys, Bette felt "attracted to a more holy, quiet life" and "a strong connection with Christ, a call to follow him to a deeper union." Her parents thought she was too young to enter a convent and insisted that she finish college. As if discussing putting off a beloved suitor, she says, "I had to wait." Finally, at twenty-one, she joined the Franciscans as an active nun, most of whom, during the 1950s, taught in burgeoning Catholic schools.

In certain respects it was an inauspicious time for young Sister Bette to embark on her spiritual path. She smiles as she recalls her first meeting with her mother general. Bette explained that she had become a nun because she wanted a life of prayer. "Mother's response was, 'When you come to the convent, obedience is the most important thing,'" says Bette. "'You do what your superiors tell you. That is the greatest prayer.'" Like the other ACS sisters, Bette doesn't dwell on life's vicissitudes. With an oh-well sort of laugh, she says, "That was the spirituality of the time! It seemed so off that I didn't know whether I should laugh or cry. But I did what I was told." Of her tenure as a first- and second-grade teacher in South Dakota, she says, "It was a learning experience!"

When Bette joined the Franciscans, many Christians were—and they still are—unaware of their own religion's mystical tradition. In modernity Jesus has been most often portrayed as a moral teacher and social reformer. The Gospels, however, portray another side of Jesus, expressed in his frequent retreats into prayer. He described his contemplative disciple Mary, rather than her hardworking sister, Martha, as having chosen "the better part."

The church has long put forward its Marthas, but from its earliest days it has included contemplative Marys. Institutional religion is wary of mystics and the importance they place on direct personal relationship to the sacred. A wily pope thought to control the hugely popular mystic-reformer Francis of Assisi by offering to ordain him, but the equally canny lay saint refused the honor. From the medieval period, the church increasingly downplayed individualistic, experiential spirituality in favor of ecclesiastical tradition, a condition exemplified by its preference for the intellectual Thomas Aquinas over the mystical Meister Eckhart. When the Reformation split the church in two, Protestantism stressed the primacy of scripture over both personal spirituality and institutional authority. Rome, too, clamped down hard on potentially unorthodox mystics, subjecting even its great saints Teresa of Ávila and John of the Cross to inquisitions. By stifling Christianity's ancient contemplative strain, both Protestant literalism and Catholic authoritarianism helped create the postmodern spiritual hunger that has pushed many thoughtful Westerners toward the East.

It was not until the 1960s that Christian mysticism began to emerge from the shadows. The Second Vatican Council not only ordered the "renewal," or reform, of the monastic contemplatives' way of life but also emphasized the importance of personal spirituality for laypeople. Suddenly the Cistercian contemplative Thomas Merton became a bestselling author.

In the sixties, Bette's life, too, began to change. Her college background in music and Spanish was her passport to a missionary's life in Costa Rica. She promptly fell in love with that beautiful country and its people—and, thanks to a shortage of priests, with a freer, more varied vocation. She traveled among villages, not only teaching religion, music, and English but also functioning as an ad hoc religious minister. "The priests there were so much more down-to-earth and informal," she says. "The sisters did all the preparation for baptism, mass, marriage—everything." Bette played her guitar at liturgies and devised ways to make sacraments such as reconciliation and healing more accessible to the people. "There was a lot of singing," she says, eyes alight. "Just a much warmer kind of faith—and a totally new world and experiences! Those were probably the happiest days of my life."

Nonetheless, Bette wasn't entirely suited to the busy life of the missionary either. "There was such a lot to do," she says. "I was on the road all the time." Travel's imposed solitude also developed what she calls her "contemplative leanings. I began to question why I needed space and quiet time to pray." In addition, Bette had grown increasingly troubled by the connection between Central America's terrible poverty and her own nation's imperialism. It began to seem to her that such problems were rooted in something more fundamental than politics or economics. "Jesus' heartbeat was lost," she says. "There's no beat of Christ's love, life, mercy, heart in the world. I felt that there was no way to change the situation without prayer, without entering into deeper realms."

In 1971, after eleven years as a missionary, Bette returned to the United States to explore her "prayer hunger." She worked in one of the new Christian communities that combined civil rights and antiwar activism with experiments in spirituality; it was exciting but also draining. "I never got a chance to regroup after Central America," she says. "I was just exhausted." She finally sought peace and quiet in a Canadian center for conscientious objectors that also provided for solitary retreats. There, she says, "I really began the discernment for my eremitical life."

Many nuns in the ACS, including Bette, discreetly make clear that the "call" to their vocation was quite unmistakable—indeed, very like a marriage proposal. In contrast, Bette says the decision to become a hermit was based "much more on trial and error. You try it, and if it isn't right, the Spirit will tell you. It's a process. I started out with a day, then two days a week, then a week each month, then a month, and so on." Along this much-less-traveled road, Bette had important mentors, especially the abbot of the Cistercian monastery in Snowmass, Colorado, who had himself lived the solitary life. "His thing was to keep it as clean and simple and empty and free as possible," says Bette. "He got me in tune with how to practice."

After her spiritual preparation was completed, Bette sought permission from her religious superiors to become a hermit; this isn't easy to secure, especially for a woman. Aspirants must be certified as mentally and physically healthy, truly suited to such a life, and self-supporting. Some Franciscan friaries have hermitages and accept women for short periods, but Bette, inspired by a few female Franciscans in California and West Virginia, persisted in getting a permanent home of her own. Looking back, she says, "You take tiny steps and get little glimpses. That has been my whole journey to Maine."

Like women in all religions, Bette wishes she knew more about her predecessors down through the centuries. "Here and there, you find names of Christian female hermits," she says, "but they're just given in passing, like 'Sarah from such and such a place.' Men kept the records, and they just didn't keep good records of the women that preserved their identities."

Like any other, a hermit's life has its ups and downs. A yurt in Maine without electricity, plumbing, and central heating is one thing in summer and another during a severe, prolonged cold spell. "I use up all my energy just trying to keep warm," says Bette. "You can't do another thing. But I'm learning that I can be joyful in those darker times, too, because I know that it's okay. It's just a time to rest and stay warm. Whatever is, is, and one is with it. Then, on the warmer days, I enjoy being able to work like mad. And do I appreciate the sun and warmth and light after winter? That cycle is very purifying. You go through it and realize, That's life."

"Work and pray," decreed St. Benedict, the founder of Christian monastic life. Weaving on a loom placed by a window overlooking the sea allows Bette to do both at the same time. Earnings from her scarves, shawls, and hangings, often made from yarns she has spun and colored with natural dyes, supplement her social security income; nonetheless, she says, "it gets pretty lean toward the end of winter." One wrap on display at the convention might be a late-Monet interpretation of dusk, painted in blacks and blues and grays by silks and wools from llamas and various breeds of sheep. Bette says that the piece incorporates a lot of yarn from a sheep called Blue that "has a blue touch, a tremendous light in it. It refracts very well."

When she talks about her chop-wood, carry-water life, Bette sometimes can't help sounding like a poet. "Silence is my music now," she says. "My language is solitude, and the solitude speaks." But even a hermit must have some social life to stay well-balanced. "I don't tend to get pious," she says, "but I can go to an extreme where everything seems very clear and simple and directed, and I lose flexibility." She allows one day a week for errands or seeing visitors, "but I get very careful about doing more than that," she says. Even churchgoing is limited to once or twice a month, sometimes on a quieter weekday. "When I feel I really need a faith-community experience," says Bette, "I plan for it and go to a particular parish where I know there will be rich liturgy and nourishing people."

During Maine's long winter, Bette exchanges greetings with neighbors at the post office or on walks. "We might talk about the conditions of the road or whatever," she says. "It's very right on and grounding. They're like, 'If you need water, the spigot is over there. Just don't turn it off too tight.'" Sometimes neighbors ask how Bette copes with winter's rigors. "I try to answer in a way that lets them appreciate their own struggles," she says. "Like, 'It's hard, but we get through it, and afterwards we feel more free.'"

To Bette, the most onerous aspect of a hermit's life is that it's so widely misunderstood. Many pragmatic Americans, including Catholics, question the utility of a solitary life of prayer as opposed to one of service and "good works," such as she herself led as a teacher, missionary, and activist. Looking strained at the thought of being considered some sort of wifty daydreamer, she says, "I just don't let that American mercenary way of judging influence me. I can't just tell *anybody* that I'm so conscious of the depth of the power of God within me working that I have no real control over how it is or what I'm going to do. I just have to live in faith. It can be very dark, especially when I get a lot of criticism." As if reminding herself, she says, "When it's hard, God is closest, although it doesn't feel that way at the time." Then she grins. "I just have to hold people in my prayer and love them and smile and treat them as if they're doing the best they can."

Like many sisters here, Bette feels that ours is a time of transition. "The whole world is much more globally connected," she says. "That means we're aware of our neighbors as being fully human just as they are, not as we think they should be. We can't go backwards from this point. We've got to move forward." She feels not only that "religion as is will have to change" but also that the Christian contemplative vocation is "about to leap into something new. No one is entering the old cloistered forms anymore, so it will have to change to survive. It's not there yet, but in the process." As the ACS founders might have said of her, Bette says, "The next generation will create their own structures, but I can't tell you what their way of keeping alive the spiritual life—the journey— will be like."

The future may be unclear, but Bette is sanguine about it. Signs ranging from the Dalai Lama's prestige to the plethora of religious sites on the Internet convince her that society increasingly values the spiritual life. Sounding like a prophet, she says, "The awareness that comes out of prayer and the stillness of listening to the Spirit is releasing an energy for a new beginning. For now, we're in that place where we're groaning with all creation to be born anew."

Recently, her Maine town asked Bette to contribute to its website. "I wanted to do something about the connection to the sacred in the earth, which my presence here is about," she says. "And they said that that's what they'd like." Over time, she says, "I've learned that if you keep doing your thing, people will gradually understand. If you're constant in your practice, it shows, it shines."

· : · : · : ·

The next morning at Eucharist, a lovely old priest lingers over the Gospel's assertion that "the kingdom of God is at hand." He says that "at hand" means the kingdom is "so near that it's in us."

· : · : · : ·

When Sister Rosalie Bertell, the ACS's droll Canadian president, calls the group to order one evening by rattling a tribal "rainstick," witches come to mind again. Sister Rosalie is a Grey Nun of the Sacred Heart and an internationally recognized scientist who specializes in the health effects of environmental pollution. But for her peculiar gavel and necklace of beads and animal totems, however, the frail-looking seventy-one-year-old dressed in a skirt and jersey might be the nice grandmother next door. She reminds her listeners that they can choose just two of the five prayer workshops, each of which meets for two sessions. "If you listen to your head, you want them all," says Rosalie. "Go with your heart. With your desire. John of the Cross said that God gives us our desires."

Rosalie is not only greatly respected by her sisters but greatly loved. Bidding them good night, she gently touches on the conference's multifaith perspective. "The heart of our meeting is listening to the women of prayer who've joined us here," she says. "Our God is an immense God. A most amazing God, who is intensely loving and jealous, yet who sets us free."

· : · : · : ·

One morning Leili Kaye First introduces a circle of Christian sisters to Sufi meditation. The only suggestion that this slender white Californian is a Muslim is the small shawl she drapes around her shoulders. In a soft, pretty voice Leili explains that she was brought up in an educated family that provided her with an ethical, but not a spiritual, foundation. Ten years ago, despite her achievements as a chemist, she felt that something important was missing. After a search she found it in Sufism, or Islamic mysticism. Because it stresses the individual's innate inner knowledge of the divine over rituals and dogma, Sufism increasingly attracts the same sorts of Westerners who are drawn to Zen.

First, Leili fields a predictable question about Islam. She explains that abuses of women in Muslim nations such as the Taliban's Afghanistan are caused by a politics that twists religion to suit its own ends. Islam, she says, teaches justice and respect for the human being and does not condone oppression. When his daughter Fatima, a scholar, entered the room, "Mohammad himself rose and gave her his chair."

Next, Leili explains that while Sufis pray five times daily, they don't necessarily go to mosques. The tradition they follow is less a religion in the conventional sense than what she calls "a process of discovery of the true self, which is a spark of the divine." Teachers merely help a person to mine this inner knowledge "by whisking clean the inner path," she says, and "preparing the heart." She offers some advice from her own Iranian teachers: "Pray to make your question clearer, then the answer will come."

Sufism centers on what Leili calls "praying with the heart, not just the brain and lips." Popular metaphors for this practice include the lover who sits silently, thinking only of the beloved, and the unborn baby resting in the mother. Face alight, a Redemptoristine nun says that her order's foundress had a vision in which God told her, "Live like a child in my womb."

The Christian sisters, several of whom have spent decades in monastic life, prepare to meditate Sufi-style. Leili says that specific Arabic words and sounds and gestures have "energy" and suggests they repeat a short mantralike prayer. Their goal, she says, is to "release all mental activity and gather outer-directed energy into the self. As you say the prayer, breathe out emptiness and breathe in Allah—God. Concentrate on your heart as a point of light in the center of your chest." The sisters close their eyes, bow their heads, and silently repeat, *"La Illaha Illa Allah."* There's nothing but God.

· : · : · : ·

The next morning, as dawn's light just penetrates my room, a woman's soft but impassioned singing floats through the open window. What first sounds like a love song turns out to be "Alleluia! Alleluia!"

· : · : · : ·

Part of the ACS meeting is devoted to organizational matters. The most important issue to be settled is whether men should be allowed to join the association. Before the vote Gert Wilkinson, one of the group's five "founding mothers," urges members to undertake a careful process of "discernment"—a word much used by the sisters to describe listening for God's voice in human affairs. "We must have faith that God is in us and in each other," says Gert. "We must center down and be still so we can listen and be open." Casually borrowing from Hinduism, she says, "When we're free from fear and desire, that's nirvana."

Gert might be a successful businesswoman who's the country club seniors' golf champ. Yet this tweedy lady in slacks once dressed in the literally stunning long red and blue habit formerly worn by Redemptoristine nuns. When the ACS was founded in August 1969, Gert was the prioress of the order's monastery in Esopus, New York. She was one of 135 nuns from fifty-three cloistered communities who agreed to meet for the first time at a Jesuit seminary located, fittingly for that "summer of love," in Woodstock, albeit Woodstock, Maryland.

In hindsight, these cloistered sisters' courage seems astounding. They were still living according to guidelines established in the Middle Ages, in monasteries governed by autocratic bishops. Measures initially meant to protect women's communities in violent times had become entangled with notions of piety, so that many nuns were almost unimaginably sequestered, sometimes behind high walls, even bars. Most groups had little money or other material resources. Moreover, they had little knowledge of the outside world, even from newspapers and radio, or of each other's communities. When the American Carmelites tried to form a federation, Rome refused to allow it.

With Vatican II, however, the church, as Pope John XXIII put it, let in some "fresh air." The Jesuits, supported by their local bishop, supplied the nuns with accommodations for their meeting, some funds, and their inimitable expertise, including translating Latin correspondence to and from the Vatican. After the sisters received a letter stating that the church hierarchy "would prefer" that they not meet, their assembly took on new import. Their original motivation had been to share ideas about how to implement council-mandated changes in their way of life. Hierarchical opposition, however, helped turn a simple gathering of cloistered nuns into an association that supported all women "called to a contemplative response to the Spirit and who live this call in a diversity of lifestyles."

Gert Wilkinson's genius for finding her own authentic spiritual path peculiarly illustrates the ACS's evolution. She left the Redemptoristines and became an insurance executive and aficionado of urban life and, recently, an early retiree in her Wisconsin hometown. There, Gert "does what's dearest to me," she says, including serving on the board of a Lutheran home for the elderly, volunteering with the Girl Scouts, and teaching, preaching, and acting as "an ear" at her Catholic church. For several months after the pastor died suddenly, Gert ran the parish. "It was a marvelous time," she says, "and then we got a priest."

Describing herself as "my own woman on a pilgrimage, a search, for the life of God within me," Gert says, "I've tried to be faithful to what I discern as God's desire for me at the time. I don't set out saying, 'I'm going to be or do X and that's it!' I don't *have* to be anything but independent." Looking back, she shakes her head wonderingly and says, "I never could have planned this life."

Contemplative life is "better described than defined," says Gert, "because it's different for everyone. To me, it means living in a way that's propelled by God's spirit . . . in a way so that others will come to know God better through me." She recalls a "transformative, liberating moment" in 1967, when she and a dozen nuns met with Thomas Merton at his Trappist monastery. Alluding to the monk's struggles with alcohol and a love affair, she says, "It was the year before he died, and he had been through a lot. He told us not to tie the contemplative life to rubric and ritual."

Gert is proud of the venerable "public witness" of traditional women's contemplative religious life: "It has existed this long." She also feels, however, that it must evolve to survive: "It shouldn't exist just to exist, but to fill the needs of its members and nourish their communities." To her, however, the point of the life will always be that "in some way we'll be better together because I do this in solitude. In some way we'll be enriched because we've become more whole."

Many idealistic organizations that sprang up in the sixties have faded into oblivion. Gert attributes the ACS's vitality to its diversity. "We're a diamond with more than three hundred facets," she says. "There's no 'typical member.' Every experience a woman could have is represented here." At this assembly she sees the same desire to learn from and support each other on the contemplative journey that inspired the sisters' first meeting. "The ACS began as a web of relationships and has stayed that way," says Gert. "There has always been an emphasis on sharing stories."

· : · : · : ·

Over dessert one night, Sister Mary Lavin, a piquant Carmelite, discusses the morning's workshop on Kabbalah. Sandy Buttler, a Jewish writer and teacher, had asked participants to consider "What is the question your life is the answer to?" Mary says she hopes that her life will help one person answer the question of how to come to know God.

The conversation shifts to memories of Catholic girlhood back in the pre–Vatican II days of black-and-white morality and harsh confessors. Mary has strong opinions about the sacrament once called penance, now reconciliation. The rite, she says, should be modeled on the story of the prodigal son, in which the father celebrates the son's decision to return home. "He didn't blame," says Mary. "He just welcomed!" She smiles over her pineapple upside-down cake, helping one person to know God. "Love, love, love and acceptance!"

· : · : · : ·

Like Hasids and Sufis, the sisters like to express the transcendent through stories. Each day the group listens to one member narrate her life, which invariably reveals a mystic disguised as the woman next door. A nun who lives in a slum riddled with drug abuse and crime offers an impassioned apologia for downward mobility. "I want to know how the poor experience God," she says. "I want to be in on God's bias toward the poor by being poor, too." A divorced health-care professional describes family and health problems, culminating in cancer, of such proportions that, led by the narrator, the audience can only shake their heads and laugh. She ends her talk by reading a poem about a two-headed calf that, because of its problem, sees twice as many stars.

One afternoon a Franciscan who hopes to start a farm that will offer retreats and hermitages for women describes her practice of looking for God in everyday life. One day in a laundromat, she says, during a period of caring for her elderly father, she was going about her sorting and folding, feeling burdened and downcast. A strange man approached. "You must be a minister's wife!" he said. "You don't even have to open your mouth! *You just have Jesus written all over you!*" Joining in the laughter, the merry nun says matter-of-factly, "Of course, he *was* Jesus, relieving my discouragement!"

When she smiles it's easy to see the vivacious New Orleans belle that Sister Angele Sadlier must have been when she joined a group of "active" Carmelites who work in social ministries. She begins her own story with a sage's tale about a deer who frantically pursues the scent of musk until, exhausted, he stumbles and falls off a mountain trail. Only when he's bleeding to death does the deer realize that the musk he sought lies in a sac in his own torn chest. Since the sixties, Angele says, she has experimented with Zen, yoga, tai chi, Transcendental Meditation, and long retreats: "Doesn't that sound like the deer? In many ways that's my story, except that I hope it's not too late."

After decades of religious life Angele concludes that being a contemplative is largely a matter of "paying attention" and "being present to the moment that's pregnant with God." Struggles as diverse as anxiety, falling in love, and burnout while working for the poor have taught her three key things, she says: "The importance of feeling what's really going on in my mind, heart, and body. Of being honest with God about what's going on. And of surrendering in faith."

Angele tells the story of a dark period when she wrestled with religion's thorniest problem. She could no longer reconcile the world's evils—child abuse and old people eating from trash cans—with the existence of God. She went on a retreat. After a week of intensive prayer centered on the Gospel of John, a voice inside her asked: "Do you want to be a woman of faith or not?" Angele went for a run, decided to persevere without any easy answers, and gave herself up to silence. She narrates what followed in the same straightforward way her listeners receive her account.

During an "inner communing," Angele says, Jesus explained John's Gospel to her, stressing that "It's about God's love. 'When I say that I call you "my friends,"' he said, 'I really mean that. And I mean my friends to be my presence in the world.' It was so strong! I kept exclaiming, 'Wow! Wow!' I said to Jesus, 'I knew this stuff before, but now I *know* it!'" When Angele confesses that she celebrated this event with cookies and milk, the sisters nod and chuckle, as if this were the standard response to divine revelation.

As an aid to "being attentive," Angele recommends the daily practice of centering prayer. In this increasingly popular Christian form of contemplative meditation, she explains, one stays open to God's presence by quietly allowing a word or short mantra to "lead one into silence." As he advanced in his ministry, Angele says, "even Jesus had to learn to go to another place—to a deep level of consciousness where God is ever transforming us—which is accessed by prayer." Like Jesus, says Angele, we must struggle to move awareness from the head to the heart, over and over again, through conscious decisions to return to God. "The mystery of dying and rising is what we're about," she says. "God speaks to us in every moment, so we must take time to become disposed to hear."

· : · : · : ·

The vast majority of American Catholics of both sexes support female ordination, which Rome still refuses to permit. None of the sisters can actually say mass, but they've designed a special Eucharist for their convention. Father Tom, the celebrant, winningly introduces himself as "your appointed priest" and compares the mastering of his part with "learning to say mass for the first time." More seriously, he adds, "I hope that a priest will emerge from your ranks in our lifetime."

The most moving aspect of the eclectic two-hour service for me isn't its innovations but the effortless way in which a hundred women from around the country fall into natural harmony whenever it's time to sing. The sound might be their serene confidence about their rightful place in their church set to music.

· : · : · : ·

After dinner one night Sister Rosalie Bertell settles down in the garden, seated in a cleverly designed walker that converts into a chair. She's recovering from surgery to repair a birth defect in her foot. "Just think, at seventy-one!" she says cheerfully. She begins her story by identifying herself as "a Carmelite in the tradition of Elijah." Like that discomfiting prophet, this jet-propelled contemplative travels around identifying evil—in her case, environmental health hazards from nuclear waste to chemical toxins—and then retreats to solitude and prayer. "I go all over the world," she says, "and then I have to go back and hide out alone in Horeb, as I call my apartment." Like Elijah, Rosalie has a genius for combining mysticism and activism.

As with many sisters here, there was never any question of what young Rosalie would be when she grew up. "I knew very early that I would be a virgin and a contemplative," she says, "and I made those vows on my own. I wasn't sure I wanted to do it, but I was clear about the fact that that was what God was asking. I knew because of an experience of God, so there weren't any doubts."

She describes herself as a Carmelite, but technically Rosalie is a Carmelite dropout. As a young woman she spent six years in what she describes as "a tough Carmel that supported itself with hard manual labor. I entered right after college, not knowing that other Carmels did sewing and made altar bread. I just physically couldn't do it." After Rosalie suffered a heart attack, her superiors advised against final vows. Despite this setback, she says, "I was okay personally, because my vows, which I made on my own, didn't have anything to do with being in the convent." After a two-year convalescence, she joined the scholarly Grey Nuns of the Sacred Heart.

As a Grey Nun, Rosalie earned a doctorate in mathematics and did graduate work in biology and biochemistry. She seemed destined to continue as a professor in one of the brainy order's colleges. In 1973, however, she had another heart attack. Ever since, she says, "people leave me alone!" Rosalie's subsequent career evolved from her science background. While doing some research for a hospital, she became aware of the correlation between pollution and health. "The more I learned," she says, "the more horrible it got. It upset me."

Rosalie got particularly upset when the U.S. Congress investigated the misuse of diagnostic X rays and her supervisor at the hospital forbade her to testify. Rosalie was outraged by this firsthand evidence of corporate vested interest in opposing the public good. She left the hospital and offered evidence that helped stop then common abuses, such as using X-ray machines to check the fit of new shoes.

Since becoming an activist, Rosalie has published more than a hundred scientific papers about the connections between pollution and cancer and birth defects. Her five books include *No Im-*

mediate Danger, an analysis of risks posed by low-level radiation, which was hailed by the prestigious science journal *Nature* as "brilliantly written."[1] She has done research all over the world, including Bhopal, India, after the chemical disaster there, and Chernobyl following its nuclear crisis. To help educate the public, Rosalie founded the International Institute for Public Health, a nonprofit organization that collects and publishes data on environmental crises around the world. Her specialty, however, is helping communities organize to document their own health problems. "There are things in the air and water and lifestyle—usually a toxic waste dump or an industrial disaster or nuclear weapons testing or your friendly nuclear power plant—that make us sick," she says. "When people find these things themselves, they can use their data for political and financial leverage, which is much more effective in creating change."

The California evening has turned chilly, and Rosalie suggests returning indoors. She slowly rolls her walker to her room in the retreat center's handicapped area, chortling over its extra bells and whistles. When she's comfortably resettled and asked to talk a little about religion, Rosalie continues to discuss the environment.

A mystic might be defined as someone who sees a whole where others see parts. To Rosalie, environmentalism and religion aren't separate things. "If you care about creation and about God's people," she says, "the environment is very central. Once I realized the pollution that was going on, I couldn't just try to forget it, to pretend things were normal. Once your consciousness is raised, you have to do something."

Rosalie's near equation of insight and action strikes deep. One of my children has had cancer, and I confess to Rosalie that I can barely think about the cause, much less "do something about it." After a few minutes of wondering *Was it the water I gave him to drink? Our neighborhood's air? The playground's soil? Something in his room?* my mind just shuts down. It's simply unbearable. "I know," says Rosalie. "It's paralysis. I remember talking to this woman near Three Mile Island who was just distraught. 'I was so careful,' she said. 'I have all my medicines and cleaning stuff locked up, then they put that thing in my backyard.' She's right." Rosalie's eyes fill with unshed tears. "You're so careful, and they're not. They don't warn people."

That's the work of prophets. Empathy notwithstanding, Rosalie, like Elijah, tells it like it is. "If I were going to be really frank," she says, "I'd say the reason why you can't do anything about the wrongs you see is that your roots aren't strong enough to reach out. If you really want to do something with your life more than maintaining it with sustenance, retirement funds, vacations, then you've got to have the depth that enables you to reach out."

To Rosalie, contemplatives don't escape from the world but develop a different style of engaging with it. Because of the way they live, she says, "they're not too busy to hear." As a scientist, Rosalie has some unusual insights into the source of contemplatives' special strength. Research on brain waves shows that most people spend most of their time in the very fast beta-wave level, which is geared to attending to external sensory stimuli. Contemplative practice accesses the more reflective alpha state, which is best suited to creative problem-solving.

"Ask someone a hard question," says Rosalie. "They'll look up, like they're going to see the answer in the air." She raises her arm straight out and up at a forty-five-degree angle and focuses on her hand with the same upward gaze that symbolizes prayer. "When you look up like this," she says, "you put your brain into an alpha state. That's where you do get your answers—from alpha, not your senses, which get in the way."

No religious elitist where contemplative problem solving is concerned, Rosalie cites Bill Gates as an alpha-state role model. "He's in trouble for running a monopoly," she says serenely, "but *I* like him. He was a dropout at Harvard who went off and did something good for society, instead of making weapons, as our best students often end up doing. We use their fine minds to build a death-producing society with castoffs from the military—things like nuclear power, pesticides, and chlorine, which was a poison gas used in World War I."

Trust in humanity's capacities to sense what's right and solve problems—and a belief that "when push comes to shove, life is stronger than death"—makes Rosalie optimistic about the future. "I expect the human race to find a way out of this environmental mess," she says, "even if we have to go sideways. It's not going to be an obvious solution, and it will certainly be the reflective people who find the way out."

Rosalie is similarly sanguine about the future of the contemplative life. "I do think we're all connected," she says. "When a part of society does something special, there are ripples." She dismisses criticism of monastic tradition as anachronistic, saying, "Many things that people say are useless are being kept for a time when they'll be needed. Because contemplatives have kept their way of life alive over the centuries, it's out there now, available to people, when it's so important." However, Rosalie's definition of a contemplative isn't confined to the traditional one. To her, the term means "a person who's able to touch both the depths of life within and the bigness of life without." As examples she brings up young people in the ranks of the increasingly influential nongovernmental organizations that work for peace and other good causes. "Many of them really embrace a very austere, almost monastic life," she says. "If I were nineteen, I'd be out there, too!"

Rosalie's next project, which she claims "will probably be my last," will be to mentor young environmental activists within the University Without Walls. "We underestimate the young," she says. "We need to respect their on-the-job life experience and give them the degrees they need to function in our paper-oriented society. And at my age, I want to teach them how to handle these problems."

Rosalie talks about death easily, employing the imagery of physics. Despite the difficulty of picturing an afterlife, she imagines "a dimension in which whatever has been—although it might not look the same—still is." In her view, "having existed is enough to exist, to be. You were created, so you just are. You lived, you have a history, a story, which you still are. After death it doesn't change anymore. It's a whole—an entire life, seen at one time, that always is and always will be. Nobody can change or touch it. It's just there."

This is heady stuff, and Rosalie amplifies a bit. "We see a life only in a personal way, by slices of time. But it seems to me that there's another dimension whereby a life goes out sideways instead of going on along the same time line. It's real, there. But we can't see it, because we're still moving on a time line and it's not, anymore."

Looking back at her own life, Rosalie remarks, as do many sisters here, on her surprise that she has done "the right things all along, although at the time they seemed offbeat. I have ended up with just what I need. It's quite amazing. As a kid, could I have planned this life? To think, I'm going to enter Carmel, then I'm going to leave, but I'll need that contemplative experience years later in Malaysia, when I take on the Mitsubishi company. I've had what I needed because of the past. You have to reflect on your life, or you don't see that."

Having reflected more than most, Rosalie believes that "life is a gift from someone who wants to be loved. There are lots of ways to give back that love. Certainly in marriage, when love produces children—a beautiful way to return it. And I'm doing some things, too. Now I'm going to have some red wine, because I sleep better when I do."

· : · · : ·

Like other revolutionaries, the ACS's old guard cherish a romantic nostalgia for their movement's wild early days. Like graying hippies remembering Bob Dylan and Che Guevara, they enjoy reminiscing about that summer of '69 at their own private Woodstock, when their founders were slender young zealots who eagerly embraced monastic renewal. "Oh!" they exclaim. "You should have seen Connie, with her long black hair!"

Thirty years later, in the retreat center's chapel, Sister Constance Fitzgerald has short, silver hair, but she has remained a revolutionary. She's now a well-known scholar of Carmelite spirituality in the male-dominated world of Catholic theology. Her presentation centers on Western contemplation in the tradition of St. John of the Cross. The great sixteenth-century Spanish Carmelite mystic famously put a name to the "dark night of the soul"—a period of spiritual aridity during which God seems absent. John taught that this experience, though painful, is a positive step in religious development. The egocentric self is compelled to recognize first its own emptiness, and then its utter dependence on God and God's creation.

Although it feels like doubt, says Connie, persisting in prayer that provides only the humbling "no-experience experience" is a "faith posture" that particularly suits our time of transition. The holistic worldview increasingly described not only by mystics but also scientists calls for less ego and more compassion. When we truly identify with the shared human ordeals of dark nights, pain, and despair, which even Jesus experienced on the cross, "We no longer think of 'the poor,' but of 'we poor,' " says Connie. "This is how divine wisdom works in the world—by subverting our usual vision of reality. The destitute, the sick, and even the ravaged planet itself take on a new significance as imprints of the crucified one. God's and the person's desire for the world become the same." Connie pauses for a moment, then says, "Think what you'd do if you really believed that."

After the lecture, a comment offered by a much respected Carmelite hangs in the air. "You don't have to concentrate on the dark night or suffering," she says. "Just let it do its work, and you do your work."

· : · : · : ·

Early one morning Judy Walters, a nurse who spent twenty-two years working with women in Bangladesh, one of the world's poorest, most populous countries, leads a yoga class. Everything about her is soft and gentle, from her long gray hair and gauzy *salwar kameez* to her eyes and voice. Judy explains that yoga was designed to prepare the body and mind for contemplation, then almost whispers instructions to the sisters, some of whom are old, stiff, and unfamiliar with yoga. Each stretches and bends as she is able, open to receiving whatever the ancient sacred postures might have to give.

Judy has come to the ACS meeting with her old friend Sister

Pascaline Coff. A Benedictine contemplative nun, Pascaline is the founder and director of the Osage Monastery, Forest of Peace, which is a "monastic ashram" in Sand Springs, Oklahoma. She and Judy are presenting a program called "Hindu Meditation and Ashram," which focuses on the basic technique of Hindu prayer: the use of certain sounds, from the breath to chants and mantras, "to go beyond the mind through a disciplined path," as Pascaline puts it. The pair also draws on personal experience to describe life in an ashram, where such spiritual disciplines are taught.

Pascaline is a serious, good-looking woman whose tan and cropped white hair are set off by a vaguely Asian-looking uniform of white skirt and top with sandals. She looks perhaps fifty-five, but says that she's about to celebrate her fiftieth anniversary as a Benedictine Sister of Perpetual Adoration. Her twenty-fifth anniversary—and fiftieth birthday—was celebrated in South India, where she spent a year at Father Bede Griffiths's Ashram of the Holy Trinity. This experience not only changed one nun but has expanded the palette of the traditional Christian contemplative life in America in ways that would have astonished the ACS's founders and that presage its future. Like her mentor, Pascaline has a genius for upholding her own tradition while learning from other religions.

Pascaline's interest in Asian religion dates to the time of Vatican II. One of the council's most important accomplishments was its public proclamation that other religions also possessed "truth" and that their spirituality and morality should be respected, even promoted, through dialogue and collaboration. Pascaline, then the superior of her monastery, already knew a little about Father Bede and his work in India, because her fellow Benedictine had been featured in their order's magazine. Based "on no real information," she says, rolling her eyes at the memory, "but on a sense that India had a deep, interior spirituality I wished to learn from," she set her heart on visiting his ashram when her term of office expired.

If it was considered adventurous for young hippies to visit India back in the seventies, it's hard to overstate the courage required of a middle-aged contemplative nun. It was only recently, Pascaline recalls, that sisters had been allowed to visit their families' homes, much less Asia. Semicloistered Pascaline quailed when she saw pictures of Indian *saddhus* wearing, as she says, "nothing but oil and a diaper." Nevertheless, she wrote to Father Bede, who replied that she would be welcome to stay for a dollar a day.

Father Bede was willing, but Pascaline's abbot primate was not. After all, the Oxford-educated, philosophical British monk had written a book called *The Marriage of East and West* and lived in an ashram—an unusual orientation for a Western clergyman at the time.[2] One day, recalls Pascaline, a nun who had agreed to accompany her to India said, "Are we going to let men run our lives forever?" The two sisters, dressed in their heavy garb, set out for India. On their way south they stopped at a Bangalore convent whose nuns fashioned them more comfortable skirts and loose tops in the orange color worn by *sannyasins*, or Hindu ascetics.

As E. M. Forster's Mrs. Moore learned, Westerners who book a passage to India often find themselves on an inner journey. Pascaline and many other visitors attest that Father Bede was staunchly Christian, teaching that God is love, for example, and that evil is the result of willful sin, not inexorable *karma*. However, he asserted that, despite external differences, the great faiths converge at their deepest level into what he called a "religion of the Holy Spirit"—a shared spiritual awareness that could unite diverse traditions against their common enemy: the social and ecological crises wrought by scientific materialism. He also presciently observed that Christians could use Eastern philosophy and religious practices, such as meditation, to understand better their own faith. To Pascaline, Father Bede was "a teacher who loved and respected Hinduism and experienced it as a light on his own Christianity."

As Pascaline describes life at the ashram, which continues to flourish after Father Bede's death in 1993, his creative ideas spring to life. There are several Christian services daily, including mass, the recitation of the divine office, vespers, and homilies. But Father Bede strongly opposed packaging a universal religion in Western culture. The mantra is India's form of prayer, so a sign over the meditation center's doorway proclaims: "Om Nama Christaya." Inside a statue of Jesus sits cross-legged, eyes closed like a *saddhu*. In terms of food, housing, and the particulars of daily life, the ashram follows the simple Indian agrarian style. Pascaline calls her year there "very opening and stretching. I really learned that being and doing go together. We need to learn how to go deep to keep our attention on the Lord and be in the sacrament of the Lord's presence."

Pascaline returned to America as "a Christian contemplative who's very open to people of any or no religious background," she says. "I respect all religions and feel very grounded in my own." Her year in Asia had convinced her that contemplatives, who have much in common across religious boundaries, are Christianity's "natural bridge to the East." Her desire to share insights into the life of prayer across cultural divides, combined with the church's desire that its monastic orders "return to their sources and simplify," started her on the path to Osage, which she calls "a true Benedictine monastery that embraces ashram spirituality." After searching for a suitable property in the domain of a enthusiastic bishop, she found both in rural Oklahoma.

The goal of Osage, says Pascaline, is to provide a place "where people can know the Lord." Four Benedictine nuns live at the monastery, and they'll soon be joined by a permanent priest. Fifteen guest cabins, including a hermitage, shelter a motley crew of retreatants: male and female, Catholic and Protestant—even a few ministers. Guests can set their own schedules or follow the Benedictine regimen, which begins each day with prayer at 5:15 A.M. In keeping with the ashram sensibility, "there's an atmosphere of silence," says Pascaline, "and accommodations are simple—no air conditioning!" She proudly says that Father Bede visited Osage five times and declared it "the most peaceful place I've ever been."

Her unusual combination of long experience as a Christian contemplative and in-depth exposure to another spiritual approach gives Pascaline's speculations about the future of contemplatives a special weight. Concerning traditional communities, she says, "Vocations will come if we do our homework." Like Osage, monasteries will be "smaller, but more serious about discipline, training, and practice." Regarding contemplative life in a more general sense, Pascaline believes that, far from subverting interest in Christian spirituality, Asian religions have highlighted some of its long-neglected elements. Pointing to the renewed interest in Meister Eckhart, say, and the mysticism of the Orthodox church, she says, "The Eastern light is showing us what we have."

In the past contemplatives lived behind high walls and prayed for others. In the future, Pascaline says, they must "reach out much more to other people who want to learn to pray. As Father Bede said, 'My monastery is the world.'"

· : · : · ·

After dinner Sister Rosalie, contemplative and mathematician, sips some wine. "I just don't get reincarnation," she says, "because there's an exponential growth in the population. I can't figure the numbers! How do you get from a hundred people to a million people?"

· : · : · ·

The word that repeatedly comes to mind when thinking of the ACS in general and many of its members in particular is *openness,* both intellectual and emotional. Unlike many organizations, particularly the religious sort, this one has a genius for combining respect for a spiritual tradition with the desire that it evolve to meet changing needs in a mysterious future. The group continues to represent the Christian contemplative nun in her many facets—solitary Sister Bette, activist Sister Rosalie, ecumenical Sister Pascaline—while welcoming a new kind of "sister," who's not one at all in the conventional sense, and whose numbers already make up two-thirds of the membership.

When she first arrived to work in Bangladesh, Judy Walters recalls, her Christian faith was "rocky" and her prayer life was a "dead end." The Muslim women's lives were so harsh that she wondered how they could rise each morning. In time, however, she saw that they had "the tremendous capacity for joy that comes from a deep spiritual connection. They prayed five times a day wherever they were—that's what kept them going. They gave me back the gift of faith."

During her time in Bangladesh, Judy heard about Father Bede's ashram, spent a restorative month there, and returned frequently. She and Sister Pascaline, whom she smilingly calls her guru, missed each other there but, at the monk's urging, finally met back in the United States. Judy's first jaunt to Osage ended up lasting a year.

Judy has never joined a religious order. After her long service in Asia, she has returned to America to care for her elderly mother and work as a nurse in a hospice. In coming home, Judy has also come back to the spiritual future. "I kept looking for some group that would help me with contemplative life," she says. "Then I realized, This is it—here and now. It's just part of who I am."

· : · : · ·

At breakfast on the day I leave the ACS meeting, a Carmelite says that when her monastery's address somehow got posted on the Web, the sisters were "deluged" with requests for prayers. She seems surprised.

9. DOCTOR

⠂⠒⠒⠒⠒⠒⠒⠒⠒⠒⠒⠒⠒⠒⠒⠒⠒⠒⠒⠒⠒⠂

The southern city of Madurai is one of India's major pilgrimage sites. Many visit the spectacularly carved Technicolor temple of the goddess Meenakshi, from whom they beg various favors. Just across the Vaigai River, a nondescript complex of modern buildings known as the Aravind Eye Institute attracts pilgrims who all seek the same miracle. Each year, for little or no cost, nearly one hundred thousand of the blind will regain their sight here, and many more will be treated for lesser vision problems. Aravind operates like a factory, but it, too, is a temple—one that's built on the down-to-earth spirituality of Dr. Govindappa Venkataswamy, a legendary eye surgeon known as Dr. V.

The first things one notices about Dr. V, who's now an octogenarian, are his hands. When he was a young man, a bout of rheumatoid arthritis skewed his fingers at such seemingly impossible angles that for a while he couldn't even hold a pen. Marshaling the combination of determination and disregard for conventional wisdom that has characterized his remarkable career, he developed his own way to handle a scalpel and the other tools of the delicate trade of ophthalmology. In time, Dr. V was performing a hundred cataract operations a day (the average eye surgeon does five to ten). By the time he stopped operating a few years ago, he had conducted more than a hundred thousand surgeries.

The second thing one notices about Dr. V is his gaiety, which is particularly remarkable considering the amount of human misery he confronts. Blindness is bad enough, but in the Third World it's often synonymous with the direst poverty as well. Nevertheless, it seems impossible to come up with a subject, including blindness, that doesn't make Dr. V smile, albeit in a cosmic way. When I observe that in India alone there are 14 million blind people—almost half the world's total—which makes the affliction a staggering national as well as individual burden, he gives a Cheshire cat grin. Eighty percent of the blind suffer from cataracts, he says, and that's a readily curable condition. "No one should be blind if it can be helped," he says, smile widening. "Just as we have eradicated other global health problems, like polio, that were once common, we can eliminate blindness. We can do it now."

An iconic photograph hanging on the wall behind Dr. V's desk, seemingly perched on his shoulder, represents one source of his indefatigability and humor. Sri Aurobindo (1872–1950) was a Cambridge-educated Indian intellectual whose interest in religion began when the British jailed him as a freedom fighter. Aurobindo left behind politics but not pragmatism. He founded Auroville, his famous self-supporting ashram in Pondicherry, where he taught that people should try not to "rise above" the world but to transform it by "bringing down" divine energy and allowing it to work through them for the greater good.

The young Dr. V, who was already working at a medical center in Madurai, frequented Aurobindo's ashram during an era of extraordinary national idealism inspired by Gandhi's search for a better life for his people. Dr. V met the great visionary several times and remembers him as "very simple" yet possessing "a special . . . *radiation*." Inspired by the complementary hands-on spirituality of Aurobindo and Gandhi, Dr. V decided to unify his professional and religious lives. He concentrated on becoming an agent of divine energy that would focus like a laser on eliminating blindness in the entire Madurai region. "I found that the more I worked for this goal," he says mildly, "the more help I got." In response to his local success, he set about vanquishing blindness in all of India.

In 1976 Dr. V reached the mandatory retirement age of fifty-eight, relinquished his post at Madurai Medical College, and started working toward a new goal: the elimination of blindness not just in India but worldwide. To that end he began organizing the special medical community that, in honor of Aurobindo, would be called Aravind. The new retiree remortgaged his house, tapped his government pension, and drew medically trained relatives into his benign web. "We had no money," he says, laughing at the memory. "But we had eleven beds and three doctors. We just began working."

More than fifty years after taking up the real-world spirituality of Aurobindo and Gandhi, Dr. V is still at work in what has become the world's busiest eye hospital. With its affiliates, Aravind performs 200,000 operations per year and brings 1,500 mobile "eye camps" to Indian villages. Increasingly the institute reaches beyond India's borders, particularly into Nepal, Cambodia, and Bangladesh. Dr. V's scope has become greater, but his objective remains the same down-to-earth miracle. "To be able to see your family, your food—it's not a small thing," he says, smiling. "I eliminate disabilities. This is my spiritual practice."

· : · : · ·

For a Western visitor the Aravind complex dizzyingly juxtaposes familiar medical technology and an unimaginably foreign setting. The overriding goal is supplying high-quality care to the greatest number of patients for the least expenditure of time and money. Each day twenty times more patients are treated here than in a U.S. eye hospital. The hubbub created by patients ranging from the simplest villagers to urban professionals, their relatives (an Indian invariably enters the hospital with an "attender"), medical personnel, housekeepers, and vendors is tumultuous, even for India.

Aravind runs on a kind of Robin Hood economics. About 60 percent of its patients, who can't afford health care, are treated in the "free" hospital building. Their costs are subsidized by the modest fees charged at the "paying patients" building right next door. In keeping with this philosophy, Aravind's most expensive operation is the surgery that allows the vain to dispense with spectacles; as a concession, this treatment is provided in a delightfully air-conditioned suite.

By American standards, Aravind's facilities are no-frills: simple, sterile, and organized for maximum efficiency. In the paying hospital, patients stay in private or semiprivate rooms equipped with the usual hospital beds. In the free hospital, they stay in open men's and women's wards, where they sleep on straw mats. What matters most is that every day three hundred to four hundred patients on gurneys disappear into a door on one side of the surgery and emerge bandaged and cured on the other. The obvious comparison to an assembly line delights rather than affronts Dr. V, who claims McDonald's as a cherished model of good, cheap, reproducible service. By emulating the mass-production expertise that cranks out millions of reliable hamburgers, he says, Aravind can perform for ten dollars a cataract operation that costs fifteen hundred in the United States.

A tour of Aravind makes plain that treating patients is just one step—and not the most challenging—in the war on blindness. Several of Aravind's most important weapons are housed in a modern high-rise building named for the International Lions Club, one of the institute's greatest supporters. In a sophisticated factory called Aurolab, technicians inexpensively manufacture drugs and surgical equipment that would otherwise have to be bought from Western companies at vastly higher prices. For example, Aurolab produces interocular lenses, which eliminate the need for thick corrective spectacles after cataract surgery, for $8; Western suppliers charge $50. Similarly, a small vial of medicine that costs $250 when purchased from conventional manufacturers costs $50 here. Access to these affordable supplies, which are now used in seventy-five developing countries, can mean the difference between sight and blindness for the world's poor.

The Lions building houses another crucial if under-remarked tool in the battle against blindness. Aravind's training center for health professionals draws technicians, researchers, and hospital administrators from around the world. Health administrators in particular seem to constitute one of Dr. V's favorite groups. If a hospital wants to attract the paying patients it needs in order to treat the poor for free, it must be well-run. Then, too, he says, "Without administrators, doctors have to manage a business, when they could be eliminating blindness."

One striking feature of the institute's campus is the workers' high seriousness and fierce concentration—hallmarks of the proud "Aravind culture." Aurolab technicians swathed in surgical scrubs seem never to look up from their microscopes and lens-crafting machinery. Aravind's international reputation attracts talented doctors willing to work much harder for less; a typical surgeon here, for example, will perform two thousand cataract operations per year, in contrast to an Indian peer's average of two hundred. Workers ranging from housekeepers, who traditionally come from society's low rungs, to top surgeons treat each other with an even-handed respect remarkable in a still caste-minded culture. To these troops in his battle against blindness, Dr. V is known simply as Chief.

· : · : · : ·

Aravind's constantly expanding scope is fed by Dr. V's indefatigable curiosity. His appetite for new information is such that when he's being interviewed he, too, takes notes, lest he forget any interesting tidbit that might emerge. When I return to his office after my tour, he hands me a reprint of an article that supports one of his long-held convictions: that it's possible to do well by doing good. Producing necessary goods and services for the poor isn't just moral, claims Dr. V, but profitable.

There's nothing Dr. V loves more than a win-win situation in which spiritual and material goals are simultaneously met. In India the rich constitute a tiny minority of perhaps 10 million. Rather than cater to them, he says, companies can make much larger profits by supplying large quantities of low-cost products, from ice-cream pops to Internet access, to the hundreds of millions of the poor. Indeed, by providing inexpensive health care to the masses, Aravind has proved not only that "the basic elements of a good life can be marketed to the poor," he says, but also that such an effort can "create a positive industry based on caring, supporting, helping."

In his ongoing study of poverty, Dr. V has also been impressed by the success of new income-generating strategies for the poor, such as microlending organizations that supply very small loans to cottage industrialists. In one such booming "industry," for example, everyone benefits when a poor woman borrows enough money to buy a cell phone, then charges previously deprived neighbors reasonable fees for its use. New collaborative enterprises, such as India's dairy cooperatives, allow owners of limited resources, such as a cow or two, to pool their products for processing and marketing. This new small-is-beautiful economy particularly helps India's hard-pressed women to realize their capacities, says Dr. V, smiling. "Once they do, they say, 'Don't bother about husbands!' "

It is not surprising that Dr. V is especially interested in the connections between poverty and blindness. He remarks on the high incidence of vision problems in Africa and says, "It's even poorer than India! One way to eliminate poverty is to eliminate blindness, which afflicts at least thirty million people around the world." In largely rural developing areas like Africa and the subcontinent, he points out, ignorance is often the greatest obstacle to achieving medical goals. "Doing surgery is the easy part," says Dr. V. "The real problem is getting the patients to come to the doctor. In the villages, people may think they're too old for an operation. They may not know where to go for help. They don't understand hospitals, towns, transportation. Someone might remain blind because he thinks, How would I get to a doctor?" The very thought elicits one of Dr. V's cosmic laughs.

By combining Indian spirituality and Western know-how, Dr. V has accomplished seemingly impossible feats. Who's to say that his practical religion can't eliminate poverty as well as blindness? For a few moments in his office, his latest objective seems possible, even inevitable. He smiles as he says, "There's just no need for child beggars and blind people slumped in the streets."

· : · : · : ·

Each Aravind building contains a small, simply furnished meditation room. Hanging on the walls are the same pictures of Sri Aurobindo and the Mother, his spiritual partner and successor, that appear in other prominent sites around the campus. With his flowing white locks and magnetic eyes, Aurobindo looks like a sage sent from Central Casting, but he never fit the mold of the celebrity guru. He lived in deep seclusion and held *darshan* just four times a year; despite many visits to his ashram, even Dr. V actually saw Aurobindo only once. Then, too, his teachings seem less concerned with conventional religion than with a process of human evolution. Its end product, Aurobindo predicted, would be a different kind of person who possesses a higher kind of consciousness.

One afternoon in his office Dr. V points out that our species has made this sort of developmental quantum leap before. Our animal ancestors slowly advanced from the lower physical and emotional levels of existence, he says, until there was a point "when mind came down and created a new being—the human being." This advance in human evolution was intellectual but, according to Aurobindo, the next will be spiritual. Already, he taught, a small, hardworking elite is working to bring about this transformation by practicing what he called supramental consciousness.

Twice each day Dr. V cultivates this higher state of awareness in one of Aravind's meditation rooms. During what he calls a "silent talk with God," he asks to become a "a better tool, a receptacle, for the divine force." But supramental consciousness isn't achieved merely by sitting around meditating, any more than Gandhi's nonviolence meant withdrawing from the world. To attain this state, a person must practice what Dr. V calls a "discipline for creating peace" while remaining on the job, whether raising a family or treating the sick.

First, says Dr. V, one must learn to become aware of thoughts that feed anger and hatred, and then to squelch them. "If an intuition creates peace and calm, keep it," says Dr. V. "If not, don't." Over time this habit of mind brings not only equanimity but what he calls "an immense capacity to work with concentration. You work on your work, then supramental consciousness works through you."

It's easy to dismiss unfamiliar religious teachers and their language as exotic, but Aurobindo's down-to-earth brand of spirituality— even some of its imagery—exists in every religion. Soon after talking with Dr. V, I come across Paul's letter to James: "Every generous act of giving, with every perfect gift, is from above, coming down from the Father of lights, with whom there is no variation or shadow due to change. In fulfillment of his own purpose he gave us birth by the word of truth, so that we would become a kind of first fruits of his creatures. . . . Let everyone be quick to listen, slow to speak, slow to anger. . . . Be doers of the word, and not merely hearers who deceive themselves."

· : · · : ·

My visit to Dr. V occasioned some reflection on the third element of spiritual genius: charisma, or the ability to inspire others. Both the laconic physician and, say, the emotive Mata Amritanandamayi are holy, or intensely aware of a transcendent reality, and good, or compassionate. Compared with hers, however, Dr. V's charisma is a slow burn that derives less from innate personal magnetism than from the gradually dawning awareness of how immense his work is and how he does it. Then too, one's response to a spiritual genius, as to any other individual, depends on the chemistries of the two people involved. Ammachi's *shakti* could put off pragmatic types, just as the naturally contemplative might be alarmed by Dr.

V's workaholism. Before arriving in Madurai I had an experience with a guru widely regarded as a living saint that suggests how much spiritual genius can depend on the eye of the beholder.

The ashram of Yogi Ramsuratkumar, just outside the south-eastern town of Tiruvannamalai, looms above a landscape of pastoral fields, trash dumps, the villas of Western spiritual seekers, and the shanties of the Indian poor. Twice each day the yogi gives a two-hour-long *darshan* in a huge concrete building that looks like a cross between an airplane hangar and a sports arena. This grandiose setting is a stark contrast to the guru's former milieu. For many years he lived as a beggar on Tiruvannamalai's streets, where he continuously chanted his mantra to the god Ram. Over time he began to attract devotees, who felt peace and joy in his raggedy presence. Talk of *siddhi*s attracted more followers, who eventually enshrined him in his own ashram. The yogi's attractively simple teaching, however, remains the same: the cultivation of constant awareness of God through chanting the divine name.

When I entered the vast ashram building, devotees were prostrating themselves before a huge messianic-looking bronze sculpture of Yogi Ramsuratkumar. I was puzzled to see that, off to the right, the white-bearded yogi, now in his eighties, was slouched in a chair, smoking a *beedi,* or cheap Indian cigarette. He strongly resembled a world-weary old beatnik. Several hundred men and women seated before him on brightly colored cotton spreads on the ground sang rounds of *bhajan*s. Overhead, the legend "Long live Yogi Ramsuratkumar" twinkled in turquoise fairy lights. A gleaming white Ambassador sedan was parked against a nearby wall, and an open-sided hut with a thatched roof stood a short distance from the yogi's chair. All told, the sanctuary had a wacky tropical ambience reminiscent of a Polynesian theme bar.

Those who seek Yogi Ramsuratkumar's personal advice or intercession can leave written requests at the door before *darshan.* The guru's aide took up a sheaf of these notes, then began to call out names in groups of four. The chosen devotees came forward, prostrated themselves, then sat on plastic garden chairs near the yogi, with whom they earnestly conversed. When the *darshan* was nearly over, the aide held up my request and called out my name alone.

Nervously I approached, bowed, and took a seat. The yogi and his aide, both of whom spoke English, seemed stunned that Winifred was not a man. "You mean it's a woman?" said the yogi. "Yes, a woman," said the aide, waving helplessly toward me. I looked on, obscurely embarrassed, as they continued to study my signature and shake their heads.

Eventually Yogi Ramsuratkumar looked up at his aide and said, "What does she want?" As if translating, the aide turned to me and repeated, "What do you want?" Before I could answer, however, he returned to his study of my petition, then announced to the yogi, "She wants a blessing." Suppressing a yawn, the yogi handed me a small banana.

By this point it was clear that I had nothing to lose. I straightened my spine and asked the yogi for a teaching. The aide said, "She also wants a teaching." The yogi looked at me briefly. "Keep saying God's name," he told the aide, who told me. Clutching my banana, I bowed and withdrew.

When I left the building, the doorman congratulated me for having enjoyed such an extensive consultation with the yogi. A woman in a fine silk sari, carrying a beautifully dressed child of about five, hurried toward the door. As they came closer the boy was revealed to be terribly disfigured. His mother's face was pulled taut by the battling forces of despair and hope in Yogi Ramsuratkumar.

Despite my expectations, I didn't experience what his devotees do in the presence of Yogi Ramsuratkumar, much less anything like what that desperate mother desired. Nevertheless, I got some perfectly good advice—and a piece of fruit, too.

· : · : · :

Early one morning in his office, Dr. V invites me to his home for breakfast, which he takes after meditation. In India the proprieties must be observed, so I sit in the backseat of his car while this aged bachelor drives the few blocks at a stately five miles per hour. In classic Indian style, Dr. V toots his horn all the way—one of many customs that would drive one mad at home but seem rather merry here.

Dr. V leads the way through his large, plainly furnished modern house to a roomy kitchen. While a smiling young woman makes eggs and coffee, he cruises through the morning papers, which, like most things, make him smile. He taps an article about America's soaring medical costs and insurance crisis and says, "Everyone in medicine wants to get rich! Doctors don't want to do lots of cheap surgeries for the poor but a few operations for the wealthy."

Dr. V next inquires about my tour of Madurai's spectacular Meenakshi temple on the previous afternoon. In its vast precincts, the membrane between sacred and secular India seemed especially permeable. Office workers stopped in for a quick prayer. Parents carried newborns on their first outings. Honeymooners lolled by the inner pool. Pregnant women hoping for easy labor poured oil on a graphic relief of a goddess giving birth. Visibly downcast individuals offered ghee to skull-bedecked Kali, whose fearsome aspect belies her mercy to the hopeless.

It's hard to overestimate how thoroughly religion saturates Indian life, from diet to art, from ablutions to the sacred cows wandering the streets. There's hardly a jungle clearing that lacks a shrine and a *saddhu* or two. Dr. V says that Hindus' easy access to temples and spiritual teachers over many centuries accounts for the fact that "*dharma* is ingrained in our people. Since the Buddha, saints and seers have been working on India's spiritual development." Despite India's terrible poverty and related problems, life there often has a joyousness that comes when there's little to buy and less to buy it with, so that happiness floats free from the material realm. As Dr. V says, "Here, even a poor person might not be *spiritually* deprived. India is a spiritual teacher for the whole world! We must preserve and build on that heritage, not out of a sense of superiority but as America does with its science and technology."

By combining Eastern spirituality and Western know-how, Dr. V has pioneered an important approach to some complex global problems of the twenty-first century. He's certainly aware of the challenges ahead but is also encouraged by recent progress. In his own field he points to the enormous strides made in curing blindness, which can be eliminated "now, today." In the larger world, the human rights movement and the Internet, which permits the nearly free sharing of information, strike Dr. V as signs that the higher level of evolution predicted by Aurobindo has begun. Always a realist, he smilingly allows that "its completion may take millions of years!"

Perhaps because we're sitting in his kitchen, Dr. V talks a little about his personal life. He has never married and has no children but has enjoyed "lots of support," he says. "From my family alone there are more than a dozen doctors who work with me." He chivalrously professes that mothers are beset with anxieties that he has been spared, yet with his usual lack of pomposity, he admits to "a lot" of worries. When the world he's trying to save is too much with him, he reads some Aurobindo, he says, and tries "to see the anxiety as an object that's apart from me—detached." He laughs. "Of course, that's easier to say than to do."

Dr. V has a genius for show-not-tell religion, which is of inestimable importance at a time when many are skeptical about the dogmatic, institutional sort. Before I visit Madurai's Gandhi museum at Dr. V's insistence, I ask this frail, elderly man with the twisted hands how he continues to accomplish so much. "When you're in contact with the soul," he says simply, "you have energy. You don't have to be 'religious' to serve God. You serve God by serving humanity—by being more generous and less selfish in what you do." He gives his cosmic smile. "I just want to eliminate the world's blindness."

10. INTERPRETER

·:::::::::::::::::::::::::·

It's very early on a hot August morning at Omega Institute, a large "holistic learning center" nestled in the manicured wilds of the Hudson River valley. A tall, white-bearded, bare-chested man emerges from the mist like a prophet, slowly turning into Huston Smith, a philosopher by training who is America's pioneering scholar of comparative religion. The biblical image suits Huston in both its anticipatory and its admonitory senses.

Forty years ago, Huston sensed the West's imminent encounter with cultural pluralism and responded with *The Religions of Man*. This scholarly yet highly readable bestseller, now titled *The World's Religions: Our Great Wisdom Traditions,* remains a powerful influence for religious tolerance and resource for eclectic spiritual seekers open to insights from diverse traditions. Increasingly, however, Huston exercises the prophet's other, darker prerogative. His jeremiad is directed at an academe that encourages society's "brightest and best" to spurn religion's philosophical and moral riches because religion disagrees with science about what Huston calls "the big picture." Science claims that reality begins and ends with nature. What Huston calls the "wisdom traditions" regard nature as part of a much greater transcendent reality, called big mind, God, or other such terms. In Huston's view, religion and science simply offer "very different windows onto reality." Stressing that many scientists have observed that it's as reasonable to conclude there's a God as not, he says, "Nothing in the modern or postmodern eras has disproved transcendence. We have simply lowered our gaze."

Huston has traveled here from his home in Berkeley, where, as his card says, he remains a "some time visiting professor" at the university, to teach a weekend workshop called "Applied Wisdom: Universal Truths of the World's Great Religions." Most of his students are still asleep, but Huston, who recently celebrated his eightieth birthday, is returning from a swim and some tai chi. This seems only fitting for the man who blazed the trail for the many Americans who now study yoga at the YMCA or meditation at the local zendo. Way back in the fifties, Huston was demonstrating the lotus posture on public television and seeking *satori* in a Japanese monastery. His contagious enthusiasm for and personal involvement with Hinduism, Buddhism, Confucianism, Taoism, Judaism, Christianity, Islam, and the tribal traditions have made him a popular teacher and author, and the subject of a public television series. To conservative critics, however, the apostle of religious pluralism, who refuses to prioritize the eight great traditions he has worked with, is a promoter of postmodernity's fashionable, feckless "shopping cart" or "salad bar" spirituality.

At 9:00 A.M. about seventy people from as far away as Louisiana, Arizona, and even the United Kingdom settle down in one of Omega's cluster of one-room schoolhouses. The diverse group includes Buddhists, Jews, Christians, Hindus, and some who seem to be all or none of the above. Everyone is younger than Huston, and in a society that mostly ignores its elders, their palpable excitement is striking.

As I watch Huston prepare for his presentation, I realize that he actually looks *better* than he did three years ago, when we first met

in California. A certain Confucian air of calm benignity, rein-
forced by a drooping silver mustache, high "scholar's brow," and
small, slippered feet, gives this very tall, blue-eyed WASP a subtle
resemblance to an Asian sage. In fact, Huston, the son and grand-
son of Methodist missionaries to China, lived in a small village
near Shanghai until his college years. This rare life experience
has made him especially adept at interpreting Eastern religion for
Westerners.

When I arrived at his Berkeley home for that first interview, I
privately hoped that Huston could help me navigate around
Christianity, acquired by the accident of birth, to the Buddhism I
intellectually preferred. He has been strongly associated with Zen
since it came to America, and I had just finished a *sesshin*. This rigorous retreat had been a wonderful experience but left me troubled. As greatly as I valued Zen practice and principles, I just didn't
feel Buddhist. With an embarrassed shrug, I told Huston that I
couldn't quite give up the notion that, like someone who enters a
room soundlessly and out of sight, Jesus just sometimes seemed *to
be around*.

In the strong sunlight flooding his parlor, Huston cocked his
head at me. Time slowed down, and the air thickened. With a very
direct, unblinking blue look, he said, "I think that's wonderful.
You're fortunate."

From that moment I gave up brooding about religious labels. I
accepted my conflicted Christian heritage—who knows, maybe
it's genetic—and also continued to do Zen meditation, study with
rabbis, and pursue other kinds of religious insight. It was then, too,
that I really began to notice men and women who, like Huston,
could see the way things really are and help others see, too. References to these spiritual geniuses and the epiphanies they effected
began to appear in my notes.

Huston has spent most of his career teaching at universities,
and he calls us to order with the easy authority of the academic
lifer. He enjoys teaching, he says, "and that's very important, because joy makes us more open to learning, and learning makes us
joyful." Then he presents us with his sketch of the big picture

shared by the great religions, in which God or Allah, Buddha nature or the Tao are among the names for a transcendent reality of which our world is just a part and reflection. "Every great sage," he says, "has seen reality as a vast hierarchy presided over by perfection at the top."

Religion's vision of reality differs greatly from our view from the trenches of daily life. First of all, says Huston, in its big picture, "things are more integrated, unified, whole than they seem to us." Cosmologists such as Stephen Hawking now search for a single principle that explains the universe. Religion, however, has long proclaimed its grand unified theory in declarations such as the Sufis' "There is nothing but Allah" and the Jews' "*Sh'ma Israel! The Lord our God is one!*" Unlike the great sages, says Huston, we're distracted from ultimate reality's wholeness by the "tiny egocentric hot spots" that are sparked by life's vicissitudes. Religion sees a great seamless tapestry, while most of us see only "the threads and knots on its back."

According to religion's big picture, reality is not only more unified but better than it seems to us. As God told the medieval mystic Dame Julian of Norwich, "You will see for yourself that every sort of thing will be all right." Although such an assertion is nonsense in everyday terms, Huston is "absolutely sure" that this mystical vision reflects true reality, of which our usual view is only a "postcard." In other hands, sublime abstractions such as transcendental unity and perfection can seem chilly and dull, but Huston's almost ecstatic delight in them is contagious. "We just can't comprehend the glories of existence," he says, "except when we're in what the Celts call "a thin place" between this world and another, and the clouds part."

The wisdom traditions' third common insight into reality is easiest to grasp: things are more mysterious than they seem. "*Mystery* is a debased word today, as in *mystery novels,*" says Huston. "It really refers to a unique problem, wherein the more we advance in comprehending it, the more we see about it that we don't understand." Long after the first philosophers and priests brooded over life's mysteries, each of us is still wrestling with the same questions: Why is there something rather than nothing? Is this all there is? "We are born, live, and die in mystery," says Huston. "No matter how much information we acquire, that's not going to change. The larger the island of knowledge, the longer the shoreline of mystery."

This workshop is supposed to be about religion, but Huston's discussion of reality—specifically, its unity, goodness, and mystery—seems more like philosophy. A hand shoots up. Huston stalks over and, like a benign great heron, bends almost in half to peer into his questioner's face. A hearing problem only partly explains this behavior; Huston treats each interlocutor like the only other person in the world.

The young man asks, "When did your focus switch from the strictly intellectual to the religious?"

Huston smiles at a question that allows him to explain his conviction that religion primarily concerns what to *think* rather than, more conventionally, what to *feel* or *believe*. "One evening when I was twenty-four," he says, "just before I finished my doctoral dissertation in philosophy." The catalyst of his transformed worldview was Gerald Heard's book *Pain, Sex, and Time,* an avant garde treatment of mysticism, which focuses on intuited truths that elude conventional understanding and teaching. "It was the only time in my life that I read all night long," says Huston. "I said to myself, 'This is what the big picture looks like.'"

Presenting the mystic's great intuition, Huston says, "What does human life lean toward? Something *more.* Hidden. Lost. Undiscovered. In those 'thin places,' we all experience intimations of this deep reality, which relativize the mundane in comparison and make us feel like we've emerged from a dark cave into sunlight."

Emerging from academe, the impoverished young philosopher hitchhiked to Los Angeles to meet Heard and his friend Aldous Huxley. The three men hiked in the Mojave while Huxley talked of the early church's mystical desert fathers. Huston recalls that Huxley remarked that "like a snowy landscape, the desert subtracts details and stresses unity."

The austere beauty of a snow-covered or desert landscape symbolizes Huston's vision of the big picture. "Religion's question isn't What revs us up or makes us feel good?" he says, "but What's true?" Cultural differences notwithstanding, the traditions respond to that query with independent verifications of a transcendent reality "so different from the humdrum sort that accounts of it suggest divine revelation," says Huston, "whether the revealed truths descend on us or bubble up within us."

Many faces around the room still look surprised at the idea that, contrary to the conventional assumption, religion is actually about reality. The matters Huston discusses seem so basic that to many ears they don't even sound "religious."

Someone raises a hand to ask, "Is God an objective reality for you?"

"Yes," Huston says, "but my head sees further than my emotions." Increased idifference to and distrust of religious institutions have made personal spiritual experience postmodern spirituality's sine qua non. Huston, however, regards these affective states, including ecstasy, as mere signposts. "Bliss is when life makes perfect sense and everything is in place," he says. "It's rare, but it offers encouragement and verification." What it verifies, of course, is Truth, which has the real transformative power. "Knowing, *seeing,* that absolute perfection reigns—that what exists is, in the end, incredibly wonderful—infuses life with energy," says Huston. "One's orientation to life changes and the accidents of personality are put in a different perspective." Eschewing purple prose, he mildly compares his own religious experience with Plato's: "First a shudder runs through you, and then the old awe steals over you." He's more romantic, however, regarding the divine's experience: "The closest analogy to God's bliss, or inner life, is the sexual union of perfectly attuned lovers each of whom wants to give what the other most wants to receive."

Huston's appeal as a teacher lies not only in a fine, trained mind focused on "the way things are" but in a brown-shoe, Yankee approach to such high thinking. He scrupulously avoids stale, pious language. Noting that the blazing glory of ultimate reality can be obscured by a rainy Monday or a bad head cold, he says, "When I'm depressed, I can hear my head saying, 'Poor Huston. He's got the spiritual flu, but he'll get over it.'" He welcomes students' dissenting views, restates both positions sympathetically, offers his own opinion, and cheerfully moves on if things remain apples and oranges: "It seems we have a difference of opinion here!" Best of all, Huston is funny. When someone asks if God's existence could ever be proved by science, he says no, because, unlike nature, God doesn't have identifiable variables. That doesn't mean that God doesn't exist, of course, only that human attempts to document God are, as he puts it, "like a dog trying to prove the existence of higher math with the sniff test."

· : · : · : ·

When we return from a short break, Huston has put out some tape cassettes of chanting by the Gyuto monks of Tibet. In 1967 he was the first Westerner to encounter this primordial, oceanic music, in which a single voice produces a chord of multiple tones. "It's the holiest sound I've ever heard," he says. To raise money for Tibetan relief, he offers audiotapes of his original recording for a ten-dollar donation and sends the proceeds to the Dalai Lama. The big picture notwithstanding, God is in the details.

· : · : · : ·

Next Huston considers why the unified, perfect, mysterious transcendent reality verified by the wisdom traditions throughout the ages so often escapes us. First, he throws out a grand historical thesis that challenges our intellectual complacency. Since the Enlightenment, he says, our species has made tremendous scientific and social advances, including the "fairness revolution," or human rights movement. Where the big picture is concerned, however, he asserts that we've regressed from the understanding attained by our forebears before the Age of Reason. Modern skepticism is based on the premise that science's insights into nature refute a transcendent reality. In fact, says Huston, who knows his physics and long taught at MIT, science hasn't revealed anything that disproves the vision, shared by all the great religions, of "the encompassing and surpassing true reality beyond the status quo."

Taking in our shocked expressions, Huston says that, because we're staunch believers in progress, "It's hard for us to hear that our elders are our betters in anything." He lays the blame for our metaphysical backsliding squarely on the doorstep of postmodern society's holy of holies: the university. Lagging behind advances in physics, much of academe still cleaves to the "modern"—that is, out-of-date—Newtonian worldview, which portrays the universe not as an organic whole but as a machine that can be understood by analyzing the workings of its parts. As a result, says Huston sadly, "even philosophers analyze concepts instead of pursuing the nature of reality." This fragmenting, mechanistic mentality is particularly unfortunate, he says, considering that physics, "the same branch of science that saddled us with this reductionism, now says that the universe of space, matter, and time derives from something else that exceeds them. So science, too, is pointing to a transcendent reality larger than and different from nature of the conventional, sensory sort." Of his fellow academics in general, Huston says, "In ways, they're often the most benighted people, yet they shape the culture!"

Of course, there are personal as well as cultural reasons why we lose sight of the big picture. We're mired in the quotidian sensory world, says Huston, and "Life just comes at us, ready or not, without telling us what to think about it." Nevertheless, "it's up to each of us to see either randomness or pattern and purpose, even if elusive," he says. "That may seem harsh, but if it were otherwise, we'd have no free will." Huston is convinced that something deep in human nature inclines most of us to see meaning rather than chaos. In deistic terms, he says, there are four ways one can interpret the "great Rorschach blot of the universe." Atheists conclude there is no god; polytheists, many gods; monotheists, one God; and mystics, only God. Of course, says Huston, "there's no way to prove who's right."

At lunchtime we emerge from the cerebral equivalent of a plunge into an icy pool. At a time when educated people often feel torn between a life of the mind and a life of the spirit, it's bracing to hear an intellectual and mystic refuse to give an inch either way. We're exhilarated by the thought that God is only one name for a mysterious ultimate reality, and that religion is about this big picture and how to live according to its lights. On a deeper level, we've also been immersed in an extraordinary medium of this powerful message. More than his words, Huston's simple grandeur bespeaks the hidden glory he describes.

· : · : · · ·

Omega is a major pilgrimage site of the new McReligion called spirituality. Each weekend six hundred or so people come here to pursue subjects from yoga to feng shui, "Molecules of Emotion" with the neuroscientist Candace Pert to "Drums of Passion" with Babatunde Olatunji. Women outnumber men, but not conspicuously so. Most conferees are middle-aged or youngish adults dressed in the New Age uniform of S-M-L clothing in muted earth and jewel tones. The prevailing social style could be described as "open." Outside, there's lots of hugging amidst giant sunflowers. Inside, people say things like "Destiny is what it looks like when it's over." The combination of high seriousness and silliness, along with classes, shared bathrooms, and communal meals, makes me feel like I'm back in college, with reading glasses.

At lunchtime, perhaps intoxicated by vegetarian food of the complicated, delicious sort I never manage at home, I ask Huston about the meaning of life. "To realize with our full being the opportunity that we have been given to share in this stupendous drama," he says. "Simply to have the opportunity *to be* for even one instant is a miraculous gift. Putting God in a philosopher's terms, Plotinus speaks of the One as 'that fountain always on.' Always spilling over with the opportunity of living." He smiles. "The purpose of life is for us to fulfill what is necessary to make God God. If we were not here, there would be a hole in the cheese."

That's all very well for God, I say, but what about us? "If we just take this chunk of our life, considering all its sorrows and pains, we might say that we would have settled for not being included,"

Huston says. "In my view, that's because we see only part of the picture. The story line in all religions tells of a happy ending that blossoms as a result of ordeals necessarily confronted and surmounted. These trials add to the ultimate glory, like scrimmages leading up to victory. I believe in universal salvation—that we all make it in the end—so I think we'll look back and feel grateful to have been given the chance to be, rather than not to be. Is that too abstract?"

It's not for me. My father recently died from cancer. I want religion's "happy ending" to be true, I say, but I have my doubts.

As to what happens after death, Huston says, "The only honest answer is 'Who knows?' In talking of such matters, we are out of our depth. But it's an adventure, for sure." Both shamanism, humanity's oldest religion, of some twenty thousand years, and Plato took the spirit realm seriously, he says, "and I'm inclined to do so also." Huston says that, indeed, all religions assert that after death "we either come back or go on to new realms—and that, except in very rare cases, spiritual work continues. The intermediate realm between heaven and earth may be a real mess. Maybe the souls on the other side are as confused as we are, so we should be wary of séances!"

I confess that heaven has always struck me as a combination of church and my grandmother's parlor: fancy, but not much fun. "To associate eternity with boredom is to fail to distinguish eternity from everlastingness," says Huston. "Everlastingness goes on forever. Eternity is outside time—like freeze-frames in a movie." Moreover, he adds, "In eternity, we have an option either to behold the glory or to fuse with it, like a dewdrop entering into the shining sea. We think 'poor dewdrop,' but it would be more accurate to say that the dewdrop opens and the ocean rushes in."

· : · : · :

After lunch Huston takes up the subject for which he's best known: comparative religion. Unlike many scholars, he can clear away the flotsam and jetsam that can obscure the traditions' great truths and the similarities among them. What makes this part of his presentation unique, however, is his personal experiences of each religion.

Huston's involvement with Hinduism goes back to the 1940s in St. Louis, where he was a young Methodist minister (he was ordained but soon turned to teaching), philosophy professor—and president of the local Vedanta Society. With a wonderful economy he distills the precepts of an enormously complicated religion thus: "Hinduism focuses on the sacred within the self. It says that not only can you have what you want but, in fact, you already have it! You just need to clear away the karmic debris that obscures the divine light within."

One of the pleasures afforded by comparative religion is seeing how each tradition sheds light on others. Hinduism's four *yoga*s, or paths of spiritual advancement, for example, describe the different ways of pursuing the sacred in this or any religion. Describing the *bhakti* way of fervent devotion, Huston recalls that the swami who was his first important spiritual teacher characterized Christianity as " 'one blazing path of *bhakti* yoga' that no other religion rivals in this respect. He also believed in Jesus' incarnation more than most modernist diluted Christians—which made me see that 'missionary work' should go both ways."

No one could be surprised to hear Huston say that by temperament he's an intellectual *jnana* yogi, who pursues the sacred through cultivating what he calls "intuitive discernment, which is more like seeing than thinking. Gaining an intuitive awareness of the way things are! What could be more important or interesting than that?" To someone of his reflective *jnanic* temperament, Christianity's emotional *bhakti* emphasis is a challenge, he says: "I hope that the struggle of reconciling the two approaches will round out a flat side in my personality."

Huston has practiced *hatha* yoga for some fifty years, and there are striking recent photos of him standing on his head to prove it. With characteristic candor, however, he makes "only modest personal claims" concerning this psychophysiological path to the divine. He does his *asanas* "because the day just seems to go better when I do. Mostly I find it helps ward off the stiffness of age."

The *karma* path of seeking the sacred through service to others is as American as apple pie—so much so that our society virtually equates religion with good works. Huston, who was a founding member of the Congress on Racial Equality, has always worked for various human rights movements. He stresses that religion isn't only "the search for the real" but also "the effort to approximate one's life to it. Religious experience that doesn't increase your compassion for others is an illusion." Nevertheless, he says, the Protestant churches have "watered down Christianity's spiritual tradition and placed social concerns ahead of transcendence to the point that there's little difference in worldview between the Graduate Theological Union and UC Berkeley across the street—it's mostly Marx, Darwin, Freud, Nietzsche, and Einstein."

The secularization of Christianity and Judaism, which substitutes social activism for spirituality, helps explain why disillusioned Americans increasingly look to the more inner-directed Eastern traditions. Many are drawn to Buddhism by its emphasis on a type of meditation that Huston calls "looking at your own mind." He points out that when asked, "Who are you?" Buddha answered, "I am awake." Buddhism's popularity in America bespeaks the fact that "it's the most psychological religion, and we live in a psychological age," says Huston. He knows whereof he speaks. Kendra Smith, his spouse of more than fifty years, is a therapist who is also trained in Buddhism-inspired *vipassana* meditation. As Huston puts it, "She whose husband I am—in Berkeley, the phrase 'my wife' is considered too possessive—gives me quite a lot of psychology with my dinner."

Just as he was an early Vedantist, Huston was one of America's first "Zenists," as he says. "In my thirties, I wanted *satori* more than anything else." Daily Zen practice, which centers on a precise type of seated meditation, promotes this spiritual enlightenment, but Huston took a more dramatic approach. He undertook a two-month-long *sesshin* at a monastery in Japan, where the sleep deprivation, nearly nonstop meditation, and other ascetic rigors brought him to the verge of physical and mental collapse. Finally, in something approximating a psychotic break, he stormed off to rage at the *roshi*. The master calmly informed the crazed Westerner that he shouldn't worry about sickness and health: "Both are distractions. Put them aside and go on." Huston suddenly grasped the unity, or sameness, of these opposites, which caused his understanding to "detonate."

Satori notwithstanding, Huston sees Buddhism's unique feature in the self-sacrificing *bodhisattva* vow. "The *bodhisattva* promises to stay in this world 'until the grass itself is enlightened,'" he says. "The nobility of it! Like the image of the Good Shepherd, who sends the sheep safely through the gate before entering himself."

Huston moves from one tradition to another, highlighting the uniqueness of each. Of Judaism's prophets he says, "No other religion has this fearless band of people who will, in the name of justice, courageously confront evil right at the top, insisting that, despite its pomp, no unjust society can last. It's impossible to overestimate their influence, which can be seen from Mary's Magnificat to Martin Luther King's speeches." Islam is distinguished by its response to the one God: total submission. "That's a hard word for us," he says, "but the submission is to ultimate reality." As a Western scholar, Huston is especially appreciative of the tribal religions' stress on oral tradition. "The written word not only adds to our experience but subtracts from it—particularly from the sense of what is important," he says. "In the tribal religions, what really matters must be stored between the ears, and what doesn't just drops away."

Huston's unfeigned enthusiasm for each religion comes through in the way in which they've infused his life. Observing *shabbat* with his Jewish grandchildren—one of his daughters converted—has impressed on him that Judaism requires "pouring your life into its mold of tradition, rather than following your own trajectory. Jews were 'chosen' not for privilege but for responsibility." Five times daily Huston joins the world's Muslims to pray:

Praise be to Allah, creator of the worlds, the merciful, the compassionate, the ruler of the day of judgment. Thee do we worship, thee do we ask for aid. Guide us on the straight path, the path of those on whom thou has poured forth thy grace; not the path of those who have incurred thy wrath and gone astray.

"A mere seven phrases assert that life is not an accident," says Huston, "but divinely created by a loving God who nonetheless insists that our actions have consequences. That this short prayer contains so much that's important is almost proof in itself that Islam is a revealed religion." A more recent addition to his spiritual practice was inspired by the oral, tribal traditions: "Composting helps to ground me and phase me into nature's feedback loops without any words."

Huston's treatment of his birthplace's two major traditions has a particular charm. (Of his missionary parents' work in a Chinese village where folk beliefs in spirits and demons prevailed, he says only that they "provided a higher religion for some.") Confucianism, which stresses social harmony, and Taoism, which is more "soul-oriented," aren't really different religions, he says, but complementary parts of a whole. Spiritual progress in Confucianism is measured by ideal social relationships—from parent and child to ruler and subjects, even to the cosmos—that are characterized by *ren,* or fellow-feeling. Savoring this concept as "a great antidote to the scientific worldview," Huston describes a treasured Chinese wall hanging at home that reads, "The universe is filled with feeling."

Taoism, or "the way," summarized in the seventh century B.C.E. by Lao Tzu in the *Tao Te Ching,* stresses living in perfect balance with reality, both natural and transcendent. Courtesy of ubiquitous *yin* and *yang* jewelry and T-shirts, we're all familiar with the symbol of this Taoist concept of the interrelationship of all things. Huston illustrates with a famous tale: A certain farmer was saddened when his horse ran away. The next day, however, the seeming disaster became a windfall when the animal returned leading a herd of wild horses to its master. On the following day, though, one of the horses kicked the man's son and broke his leg. The next day, however, army recruiters spared the injured youth from conscription. The moral of the story is particularly instructive for judgmental Westerners, says Huston: "Who knows what's good or bad?"

Huston illustrates another important Taoist principle with a vignette from his boyhood. His missionary father raised bees. Despite much veiling and heavy clothing, Reverend Smith was invariably stung when he attempted to take their honey by storm. One year he decided to call a professional "bee robber." The specialist was greeted by the villagers with great respect. Rolling back the sleeves of his prestigious scholar's robe, he gently brushed the bees aside with tai chi–like grace and removed the honey without incident. Seeing is believing, and Huston says that this demonstration of *wu wei,* or behavior that wastes no energy on unnecessary conflict, so impressed him that he has no fear of bees, he says, "even if they crawl on my lips."

· ⋮ · ⋮ · ⋮ ·

At our next session Huston announces that we have a professional Jewish comedian in our number and asks him to favor us with a joke. The comic begins in the classic manner: "Two Jews were talking . . ." What they were discussing, it seems, was a plan to kill Hitler. They knew he would be at a certain place at 3:00 P.M., so they went there at 2:45, guns ready. Three o'clock passed. At 3:15, says the comedian, "one Jew says to the other, 'Where is he? God, I hope nothing happened to him!'"

Before beginning his presentation, Huston asks if there are any questions.

A woman raises a hand to ask, "Can you describe 'the Huston Smith religion'?"

Huston genially acknowledges his reputation for spiritual swashbuckling. However, he says, critics who accuse him of advocating "mix-and-match" religion oversimplify his true position and the realities of an increasingly complex global culture, which shares not just cuisines and music but religions. "As the Bible puts it, 'The Spirit bloweth where it listeth,'" says Huston. "It doesn't respect our walled enclosures and operates in an infinite number of ways."

After a lifetime Huston has concluded that, like the proverbial

Irishman's trousers, religion is "plural at the bottom but singular at the top." Because each great religion is unique and organic, he says, "Their parts aren't totally interchangeable, like a jackalope's." Moreover, many of us, including Huston, have a visceral tie to a particular faith that, like family, we often but not always acquire at birth. He has concluded the best way to develop religiously is to embrace one tradition, then add to it. For example, he says, "Christianity is my main meal, but I'm a strong believer in vitamin supplements."

Turning to his personal religious life, Huston allows that, for most of his adulthood, "I could have been described as a Vedantist, Zenist, or whatever I was exploring at the time more than as a Christian. But I never really severed the ties." He attributes this enduring connection to the kinder, gentler form of Christianity he received from his missionary parents: "I was fortunate in getting the message that we're in good hands, and in gratitude should share each other's burdens."

In his later years, Huston has re-embraced the faith of his fathers on several levels. " 'The child is the father of the man,' " he says, "and I'm now visited by my childhood's hymns, which I like. I say the creed because it connects me to my parents and grandparents, who, knowing the dangers, went as missionaries on clipper ships to China." Tipping his hat to that culture's "ancestor worship," he mischievously describes himself as a Confucian Methodist. He reads the Bible every morning and attends church every Sunday: "Worship shifts one's awareness of wonder and mystery from the peripheral to the focal."

Huston may have come full circle but, characteristically, he explores Christianity "as if it were a foreign tradition, which in many ways it is in our modern, secular age," he says. "Approaching it with openness and empathy—particularly the depths of Augustine and Meister Eckhart—strips away many stereotypes of the third-grade Christianity one hears from most pulpits."

Huston's discussion of his own faith differs from his treatment of the other traditions in that it bespeaks a spiritual struggle—specifically with Jesus, the thinking Christian's three-hundred-

pound gorilla. Regarding the nature of Christ, Huston merely remarks that the incarnation seems "mysterious, as it perhaps was
even to him. He asked his followers, 'Who do you say I am?'"
Concerning Jesus' miracles and other supernatural doings, as
Huston points out, "We moderns are hard-pressed to imagine a
culture like his, in which the other reality is unquestioned. I'm fas-
cinated by his nights of prayer, spent saturating himself in that
other reality of spirit. That's how he could do his works of metaphysical power. That was the source of a charisma so strong that
he had to teach from a boat, to crowds that followed him for
days, forgetting about meals. If the spirit wasn't real—dense—
there wouldn't be a church today."

Many educated Christians wrestle with creedal concerns, but
Huston's struggle is more personal. While he has "no problem"
with the Christian mystics' godhead, he says, he has "real trouble
with Jesus Christ, whom I don't experience very intimately."

A young man raises his hand. "Like you," he says, "I grew up
Christian, but Jesus never jelled for me."

Huston responds with what he calls "Ramakrishna's great question. 'Do you like to talk about God with qualities or without
them?'" Of course, there are not two such Gods, he explains, but
rather the visions of two different types of believers that exist in all
religions. Some are outward-oriented exoteric sorts, who see the
sacred as a person: Jesus, the *boddhisattva,* or the God of the Hebrew patriarchs. Others are inward-looking esoteric types, who
see the Other as formless form that can't be described but only
contacted or experienced, as in *nirvana.* Typically, Huston puts in a
good word for the exoteric sensibility, which is underrepresented
at places like Omega: "Like a garden hose, its narrow nozzle gives
a lot of energy. Where Christianity is concerned, I'm afraid that the
liberals would read the religion out of existence were it not for the
conservatives." Sounding almost wistful, he says, "I could never be
one of them, but they have more transcendence than the mainstream Protestant church."

Before we leave for swims and massages, Huston announces
that he has to catch a 6:30 plane from JFK the next evening and

wonders if anyone who's heading that way could give him a lift. Later, when I express amazement at this consider-the-lilies approach to travel, he says that depending on the kindness of strangers "always works out."

. : . : . : .

One evening at nine, Huston and I meet to talk. It's still very hot. Huston, who has been "on" all day, must be tired, to say nothing of jet-lagged. I offer to postpone our interview. Demonstrating a sublime courtesy that's perhaps a consequence of believing there's nothing but God, he says it's a pleasure to talk about high matters. I tell him that I've figured out one of the reasons why he has turned out so well. Recently I'd seen a photograph of Huston as an extraordinarily beautiful little boy, who must have been his mother's darling, which is often a great psychological advantage in life. Huston laughs and seems pleased but adds, "I hope all her children thought they were."

Huston's stress on the great faiths' similarity of vision has reminded me of a remark by the late, great neuroscientist Daniel X. Freedman. While conducting research on schizophrenia, he had studied LSD during its early, legal era and concluded that the uniformity of the cosmic bliss the drug evoked resulted from the fact that, by and large, people have the same brain. I ask Huston if the uniformity of the religions' big picture could be explained in the same way. He nodds but adds, "It's something deeper than the brain. It's the spirit—ultimately, the *imago dei*. We're all cast in the divine image, whether we're Eskimos or Hottentots, so we're more alike than otherwise." Although "quite open" to the idea that human nature might account for the similarity of our experiences, Huston says, "I would not allow that conclusion to denigrate or throw doubt on the noetic authenticity of what is envisioned."

The mention of LSD leads to a discussion of religion's wilder shores, including Huston's "peak experience" during legal research on the drug at Harvard in the early sixties. During three hours in a university chapel one Good Friday, he recalls, "I saw more completely than before that the religions are like fingers pointing at the same moon. The experience was also awesome, frighteningly so. I felt that if I had drawn an inch closer to God, my body would have shattered." On the one hand, Huston has no illusions about the general suitability of psychedelics or the wisdom of those who advocate indiscriminate use of them. He quotes Ram Dass, the former Harvard psychologist Richard Alpert: " 'When you get the message, hang up.' " On the other hand, Huston refuses to demonize the controversial substances categorically: "I'm too old to worry about my reputation."

In a similar way, Huston doesn't dismiss psychic phenomena, but he regards such things with caution. "It's a can of worms, a terribly messy area," he says. "Based on all of my teachers, I think there's something there that's not just made up." During an academic year in Australia, for example, he failed to find a single anthropologist in any university who didn't believe that the aborigines had telepathic powers. But, he says, "to make out what that power is is the very mischief." He approvingly quotes an Indian swami who said, "The *siddhis*—miracles—are there, but I am not interested. I have seen evil men become good, and that is as much of a miracle as I need in my lifetime."

Huston's opinions about psychedelics and psychics are somehow less surprising than his attitude about religious disciplines. For example, after many years of daily *zazen*—"I paid my dues"—he still meditates in a Zen style but no longer follows a rigorous regimen. "I was once at the stage of these bright-eyed young people—I'm all for them—who think that spiritual practice is a beeline to eternal bliss," he says. "The alternative is doing nothing, which seems to be an unwise stance, so it's the lesser of two absurdities to take on some discipline. But I make no claim about how good I am at my own spiritual practice. And I could be whimsical about how little noticeable difference it makes." Then too, he says, "and this seems humorous, considering all my venturing around, there's the fact that I am basically a Westerner. With the remaining ounces of my strength, I can make more difference if I address the tradition that has formed me. In the years I have left, I want to pour my religious energy into a deeper comprehension and realization of the Christian religion."

If Huston had to be described in a few words, they might be

"Christian *jnana* yogi." "I go to school to the minds of Augustine, Aquinas, and Dionysius the Areopagite," he says. "If these great minds could say the creed, I can, too. I won't accommodate myself to a world of shadows." Offering a profound insight into the nature of religious understanding—and not only the Christian sort—he says, "I don't affirm that the creedal truths occurred on the plane of conventional reality, but that *what happened is more like what they say happened than our secular views allow.*"

Huston may have returned to his roots, but there's a certain satisfaction in his voice when he asserts that, within Christianity, "I manage to alienate everyone. Unlike conservatives, I refuse to prioritize one of the eight faiths I've immersed myself in. Unlike liberals, I have a strong doctrine of revelation, by which God has shown Truth to different peoples, from India to Alaska, in different languages." Then too, he repeats, he has never had "that personal experience with Jesus. I'm still working toward that." Perhaps because of the combination of the heat and the late hour, I blurt out that he must be like the great mystics, who often experienced God only as not there, like an absent beloved. Huston charitably says, "I don't know. But it's a priority, and what I'm working on."

· : · : · : ·

Huston spends our final class on harmonizing the great religions' unique voices into one powerful chorus of affirmation of some basic principles. Their accord concerning ethics, virtues, and vision— "what we do, who we are, and what we seek"—is more than just "nice," he says. The global nature of the human rights struggle, the environmental crisis, the increasingly violent "tribalization" of religious and political conflict, and other problems have made their agreement intensely practical.

Concerning the major ethical issues—possessions, language, sex, and the use of force—Huston says that "the Ten Commandments pretty much tell the story." He prefers to talk about virtues rather than vices, however, "because they glow." The most important are humility, or "the self-respect of one who is fully, but not more than, one"; charity, or treating the neighbor as one's self; and veracity, or freedom from delusion. The East acknowledges these virtues by denouncing the vices that are their opposites: the "three poisons" of hatred, greed, and ignorance.

Veracity, of course, is the *jnana* yogi's favorite virtue. "Telling the truth is just the beginning of it," says Huston happily. "It can turn into a sublime objectivity that allows one to see the way things really are, which is usually blocked by self-interest." To illustrate, he tells us that one day he took a group of Western students to a Buddhist monastery in Japan so that they could try *zazen.* The *roshi,* as usual a rather severe figure, asked them why they wished to meditate. "To understand the Buddha's teachings," said one student. "No!" said the *roshi* sharply. "We do *zazen* to see reality clearly. Most of the time, we see it in a clouded mirror on which we have painted our pictures of reality, not the thing itself. Therein lies all manner of sorrow."

In earlier discussions Huston stressed the religions' shared vision of reality's oneness, goodness, and mystery. Now he concentrates on their common approach to life's darkness. From cancer to genocide, suffering and evil are, as Huston says, "the rock on which all religions and philosophies founder." Reminding us that "religious Truth is no simpler or easier than physics's truth," he offers one theological attempt to explain why bad things happen to good people: God is by definition perfect, and therefore infinitely good, thus generous; therefore, God must create something else to share with—that is, us necessarily imperfect creatures. By this route, says Huston, Augustine of Hippo came to understand that "the greater and the lesser together are greater than the greater alone."

Theological hypotheses are one thing, and experiencing darkness is another. It's not hard to imagine that someone as benign, wise, and calm—happy, in fact—as Huston seems to be has just been plain lucky in this regard. Then he describes a recent journey into the valley of the shadow of death. One of his three daughters, a wife and mother, suffered for many months from a particularly agonizing form of cancer. One reason he didn't succumb to despair during his child's terrible ordeal, says Huston, was that, despite extreme suffering, "she would tell us, 'I have no complaints' and 'I am at peace.' The only person who has the right to assert that all's well no matter how bad things seem is the one who's under fire. If you can say it then, it's real."

Huston describes entering his daughter's bedroom five minutes after her death. Even considering a father's natural bias, he says, she had always been beautiful. Despite the trickle of blood from her mouth, her face remained radiant. The last words of this young woman who loved the ocean were "I see the sea. I smell the sea. It's because it's so near." Because she was a convert to Judaism, her family kept a vigil through the night, during which they took turns reading the Kaddish around the bed and taking catnaps. For two hours Huston was alone with his child's body. "Half the time I was sobbing my heart out," he says, "and the other half, I just had this sense of her presence with me. As in the experiences of the unseen that William James reports, I could no more have doubted that than I doubt the reality of the chair I'm sitting on."

We hear Huston's words about the big picture differently now. Facing desolation, he says, "All we can do is say nothing and weep together as we experience total darkness." He tells us about a middle-aged friend who learned that she'd be completely blind in six months. She immediately called Howard Thurman, the late African American minister of renowned spirituality, who told her to come right over. Later Huston asked her what Reverend Thurman had said. "He didn't say anything," said the woman. "He took my hand and we cried together for twenty minutes." Choosing the Christian metaphor for such times, Huston says, "That's Good Friday."

Then comes Easter Sunday. The idea of resurrection per se is "hard for the modern mind," he allows, although he personally considers it "difficult, but not impossible." Theological particulars aside, he says, "Easter's main point is that death doesn't have the last word, nor does nature. When a two-year-old drops her ice cream cone, it's the end of the world for her. We're like her when something like cancer strikes. If we had the vision, we'd see our trials and tragedies as being like the upsets that a child has to undergo in order to mature. At the center of the religious life is a peculiar kind of joy at the prospect of a happy ending that blossoms from human difficulties embraced and overcome."

In the hot, quiet room, absorbing this sublime, difficult teaching elicits an almost muscular level of concentration. No one cares anymore if Huston uses monotheistic or polytheistic or nontheistic imagery. His genius has illuminated the common ground on which people of all faiths can stand and face their common enemy: the daily grind of soulless materialism. "Religion takes up where our routine reactions to life leave off," says Huston. "Blessedness is paradoxical. It brings joy in distress, even agony." He smiles, and silver bells peal. "If you open a door into a dark room, light floods *in,* not vice versa. Light has the final say."

AFTERWORD

After I finished this book, I spent some time thinking about how it came to be what it is. I must confess, however, that its evolution remains something of a mystery. My "choice" of Tenzin Palmo is a case in point. Long before learning about her, I'd decided to interview two prominent Buddhists much closer to home. When the time came, however, both were seriously ill. Then, Jakusho Kwong-roshi, the abbot of the Sonoma Mountain Zen Center, said, "I know! You should go see that nun. She lives in a cave somewhere up near Ladakh. She went on a twelve-year-long *sesshin*!" First I asked where Ladakh might be. Then I explained that such a trip was out of the question. There was no time to travel to the Himalayas. I had too many other commitments. I knew nothing about this cave-dwelling *ani*. He listened, then said, "Just go." I did, and he was right.

When I wondered aloud at the seeming coincidences and accidents that led some individuals onto these pages, my husband responded with a graphic image. "Maybe God blinked," he said, "and the flash went off and took this snapshot of what the real 'beautiful people' look like in 2001. You got to develop that picture. Maybe another blink would give another shot for someone else to develop. The faces would be different, but some things about the people would be the same."

I think Mike got that just right. The single most striking impression of my reporting is of a deep similarity that underlies the presences of these men and women. Despite often tremendous personal and religious differences, these spiritual geniuses are all on to something, and somehow, in the end, it is the same thing. The increasing interest and respect that such extraordinary souls command across cultural boundaries suggest that despite eruptions of the kind of intolerance and violence that have scarred Belfast, Jerusalem, and New York City, we human beings can indeed develop a greater wisdom and commonality that will bode well for our future.

For a writer, every book is a kind of personal pilgrimage, but the effect of this one has already been described, by pilgrims who've sought out spiritual geniuses throughout the ages. A Hindu would say these remarkable men and women give us *shakti,* and Buddhists and monotheists might say their presences confer blessings. From a different perspective, a psychologist would say that we internalize their voices. I can only say that, since I began working on this book, its subjects have a way of popping into my head at odd times, from subway rides to dreams.

Sometimes these special people appear in my mind's eye as models. What would she do? I'll wonder. What would he think? Mostly, however, they remind me of what, like other members of the meaning-seeking species, I know but so often forget: We're each part of something that's much bigger and better than what meets the eye, and if we keep that in mind, our hearts will be in the right place. Life will be all right, because its ups and downs will be seen as what they are—threads in a great fabric whose beauty depends on bright and dark colors. Perhaps spiritual geniuses are just people who remember these things more and more of the time, until the gaps of forgetting disappear.

For most of us, certainly me, our animating spirits don't lead us to spend years in a hermitage or heal thousands of the poor or unearth the meanings of sacred texts. Yet the extraordinary men and women in these pages simply personify our own potential for holiness and goodness—or transcendence and altruism—which can combine with each of our characteristics and gifts to produce a uniquely meaningful life. As a *togden* told Tenzin Palmo early in her journey, "You think we know some secret teachings that enable us to do great things, but there's nothing that I know that you don't. The difference is that I'm doing it, and you aren't."

SOURCES
AND SUGGESTED
READINGS

FOREWORD

1. Paul Tillich, *The Shaking of the Foundations* (New York: Charles Scribner's Sons, 1948).
2. Harold G. Koenig, M.D., *The Healing Power of Faith* (New York: Simon & Schuster, 1999).

1. BROTHER

1. Winifred Gallagher, *Just the Way You Are: How Heredity and Experience Create the Individual* (New York: Random House, 1997).

2. TEACHER

Lawrence Kushner, *The Way into Jewish Mystical Tradition* (Woodstock, Vt.: Jewish Lights, 2001).

————, *Invisible Lines of Connection: Sacred Stories of the Ordinary* (Woodstock, Vt.: Jewish Lights, 1996).

————, *God Was in This Place, & I, i Did Not Know* (Woodstock, Vt.: Jewish Lights, 1991).

1. Shem Tov Gaguine, *Keter Shem Tov* (Jerusalem: Ahavat Shalom, 1968).

3. EXPLORER

Tenzin Palmo, *Reflections on a Mountain Lake* (Ithaca, N.Y.: Snow Lion, forthcoming).

————, *Three Teachings* (Singapore: Kong Meng San Phor Kark See Monastery, 2000).

Vicki Mackenzie, *Cave in the Snow: Tenzin Palmo's Quest for Enlightenment* (New York: Bloomsbury, 1998).

Sogyal Rinpoche, *The Tibetan Book of Living and Dying* (San Francisco: HarperCollins, 1992).

Chögyam Trungpa Rinpoche, *Cutting Through Spiritual Materialism* (Boston and London: Shambhala Publications, 1978).

4. ACTIVIST

Riffat Hassan, *Women's Rights and Islam* (Louisville, Ky.: NISA Publications, 1995).

————, "Feminism in Islam," in *Feminism and World Religions,* eds. Arvind Sharma and Katherine Young (Albany: State University of New York Press, 1999).

5. GODDESS

Mata Amritanandamayi, *For My Children* (Amrithpuri, India: Mata Amritanandamayi Mission Trust, 1997).

Arthur Osborne, *Ramana Maharshi and the Path to Self Knowledge* (Tiruvannamalai, India: Sri Ramanasramam, 1970).

Murugan, *Sri Karunamayi: A Biography* (Bangalore, India: Karunamayi Shanti Dhama, 1997).

A. Tellegen and G. Atkinson, "Openness to Absorbing and Self-Altering Experiences ('Absorption'), a Trait Related to Hypnotic Susceptibility," *Journal of Abnormal Psychology,* 1974: 83, 268–77.

A. Tellegen, "Practicing the Two Disciplines for Enlightenment and Relaxation: Comment on Qualls and Sheehan," *Journal of Experimental Psychology: General,* 1981: 110, 217–26.

————, "Note on the Structure and Meaning of the MPQ Absorption Scale." University of Minnesota, 1992.

1. Peter Brown, *The Cult of the Saints: Its Rise and Function in Latin Christianity* (Chicago: University of Chicago Press, 1981).
2. Daniel Stern, *Diary of a Baby* (New York: Basic Books, 1990).
3. Auke Tellegen et al., "Personality Similarity in Twins Reared Apart and Together," *Journal of Personality and Social Psychology,* 1988.
4. Susan Bridle, "Otto Kernberg: The Seeds of the Self," *What Is Enlightenment?* no. 17.
5. Jerome Kagan, *Galen's Prophecy* (New York: Basic Books, 1994), p. 115.

6. PREACHER

Tony Campolo, *A Reasonable Faith* (Dallas: Word Publishing, 1983).
———, *Following Jesus Without Embarrassing God* (Dallas: Word Publishing, 1997).

7. INTELLECTUAL

Adin Steinsaltz, *The Talmud: The Steinsaltz Edition* (New York: Random House, 1989–).
———, *The Essential Talmud* (New York: Bantam Books, 1976).
———, *The Thirteen Petalled Rose* (New York: Basic Books, 1980).

8. COMMUNITY

Association of Contemplative Sisters National Newsletter, 713 East Park Ave., Suite 126, Santa Maria, CA 93454.
1. Rosalie Bertell, *No Immediate Danger* (London: The Women's Press, 1985).
2. Bede Griffiths, *The Marriage of East and West* (Springfield, Ill.: Templegate, 1982).

9. DOCTOR

Sri Aurobindo, *The Essential Aurobindo,* ed. Robert McDermott (New York: Schocken, 1973).
Harriet Rubin, "The Perfect Vision of Dr. V.," *Fast Company,* February 2001.

John Nance, "Dispeller of Darkness," *Yoga Journal,* September/October 1997.

10. INTERPRETER

Huston Smith, *The World's Religions: Our Great Wisdom Traditions,* rev. ed. (San Francisco: HarperCollins, 1991).

———, *Why Religion Matters* (San Francisco: HarperCollins, 2000).

Acknowledgments

First, I thank the extraordinary men and women in the preceding pages for allowing me to share in their lives and work.

I thank Rabbi Burton Visotzky, Dr. Ann-Judith Silverman, Kris Dahl, Susan Brown, and Michael Segell for reading my manuscript and offering splendid suggestions.

I also wish to thank the many kind people who helped me along the way, particularly Monica James, Margy-Ruth Davis, Katherine Henderson, Alok Jain, Elizabeth Lesser, Jerry Jones, and Meg Lundstrom.

And, as always, Ann Godoff.

About the Author

WINIFRED GALLAGHER is the author of *The Power of Place, Just the Way You Are*, which was a *New York Times* Notable Book of the Year, and, most recently, *Working on God*. She has also written for numerous publications, including *The Atlantic Monthly, Rolling Stone*, and *The New York Times*. She lives in Manhattan and Long Eddy, New York.

About the Type

This book was set in Bembo, a typeface based on an old-style Roman face that was used for Cardinal Bembo's tract *De Aetna* in 1495. Bembo was cut by Francisco Griffo in the early sixteenth century. The Lanston Monotype Company of Philadelphia brought the well-proportioned letterforms of Bembo to the United States in the 1930s.